MOZART
in Person

Mozart
Posthumous oil painting by Barbara Krafft, 1819. Original in the Gesellschaft der Musikfreunde, Vienna. (Courtesy Gesellschaft der Musikfreunde, Vienna.)

MOZART
in Person

HIS CHARACTER
AND
HEALTH

Peter J. Davies

foreword by
STANLEY SADIE

Contributions to the study of music and dance,
number 14

GREENWOOD PRESS
New York • Westport, Connecticut • London

TO CLARE AND MARIA

Library of Congress Cataloging-in-Publication Data

Davies, Peter J., 1937-
   Mozart in person : his character and health / Peter J. Davies ;
foreword by Stanley Sadie.
     p. cm.—(Contributions to the study of music and dance,
ISSN 0193-9041 ; no. 14)
   Bibliography: p.
   Includes index.
   ISBN 0-313-26340-X (lib. bdg. : alk. paper)
   1. Mozart, Wolfgang Amadeus, 1756-1791—Psychology. 2. Mozart,
Wolfgang Amadeus, 1756-1791—Health. I. Title. II. Series.
ML410.M9D185 1989
780'.92'4—dc 19   88-25091
[B]

British Library Cataloguing in Publication Data is available.

Library of Congress Catalog Card Number: 88-25091
ISBN: 0-313-26340-X
ISSN: 0193-9041

First published in 1989

Greenwood Press, Inc.
88 Post Road West, Westport, Connecticut 06881

Printed in the United States of America

The paper used in this book complies with the
Permanent Paper Standard issued by the National
Information Standards Organization (Z39.48-1984).

10 9 8 7 6 5 4 3 2 1

Copyright Acknowledgments

Grateful thanks are given to the following for extracted material:

"Mozart's Left Ear, Nephropathy and Death," *The Medical Journal of Australia,* copyright © 1987, *The Medical Journal of Australia,* reprinted with permission

Mozart: A Documentary Biography by Otto Erich Deutsch, copyright 1966 by A & C Black Publishers, London, reprinted with permission

The Letters of Mozart, ed. Emily Anderson, reprinted by permission of Macmillan, London and Basingstoke

A Mozart Pilgrimage: Being the Travel Diaries of Vincent and Mary Novello in the Year 1829, 1st ed., London, 1955, reproduced by permission of Novello and Company, Limited

Life of Mozart by Franz Niemetschek, trans. Helen Mautner, reprint 1966, Hyperion Press, Westport, Conn.

Lives of Haydn, Mozart and Metastasio by Stendhal, trans. Richard N. Coe, 1972, London, John Calder Publishers, Ltd.

"Mozart's Illnesses and Death," *Journal of the Royal Society of Medicine,* 1983, vol. 76, London

Reminiscences by Michael Kelly, ed. Roger Fiske, 1975, Oxford University Press, Oxford

CONTENTS

ILLUSTRATIONS

ACKNOWLEDGMENTS

This book is indebted to many talented people, especially to several of the world's leading Mozarteans.

Stanley Sadie invited and inspired my articles for *The Musical Times*, read the first and final manuscripts, and provided warm, enthusiastic, expert, provident advice. He assisted me further with his superb, encyclopedic insight into the literature, and wrote the foreword. The doyen of the Mozart world, Alec Hyatt King, in collusion with Dr. Sadie, read the early manuscripts, discovering faults, omissions, and other teething problems. Dr. King offered me astute, scholarly, practical advice. I also thank him for his assistance at the British Library. Both he and Dr. Sadie offered their input into the title.

Erna Schwerin generously provided numerous translations of German source materials. I am especially grateful for her devoted friendship and for her indispensable assistance with Mozartian psychodynamics, the date of his funeral, and the illustrations showing Mozart's skull and Mozart's ear. She collaborated with the Mozarteum in Salzburg and requested the search for the death certificate of Mozart's younger son. I also thank her for reading and correcting the entire final manuscript, and for writing the Introduction.

Dr. Rudolph Angermüller, the head of the Research Department of the International Foundation Mozarteum in Salzburg, is the most prolific writer on Mozart today. He searched the parish records at Salzburg for the death certificates of Johanna Jeanette and Maria Barbara von Berchtold zu Sonnenburg. I also thank him for expert information on Mozart's finances, Catholicism, skull, and Salzburg residences. Dr. Angermüller's friendly, courteous staff gave me free access to the library. My gratitude is also expressed to Dr. Wolfgang Rehm, the director of the Mozarteum Archives; Professor Géza Rech; and Dr. Heinz Kuschee.

I thank Alan Tyson for his many helpful suggestions and comments. Padre Rettore of Salzburg and Padre Joseph Santarelli of Loreto supplied fascinating material on the Loretto Kindl. Dr. Otto Biba, the Archive director of the Gesellschaft der Musikfreunde in Vienna, provided me with prompt, courteous assistance on several occasions. Dr. Gabriel Brenka and the Ministry of Interior of the Czechoslovak Socialist Republic kindly extracted the death certificate of F.X.W. Mozart. My gratitude is also expressed to the Mozart Museums in Vienna and Augsburg, to Dr. Alex Sakula, to Dr. Gunther Duda and to Gottfried Tichy.

I am very grateful to the British Library, especially the Department of Manuscripts, where I was privileged to examine Mozart's *Verzeichnüss*, his marriage contract, and the autographs of the last ten string quartets, the string quintets in C Minor and E Flat, and the harmonica quintet, among others. I thank Sandra Russell and the other librarians at St. Vincent's Hospital, Melbourne. I am also indebted to Marilyn Brownstein, editor of humanities at Greenwood Press, for her assistance in reshaping the manuscript.

My gratitude is extended to the editors of the following journals, for permission to reprint material from my previously published articles:

The Journal of the Royal Society of Medicine
  Mozart's illnesses and death, 76 (1983), 776-85.

The Musical Times
  Mozart's illnesses and death—I: The illnesses, 1756-90, 125 (1984), 437-42. Mozart's illnesses and death—II: The last year and the fatal illness, 125 (1984), 554-61. Mozart's illnesses: Letter to the Editor, 126 (1985), 390-91. Mozart's manic-depressive tendencies: in two parts, 128 (1987), 123-26, 191-96.

The Medical Journal of Australia
  Mozart's left ear, nephropathy, and death, 147 (1987), 581-86.

Friends of Mozart Newsletter
  The date of Mozart's funeral, No. 22, Fall 1987, 1-6. (Courtesy of the President, Friends of Mozart, New York.)

My constant companions during the past five years have been Emily Anderson's translation of the letters of Mozart and his family and O. E. Deutsch's documentary biography. While writing this book, I have been sustained by the loyalty, understanding, and inspiration of my family, friends, and teachers. On a personal note, I would like to pay special tribute to my wife Clare, who not only typed the manuscript and acted as a vital sounding board in her stimulating exchange of views and ideas, but also encouraged and uplifted me when my spirits began to flag.

This book is dedicated to the memory of Otto Jahn, Ludwig von Köchel, Alfred Einstein, and Otto Erich Deutsch.

FOREWORD

The many-sided nature of the genius of Mozart means that, as a subject for biographical study, he will not readily or soon be exhausted. The existing literature may be abundant, but there is ample room for more, especially where the biographer can bring to bear—as Peter J. Davies, a specialist in internal medicine, does—new modes of thought, the fruits of engagement in a discipline different from that of most students of Mozart. That this can produce fresh insights is vividly demonstrated in the pages that follow.

There are those who in the study of a composer would deny a place to investigations of a physical or even mental condition, and who would dismiss as morbid any inquiries relating to illness and death. But these days even our most protective and enclosed professions—among which must be numbered both those of the medical person and musicologist—are coming to accept the wholeness of human beings, the impossibility of compartmenting what they are from what they do, or how they feel from how they express themselves. If this is true of the person in the street, how much more so for the hypersensitive creative artist. There will, of course, be some, including medical persons and musicologists, who will disagree with Dr. Davies's diagnoses and judgments. Yet there is no doubting that his investigations have already helped explain hitherto problematical aspects of Mozart's life and work, and will provoke further and profitable debate. I can imagine no one better equipped, as professionally informed researcher or as sentient man, to pursue these lines of thought, and to stimulate us into a deeper awareness of Mozart, musician and man.

Stanley Sadie
Editor, *The New Grove Dictionary of Music and Musicians*
London, May 1988

INTRODUCTION

Of the many Mozart studies that have appeared since his early death, few have exhibited a probing and critically discerning viewpoint necessary to understand the composer's personality and lifestyle. Every century has viewed him differently, taking from him whatever suited contemporary needs. In the nineteenth and early twentieth centuries Mozart emerged as an idealized, stock rococo figure who could do no wrong, leading a charmed life, and who, because of the callousness of the Viennese audiences, died in abject poverty. His music, then only incompletely understood, fulfilled the longing for a better world, and a personality to match had to be conjured up. Although our feeling about his music has not changed, our conception of it and of his genius has. As a result, we are now better able to face and accept the shortcomings of his emotional adjustment and lifestyle. The enormous popularity of Mozart's music has frequently also had the opposite effect of reducing him to a media personality, severely distorting his image in popular plays and films, and thereby doing a great disservice to his genius. This has created an even greater need to clarify Mozart's true history and to better understand his image.

The reader will discover in this book a human being, realistically perceived with twentieth-century sensibility, yet retrospectively in the light of eighteenth-century mores. The author's study, addressed to the nonspecialist reader, sheds new light on the physical, mental, and spiritual aspects of Mozart's life, as they affect his creativity. Mozart is perceived as a one-time phenomenon, an innovator, and in some sense an outsider, too far advanced in his music for his contemporaries. Despite an overtly gregarious attitude, he had difficulty projecting himself into society to advance the cause of his music. His life was hectic and beset by dread of handling the practical aspects of daily problems.

This volume is not a complete biography of the composer. A chronology of his life and major compositions is provided to assist the reader. The book utilizes only authentic background material, including the letters of the composer, his family, and other contemporaries, researched with painstaking care and authority. The author avoids repetition of previously published information; yet nothing of significance is glossed over or trivialized, with interpretations always linked to relevant events.

Part I deals with Mozart's ancestry and early childhood, and explores his medical history in depth. His illnesses are traced and analyzed from the earliest recorded ones to those at the end of his life. This is also the only work that reviews *all* of Mozart's medical diagnoses from the extant literature. The reader will find Dr. Davies's enormously effective medical sleuthing, innovative ideas, and conclusions of his diagnosis of Schönlein-Henoch Syndrome fascinating and highly illuminating. A Glossary of Medical Terms at the end of the book explains technical language, when used. An overview of eighteenth-century medicine, including the essay on the smallpox epidemic of 1767 in Vienna, enables the reader to assess the dangers to which Mozart and his family were exposed. Among the incidental benefits of this chapter is a discussion of Franz Anton Mesmer's theory of animal magnetism, and his relationship with the young Mozart who later immortalized him in *Così Fan Tutte*. It was also the era of blood-letting, extensively practiced as a therapeutic tool to promote health and the management of febrile illnesses. The closeness of Mozart's relationship with his father is legend. It is further explored here with keen psychological insight, and plausible reasons are given for the ultimate split between father and son. We also learn about the great impact his mother's death in Paris had on the young composer.

The touching story of Mozart's and his family's great devotion to the small ivory statuette of the Child Jesus, known to Austrians as the Loretto Kindl, is told with poignancy, and is another facet of the composer's life not previously explored elsewhere. Despite the fact that Mozart's religious beliefs and attitudes had a profound influence on his life, this important subject has been much neglected in other biographies. It is given its due in Part II of this book. A devout Catholic, the composer had a simple trust in God which sustained him throughout his life, as can be gleaned from the correspondence, quoted liberally here. Mozart's occasional criticism of the clergy did not detract from his faith. "The Eternal Feminine," as Chapter 10 is called, held much attraction for Mozart. The women who may have caught his fancy (mainly singers and pupils) are discussed here. To his credit and contrary to prevalent unsympathetic views, the author assumes an objective and positive stance toward Mozart's wife Constanze and her part in the marriage. Mozart lovers may well have to face the sad fact that, because of his inability to manage his monetary affairs, the composer faced financial ruin despite substantial earnings. The author's elaborate and detailed research into Mozart's finances between 1784 and 1791 is one of the most important contributions to Mozart studies today. In recent years, questions have been raised in the literature as to the size of the composer's income, his debts, and possible excesses of spending. The possibility of his gambling proclivities has been considered, because Mozart repeatedly found himself in financial straits despite an income that should have guaranteed him an existence free from worries and want. The author concludes that Mozart's plight in his later years, resulting in the pathetic begging letters to Puchberg, may indeed have been the result of gambling and excessive generosity toward his friends and associates. A detailed discussion of the psychodynamics of gambling helps the reader understand Mozart's predilection for gambling and other games. He had motive (personality) and opportunity, as becomes clear in later chapters.

Part III is the heart of the book. In a detailed study, we are presented with the psychodynamics of Mozart's personality, his pastimes and stresses, culminating in the author's original and ingenious diagnosis of a cyclothymic disorder. He assigns the onset to the composer's adult life, tracing the ominous development systematically with clinical acumen and depth of insight. These plausible facts may well evoke shocked surprise and sadness in readers exposed to biographies in which Mozart's emotional problems were either left unrecognized or minimized. But the author's expert evaluation of Mozart's mood swings, flamboyant behavior at times, from the hypomanic to depressive trends, evident from the letters and contemporary observations, is indeed a pioneering study of the composer's psychohistory. The chapter exposes and interprets many of Mozart's letters to his father, sister, and cousin (the "Bäsle"), often replete with punning, word play, nonsense doggerel, scatology, and other signs of tomfoolery, which in context with "hard signs" reflect instability of mood. In contrast, the deep despair of some of his letters to his wife in his last years and to Puchberg, and his reduced creativity in 1790, are indicative of recurrent depression.

Part IV explores at length Mozart's terminal illness, the cause of his death, and his burial. The author's unique contribution in this final part of the book is his conclusion about the cause of Mozart's death, mentioned earlier. He also argues persuasively against the poisoning hypothesis advocated by other writers but fortunately no longer taken seriously in the scientific community. Also of much interest is the little known fact that Mozart had a deformed ear. This subject has been neglected in the general literature on the composer but could prove significant in explaining one of his major illnesses. Taking up the ongoing controversy about the date of Mozart's funeral, the author comes out in favor of 6 December rather than 7 December 1791 as suggested by other investigators.

The reader is also brought up to date on the current status of research on the lost and more recently alleged rediscovery of Mozart's death mask, whose authenticity is still under investigation.

Mozart was a gift to all humanity. This is reflected in this fascinating and remarkable book, in which novel ideas are backed by careful scholarly research. The author's caring about the composer is clearly evident. But regardless of the new vistas which this study opens up to us, we must also face the reality that genius cannot be lured into predictability. Thus, certain facets of Mozart's life and personality must ever elude us.

Erna Schwerin
President, Friends of Mozart, Inc.
New York

CHRONOLOGY

1719	14 November	Birth of Leopold Mozart (father)
1720	25 December	Birth of Anna Maria Walburga Pertl (mother)
1732	31 March	Birth of Joseph Haydn
1747	21 November	Parents' wedding
1748	18 August	Birth of Joannes Leopoldus Joachimus Mozart (first brother)
1749	2 February	Death of first brother
	18 June	Birth of Maria Anna Cordula Mozart (first sister)
	24 June	Death of first sister
1750	13 May	Birth of Maria Anna Nepomuzena Walburgis Mozart (second sister)
	29 July	Death of second sister
1751	30 July	Birth of Maria Anna Walburga Ignatia Mozart "Nannerl"
1752	4 November	Birth of Joannes Carolus Amadeus Mozart (second brother)
1753	2 February	Death of second brother
1754	9 May	Birth of Maria Crescentia Francisca de Paula Mozart (fourth sister)
	27 June	Death of fourth sister
1756	27 January	Birth of Wolfgang Amadeus Mozart
1761	December	First compositions: K. 1a, b, c, and d
1762	January	Three-week journey to Munich
	5 January	Birth of Constanze Weber (wife)
	18 September	Departure for Vienna

	4 October	Catarrh in Linz
	21 October	Erythema nodosum in Vienna
	19 November	Ailing
1763	5 January	Return to Salzburg
	5 January	Rheumatic fever
	9 June	Departure for the Grand Tour of Europe
	19 September	Corhyza at Coblenz
1764	Mid-February	Quinsy in Paris
	Winter	Violin Sonatas K. 7, 8, 9
	20 May	Illness in London
	August-September	Symphonies K. 16, 19
1765	August	Very bad cold in Lille
	15 November	Typhoid fever in the Hague
	December	Symphony in B-flat, K. 22
1766	12 November	Rheumatic fever in Munich
	29 November	Return to Salzburg
1767	11 September	Departure for Vienna
	26 October	Smallpox in Olmütz (Olomouc)
	Winter	Song "An die freude," K. 53
1768	September or October	"Bastien und Bastienne"
1769	5 January	Return to Salzburg
	13 December	First departure for Italy
1770	January	Corhyza and frost-bite in Mantua
	26 March	Glittering reception in Bologna
	30 March	Corhyza in Florence
	11 April	Holy Week in Rome
	April	Contredanse, K. 123
	May	Meeting with Niccolo Jommelli in Naples
	25 June	Father's injury in carriage accident
	8 July	Dubbed "Knight of the Golden Spur" by Pope Clement XIV
	Mid-November	Dental abscess in Milan
	17 December	Baptism of Ludwig van Beethoven in Bonn
	26 December	Premiere of *Mitridate*
1771	28 March	Return to Salzburg
	13 August	Second departure for Italy
	September	Tracheobronchitis in Milan
	17 October	Premiere of *Ascanio in Alba*
	15 December	Return to Salzburg
1772	January	Viral hepatitis
	Winter	Symphony in G, K. 124
	24 October	Third departure for Italy
	26 December	Premiere of *Lucio Silla*
1773	13 March	Return to Salzburg
	14 July	Departure for Vienna

	10 September	Suppression of the Jesuits in Austria
	26 September	Return to Salzburg
	5 October	"Little" Symphony in G Minor, K. 183
1774	6 December	Departure for Munich
	16 December	Dental abscess
1775	13 January	Premiere of *La Finta Giardiniera*
	7 March	Return to Salzburg
	23 April	*Il rè pastore*
	14 April-20 December	Five violin concertos: K. 207, 211, 216, 218, 219
1776	July	"Haffner" Serenade, K. 250
1777	23 September	Departure for Munich
	11 October	Arrival at Augsburg
	12 October	Meets Maria Anna Thekla Mozart (The Bäsle)
	26-27 October	Hohen-Altheim
	30 October	Arrival at Mannheim
		Falls in love with Aloysia Weber
1778	20 February	Catarrh
	23 March	Arrival in Paris
	12 June	"Paris" Symphony in D, K. 297
	3 July	Death of mother
	Summer	Piano Sonata in A Minor, K. 310
	6 November	Return to Mannheim
	25 December	Christmas with the Webers in Munich
1779	8 January	Aria "Popoli di Tessaglia," K. 316 and rejection by Aloysia Weber
	15 January	Return to Salzburg with cousin Bäsle
	23 March	"Coronation" Mass, K. 317 Symphonia Concertante for Violin and Viola in E-flat, K. 364
1780	5 November	Departure for Munich
	22 November	Corhyza and cough
	29 November	Death of Maria Theresa
1781	29 January	Premiere of *Idomeneo*
	16 March	Arrival in Vienna
	9 May	Break with Colloredo
	10 May	Minor illness
	20 June	Piano Variations, K. 352
1782	1 January	Death of Johann Christian Bach in London
	3 March	First "Lent Concert" in Vienna
	12 April	Death of Pietro Metastasio
	16 July	Premiere of *Die Entführung aus dem Serail*

	4 August	Marriage to Constanze Weber in St. Stephen's Cathedral
	19 October	Concert Rondo for Piano in A, K. 386
	31 December	String Quartet in G, K. 387
1783	2 February	Foundation of the Lodge "Zur Wohlthätigkeit"
	23 March	Academy concert in Burgtheater
	Late May	Corhyza
	27 May	Horn Concerto in E-flat, K. 417
	17 June	Birth of first son, Raimund Leopold
	17 June	Minuet and trio of string quartet in D Minor, K. 421
	June-July	String Quartet in E-flat, K. 428
	End of July	Departure for Salzburg
	19 August	Death of first son
	26 October	Great C Minor Mass, K. 427
	3 November	Linz Symphony in C, K. 425
	End of November	Return to Vienna
1784	9 February	First entry in his personal thematic catalogue: Piano Concerto in E-flat, K. 449
	15 March	Piano Concerto in B-flat, K. 450
	22 March	Piano Concerto in D, K. 451
	30 March	Piano Quintet in E-flat, K. 452
	1 April	Benefit concert in Burgtheater
	12 April	Piano Concerto in G, K. 453
	21 April	Violin Sonata in B-flat, K. 454
	23 August	Nannerl's marriage
	23 August	Serious illness
	21 September	Birth of second son, Carl Thomas
	30 September	Piano Concerto in B-flat, K. 456
	14 October	Piano Sonata in C Minor, K. 457
	9 November	String Quartet in B-flat, K. 458
	11 December	Piano Concerto in F, K. 459
	14 December	Entry as apprentice Freemason in the Lodge "Zur Wohlthätigkeit"
1785	7 January	Passage to the Fellow-craft degree under the Master Ignaz von Born
	10 January	String Quartet in A, K. 464
	14 January	String Quartet in C, K. 465
	10 February	Piano Concerto in D Minor, K. 466
	11 February	Visit of Leopold Mozart at Vienna
	9 March	Piano Concerto in C, K. 467
	10 March	Benefit concert in Burgtheater
	20 April	Masonic cantata "Die Mauerfreude," K. 471

	25 April	Last farewell to his father
	20 May	Piano Fantasia in C Minor, K. 475
	8 June	Song "The Violet," K. 476
	July	Masonic funeral music, K. 477
	16 October	Piano Quartet in G Minor, K. 478
	12 December	Violin Sonata in E-flat, K. 481
	16 December	Piano Concerto in E-flat, K. 482
1786	14 January	Headache and stomach cramps
	3 February	"Der Schauspieldirektor" at Schönbrunn
	2 March	Piano Concerto in A, K. 488
	13 March	Revival of *Idomeneo*
	24 March	Piano Concerto in C Minor, K. 491
	7 April	Last benefit concert in Burgtheater
	1 May	Premiere of *Le Nozze di Figaro*
	3 June	Piano Quartet in E-flat, K. 493
	26 June	Horn Concerto in E-flat, K. 495 (first two movements)
	8 July	Piano Trio in G, K. 496
	1 August	Piano Sonata for Four hands in F, K. 497
	5 August	Clarinet Trio in E-flat, K. 498
	19 August	String Quartet in D, K. 499
	18 October	Birth of third son, Johann Thomas Leopold
	4 November	Piano Variations for Four Hands, K. 501
	15 November	Death of third son
	18 November	Piano Trio in B-flat, K. 502
	4 December	Piano Concerto in C, K. 503
	6 December	Prague Symphony in D, K. 504
	27 December	Aria "Ch'io mi scordi di te," K. 505
1787	8 January	Departure for Prague
	19 January	Concert in the National Theater
	22 January	Conducts *Figaro*
	30 January	Death of friend Count August Hatzfeld
	12 February	Return to Vienna
	23 February	Ann Storace's farewell concert
	Mid-March	Leopold Mozart seriously ill
	7-20 April	Beethoven in Vienna
	Mid-April	Recurrence of serious illness
	19 April	String Quintet in C, K. 515
	16 May	String Quintet in G Minor, K. 516
	28 May	Death of father
	29 May	Piano Sonata for Four Hands in C, K. 521

	14 June	"A musical joke," K. 522
	10 August	Eine Kleine Nachtmusik in G, K. 525
	24 August	Violin Sonata in A, K. 526
	3 September	Death of friend Dr. Sigmund Barisani
	1 October	Departure for Prague
	29 October	Premiere of *Don Giovanni*
	3 November	Aria "Bella mia fiamma," K. 528
	Mid-November	Return to Vienna
	15 November	Death of Gluck
	7 December	Appointment as chamber musician to the emperor
	27 December	Birth of first daughter, Theresia Konstanzia
1788	24 February	Piano Concerto in D, K. 537
	7 May	Premiere of *Don Giovanni* in Vienna
	22 June	Piano Trio in E, K. 542
	26 June	Symphony in E-flat, K. 543
	29 June	Death of first daughter
	14 July	Piano Trio in C, K. 548
	25 July	Symphony in G Minor, K. 550
	10 August	"Jupiter" Symphony in C, K. 551
	27 September	Divertimento for String Trio in E-flat, K. 563
	27 October	Piano Trio in G, K. 564
	14 December	Death of Carl Philipp Emanuel Bach in Weimar
1789	8 April	Departure for Berlin
	14 April	Plays K. 537 for the elector at Dresden
	16 or 17 April	Doris Stock's silverpoint drawing
	22 April	Plays J. S. Bach's organ at Leipzig
	12 May	Benefit concert in Leipzig
	26 May	Plays at the Berlin Royal Palace
	4 June	Return to Vienna
	June	String Quartet in D, K. 575
	July	Constanze ill with a varicose ulcer
	July	Piano Sonata in D, K. 576
	29 August	Revival of *Figaro*
	29 September	Clarinet Quintet in A, K. 581
	16 November	Birth and death of second daughter, Anna Maria
1790	26 January	Premiere of *Così Fan Tutte*
	20 February	Death of Joseph II
	April-August	Illness
	May	String Quartet in B-flat, K. 589
	June	String Quartet in F, K. 590

	23 September	Departure for Frankfurt
	30 September	Constanze and Carl move into Mozart's last apartment
	9 October	Coronation of Leopold II in Frankfurt Cathedral
	15 October	Concert in Frankfurt
	20 October	Concert in Mainz
	4 or 5 November	Concert in Munich
	10 November	Return to Vienna
	14 December	Farewell dinner for Joseph Haydn
	December	String Quintet in D, K. 593
1791	5 January	Piano Concerto in B-flat, K. 595
	12 April	String Quintet in E-flat, K. 614
	23 May	Harmonica Quintet, K. 617
	June-December	Chronic renal failure
	18 June	Ave verum corpus, K. 618, at Baden
	26 July	Birth of fourth son, Franz Xaver Wolfgang
	25 August	Departure for Prague
	August-September	Illness in Prague
	6 September	Premiere of *La Clemenza di Tito*
	Mid-September	Return to Vienna
	30 September	Premiere of *Die Zauberflöte*
	October	Clarinet Concerto in A, K. 622
	15 November	Little Masonic Cantata, K. 623
		Requiem Mass, K. 626 (incomplete)
	18 November	Conducts K. 623 at the Lodge
	20 November	Onset of fatal illness
	5 December	Death
	6 December	Funeral and burial

PART I

Medical History

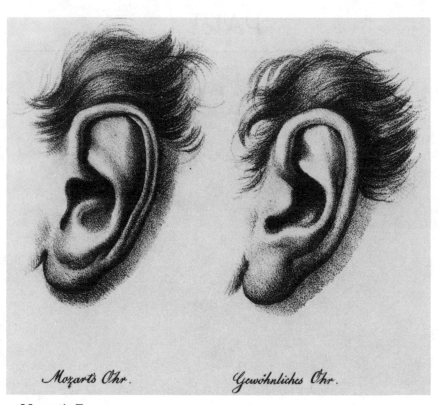

Mozart's Ear
Lithograph from Nissen's Biography. Mozart's malformed left external ear is contrasted with a normally shaped ear. (Courtesy of the International Foundation Mozarteum, Salzburg.)

ANCESTRY, BIRTH, AND
EARLY CHILDHOOD

In the district to the southwest of Augsburg lie more than thirty villages in which the name Mozart, variously spelled (Motzart, Motzhart, Motzhardt, Mutzhart, Mutzert, Motzet), traces back to the fourteenth century.[1] Two artists were born into this family in the sixteenth century; indeed, the paintings and drawings of Anton Mozart (1573-1625) are extant. Among the other remote members of the family were mercenaries, farmers, craftsmen, and builders. Mozart's great, great grandfather David Mozart (1620-85) and two of David's sons, Hans Georg (1647-1719) and Franz (1649-94), were designers, architects, and builders (master-masons). David's younger son Michael (1655-1718) became a sculptor in Vienna. The house of Mozart's great grandfather, Franz Mozart, may be seen today (Das Haus Fuggeri No. 14). Franz's eldest son, Johann Georg (1679-1736), became a bookbinder in Augsburg, whereas the younger son Franz (1681-1732) was a notable sculptor in Strasbourg.

The eldest of Johann Georg Mozart's six sons, born on 14 November 1719, was christened Johann Georg Leopold. Anna Maria Sulzer (1696-1766) was the second wife of the bookbinder, and also a native of Augsburg.

Leopold attended the Augsburg Gymnasium and was exceptionally bright. His father had lived just long enough to ensure that his eldest son would complete his education at the Jesuit school of St. Salvator in Augsburg, an expensive private school. The research of Adolf Layer has concluded that Leopold's fees were discounted because his father bound service books for the Cathedral.[2] Leopold entered St. Salvator's when he was eight years of age, which was three years younger than the average entrant. At this exclusive school Leopold received the best available education in the humanities, literature, and sciences. There he gained an expert knowledge of his mother tongue, a thorough command of Latin, a knowledge of Greek, and a solid foundation in French, Italian, and English. In his last year he studied physics and showed outstanding talent in the art of dialectics. Leopold also became actively involved, as musician and actor, in the school plays which were an important part of the Jesuit curriculum. His guardian, Canon Johann Georg Grabher, enrolled him as one of the trebles in the choirs of the Canonry of the Holy Cross, and the monastery of St. Ulrich. He was also taught the organ and the elements of the violin. Leopold left St. Salvator's in August 1736, having gained his final certificate with distinction. He possessed a microscope and two telescopes. His ambition led him to become the first member of his family to receive a tertiary education.

Leopold was enrolled in the Benedictine University at Salzburg on 26 November 1737, and there he studied philosophy and jurisprudence. In 1738, he took the Bachelor of Philosophy degree with distinction, but the following year he was expelled because of infrequent attendance at the classes for natural science. Leopold had been encouraged to enter the priesthood, but instead he chose to become a musician, entering the service of the prince of Salzburg as Valet de Chambre. Leopold made himself familiar with all styles of composition. In 1740, he etched with his own hand in copper his first composition of six church and chamber sonatas for two violins and bass, which he dedicated to his employer.[3] Leopold was also a gifted artist, later painting water colors on the back of playing cards. Subsequently, this extremely talented musician composed a wide variety of interesting and novel music.

Leopold Mozart had a handsome appearance and an exceptionally fine character. He possessed a great deal of wisdom, a dry wit, and a sarcastic humor. He was also an outstanding teacher and later showed remarkable ability as an impresario and writer. Leopold was a devout Roman Catholic and had an immense faith and trust in God. In fact, his whole life was geared to the acceptance of the Divine Will. His obsessional personality contributed to later spells of melancholia.

In 1743, Leopold was appointed fourth violinist in the court orchestra of the prince archbishop of Salzburg, and in the following year he was made violin teacher to the cathedral choir boys. By this time he had fallen in love with Anna Maria Pertl (born on 25 December 1720 in St. Gilgen). Her father, Wolfgang Nikolaus Pertl (1667-1724), was also the first of his family to receive a tertiary education. He completed law at the Benedictine University of Salzburg, at which time he was appointed bass in the choir and instructor of singing at the monastery school of St. Peter. After graduating, he entered the civil service, and in 1716, he was appointed warden of the Foundation of St. Gilgen. Following his death the family became bankrupt, and his widow, Eva Rosina Pertl, the daughter of a musician, moved with her family back to Salzburg where she had to survive on a miserable pension. In 1742, they lived in an apartment at Getreidegasse 48, not far from the "Mozart Birth House." Anna Maria was a simple, upright woman with a merry sense of humor. She married Leopold Mozart in the cathedral on 21 November 1747, and they were known as the handsomest couple in Salzburg.

Their first three children died in infancy aged five months, six days, and eleven weeks, respectively. Understandably, Anna Maria's health broke down under the pressure of this stress and sorrow, so that in the summer of 1750, she was sent to take the medicinal waters of Bad Gastein. She recovered well and on 30 July 1751 their fourth child, a daughter, was born; she was named Maria Anna Walburga Ignatia, and later was known as Nannerl. Their fifth and sixth children died in infancy aged three months and seven weeks. On 27 January 1756, at 8:00 P.M.; their seventh child, a son, was born. The placenta was retained, so that manual removal of it was performed. This procedure, done without an anaesthetic, was associated with the risk of postpartum hemorrhage, cervical shock, and also with puerperal sepsis, but happily both mother and child survived. The boy was born on the feast day of St. John Chrysostom, so that on 28 January he was christened Joannes Chrysostomus Wolfgangus Theophilus Mozart in Salzburg Cathedral. Theophilus was the Greek name for Amadeus, which means Beloved of God. In Italy, from 1770, Mozart called himself Wolfgango Amadeo, and from about 1777 Wolfgang Amade.[4] His family pet names were Woferl and Wolfgangerl.

The charming fifteenth-century house at Getreidegasse 9 had been purchased by the merchant family Hagenauer in 1703. Leopold Mozart rented a comfortable third-floor apartment from his friend Lorenz Hagenauer, who later helped finance the European tours. The apartment consisted of a bedroom, living room, study, a small spare room, and kitchen. Mozart was born in the central room overlooking the courtyard, and the Mozart family occupied this apartment until the autumn of 1773. (The Mozart museum was opened there in 1880.)

Mozart was short-sighted so that he never needed to wear reading spectacles.[5] It has been suggested that the composer was cross-eyed; however, such a dubious supposition derived from an unauthenticated painting in Stockholm.[6] The noninscribed portrait, attributed to the German school of the second half of the eighteenth century, portrays the profile of an unidentified young man wearing a wig, white shirt with ruffles, and brown coat. His eyes are brown, and the left one is squinted inwards; a left internal strabismus of about 16 diopters is present.[7] Numerous portraits of Mozart have been reproduced in the books of Bory, Valentin, Zenger, and Deutsch,[8] but only a dozen or so are considered genuine.[9]

In her letter to Breitkopf and Härtel, dated 30 January 1799, Constanze stated that Mozart disliked being painted en face.[10] It should be noted that there is a lack of exposure of his left ear in most of the portraits; on the other hand, his right ear, shown in several portraits, appears to be unremarkable. Mozart was born with a malformation of his left external ear, an extraordinary peculiarity inherited by his younger son.[11]

A fascinating exhibit used to hang in the Mozart museum at Salzburg:[12] an anonymous watercolor illustrating two ears. The original inscription read: "My ear and an ordinary ear." The "my" had been crossed out by a later hand and substituted with "Mozart's." It was considered likely that the malformed left ear in the watercolor belonged to Franz Xaver Wolfgang Mozart.[13] Recently, the Mozarteum in Salzburg has authenticated the inscription under the watercolor, to have been written by Franz Xaver Wolfgang Mozart. Descriptions of the watercolor were soon reported in three medical journals, and the German otologist Dr. P. H. Gerber's own drawing of the watercolor formed the basis for the description of the Mozart Ear in the medical literature.[14] The salient features were a large, broad, flat auricle, with loss of its attractive oval shell configuration and concavity, together with a complete defect of the lobule.[15] There was also an absence of both the tragus and antitragus, along with a filling out of the concha, so as to produce a slit-like narrowing of the orifice of the external auditory meatus.[16]

It should be noted that both the watercolor and Gerber's reproduction show an earring. There is no mention of such in the literature, nor is an earring present in any of the authentic portraits of Mozart or his younger son. It is currently held that the Mozart Ear is inherited as an autosomal dominant trait and that the minimal diagnostic criterion is a bulging of the superior margin of the pinna, owing to a fusion of the two crura of the antihelix and the crus helicis.[17]

Nissen's biography contains a lithographic reproduction of Mozart's left ear, contrasted with a normal one.[18] This lithograph is considered to be a stylized drawing of the watercolor.[19] However, there is no earring in Nissen's drawing. It differs from the watercolor in one other important respect: there is a deep groove in the vertical part of the outer rim of the pinna.[20]

Most of Mozart's deformed left ear is covered by his wig in the provocative left lateral view of the famous silverpoint drawing by Doris Stock. Yet the very lowest part of his ear is exposed, and it does show the absence of an auricular lobule. Carl Schweikart's 1825 oil portrait of Franz Xaver Wolfgang Mozart was clearly intended to draw attention to the peculiar deformity of the left ear: it shows not only an abnormal prominence of the antihelix, but also a strong suggestion of the vertical groove.

The artist of the watercolor is unknown, and there persists some doubt about the identity of the subject. It is also uncertain whether the vertical groove is an integral part of the Mozart Ear, or for that matter, whether the condition is still extant.

It has been erroneously assumed that Mozart's left external ear malformation was associated with hearing impairment on that side.[21] On the contrary, his hearing was remarkable, and he possessed the gift of absolute pitch, so that for example, he was able to distinguish a difference in tuning of half a quarter-tone on the violin.[22] Until the age of nine, he was unable to tolerate the sound of a solo trumpet.

Few other composers had such an ideal environment to stimulate the early development of their genius. Woferl spent his first six years in a stable, happy home much loved by his parents and sister. Leopold was at the height of his powers, and a few months after his son's birth, he published his famous *Violinschule*—"A treatise on the fundamental principles of violin playing." It was a tremendous success and remained a standard reference well into the nineteenth century. In 1757, Leopold was appointed court composer, and the following year he was promoted to the post of second violinist in the court orchestra. Woferl's home was full of music, and always there was a bustle of activity. The Mozarts' many friends included Father Joseph Bullinger and the following families: the Schachtners, Hagenauers, Barisanis, Robinigs, Gilowskys, von Melks, von Stumbs, von Antretters,and Barbara Zezi. The patrons of the Mozart family included the banker Franz Anton Spängler, the mayor, Ignaz Weiser, and the influential wholesale merchant and burgomaster Siegmund Haffner.

From his earliest years Wolfgang was consumed by music. Even his childish games had to be accompanied by a march or a song. He showed a keen interest in the clavier at the age of three and was delighted by picking out thirds. In 1761, Woferl commenced clavier lessons from his father; he could learn a minuet in half an hour or a new piece in an hour. Even by then he had already attempted to compose a clavier concerto. The boy made such rapid progress that he had composed his first clavier pieces by the end of his sixth year. Leopold wrote them out in Nannerl's notebook—Andante (K. la), and two Allegros (K. lb, and lc) on 11 December 1761. At times the boy became so engrossed in his music, for hours on end, that it became necessary to lead him away from the clavier. He also showed astonishing precocious talent with the violin.

Mozart never attended a school. He received his entire initial general and musical education from his father, who, as we have seen, was well qualified as a teacher. Leopold gradually phased out his other pupils so as to have more time to devote to the education of his prodigies. (Nannerl had also shown musical proficiency.) The lessons were conducted with a reasonable discipline, and Wolfgang was an obedient, enthusiastic, and highly receptive pupil. However, such an insulated upbringing likely restricted his personality development. Mozart later regretted not having had formal teaching in writing, and he was never satisfied with his own standard. (Later, when Empress Maria Theresa launched her social reforms, she stressed general education, so that by 1774, over 500 new primary schools had been established in Austria.[23])

During his lessons Wolfgang showed an expected avidity for knowledge, but outside of music he showed exceptional talent only in mathematics, a subject that fascinated him. Schachtner recalled that, when as a child Mozart was engaged in learning, he applied himself so earnestly to it that everything else, even his music, was forgotten. For instance, tables, stools, walls, and even the floor were chalked over with figures when the boy was learning arithmetic. He was also enthusiastic at drawing but later showed no outstanding talent in this art. Wolfgang became very well versed in French, Italian, English, as well as his native German, so that he later read and understood important literary works in these languages. He also studied Latin, geography, and history.

In contrast to his serious preoccupation with music, Mozart was a jolly scamp at play. He enjoyed all manner of pranks and childish games, showing a mischievous sense of humor. The boy was full of fire, and his inclinations were easily swayed, so that he was ever so ready to yield to every available attraction. His vivid, fertile imagination led him readily into profound reveries and fantasies in the wonderful world of make-believe. Thus, for example, he invented an idyllic land called the Kingdom of Back, of which he was the king. He would dictate the names of the cities, market-towns, and villages to the families' servant Sebastian Winter, who would then have to draw them on a chart. Woferl and Nannerl enjoyed many imaginative adventures in this exciting dream world.

Despite the seemingly ideal environment for his upbringing, the boy showed early signs of emotional insecurity. He spent much time in the company of the family friend, Johann Andreas Schachtner, and he would often ask him ten times a day if he loved him. When sometimes the court trumpeter jestingly replied in the negative, the boy's eyes would fill with tears until he was reassured. Mozart loved his parents, especially his father. For example, the boy composed in two parts nonsense words as an evening song from a variant of "Willem van Nassau." When bedtime came, Leopold would have to sing this melody with his son and stand him on a chair. After this ceremony was finished, Woferl would kiss his father most tenderly on the nose and then happily go to bed. The boy would not settle for the night unless this ritual was enacted, and it was continued until he was in his tenth year. These two anecdotes illustrate early evidence of dependency and obsessional traits in his personality. Wolfgang was so obedient and docile with his parents that he seldom needed to be punished, and he would neither accept nor eat food without his father's permission.[24]

Wolfgang also showed talent as an actor. He made his debut on the stage in the dramatic play *Sigismundus Hungariae Rex* at the University in September 1761. Four months later Nannerl and Wolfgang made such rapid progress in their music that Leopold took them for three weeks to Munich, where they played before the Elector Maximilian III Joseph.

Another favorite anecdote from Schachtner is worthy of repetition here. Wolfgang had been given a little violin in Vienna, and soon after their return to Salzburg in January 1763 Johann Wenzl paid them a visit. Wenzl had composed six little trios and was anxious to obtain Leopold's opinion of them. The trios were to be played by Wenzl (first violin), Schachtner (second violin), and Leopold (viola). Woferl asked if he might be allowed to play second violin. Leopold refused permission, since his son had not yet had the least instruction in the violin. The boy, however, insisted that he could play, whereupon Leopold sent him off. Woferl broke into tears and stamped off with his little violin. Schachtner, moved with compassion, implored Leopold to let his son play with him. Leopold impatiently yielded to this request and said to Woferl: "Play with Herr Schachtner, but so softly that we can't hear you, or you will have to go." Soon after the trio began, Schachtner noticed with astonishment that he was quite superfluous. He quietly laid aside his violin and looked at Leopold, who was shedding tears of wonder and joy at this scene. The boy played through the whole six trios quite accurately. Emboldened by their applause he next wanted to try his hand at playing first violin, but his attempts to do so brought much laughter.[25]

It would appear that Mozart was a most lovable child, and that his extroverted personality placed him at ease with strangers from all strata of society. Nannerl recalled that during the travel journeys, her brother made a point of advancing his knowledge through personal intercourse with the various artists he met, be they composers, painters, engravers, or whatever.

THE FIRST RECORDED ILLNESSES

During the autumn and winter of 1762, Wolfgang suffered four illnesses which seemed to have been related. These first recorded illnesses have captured the imagination of all medical writers on this subject. We will see that Mozart suffered frequent infections throughout his life, and it seems likely that his early death resulted from the complications of recurrent streptococcal infections.

Leopold Mozart together with his wife and two children set out from Salzburg on 18 September 1762 for their first journey to Vienna. After having lodged for six nights in Passau at what is now the White Hare Inn, they traveled by boat down the Danube to Linz, where they stayed at the Trinity Inn, Hofgasse 5. Woferl gave his first public recital at this inn on 1 October. Three days later the family headed downriver in the mail boat from Linz. On this occasion, however, they were unable to admire the beauty of the picturesque vineyards on the banks of the Danube, since rain squalls and high winds forced them to dock at Mauthausen. Leopold wrote that Wolfgang suffered catarrh during this journey. In view of subsequent events, this inflammation of his upper respiratory passages was probably due to streptococcal infection rather than a common cold virus (corhyza). At any rate Woferl was not greatly indisposed by it because at noon, on 5 October at Ybbs, he played the organ of the Franciscan church with such effect that the Friars were beside themselves with wonderment. Following a stopover at Stein, they arrived in Vienna on the midafternoon of 6 October. Woferl charmed the customs officer by playing his little fiddle, so that their baggage was allowed to pass free of duty.

In Vienna the boy made his debut at the Collato Palace, Am Hof 13,

where he played the harpsichord. The Mozarts were received at
Schönbrunn on 13 October by Maria Theresa and her consort, Emperor
Francis I. It was on this occasion that Woferl jumped up on the empress's
lap, hugged her around the neck, and kissed her on the cheek. Charmed
by him, she gave him an embroidered lilac suit that had been tailored for
her son, Archduke Maximilian. The Mozart children gave several
concerts which had been arranged especially for them by the Viennese
nobility and foreign diplomats.

The most sinister effects of a streptococcal infection may sometimes be
delayed for weeks or even years, as we will see. It was just sixteen days
in this first instance, when on 21 October 1762, prior to the second
command performance before Maria Theresa, Wolfgangerl complained
of pain in the region of his backside and hips. After the concert Leopold
examined the child while putting him to bed and noted a few painful,
tender, very red, and slightly raised lumps about the size of a kreutzer (a
coin of the dimensions of an Old English penny). These lesions were
distributed over his shins, elbows, and buttocks. The boy was unwell
with malaise and a fever, so that Leopold administered black powder
and margrave powder, which were among his favorite household
remedies. An urgent consultation was arranged with Dr. Johann von
Bernhard, professor of medicine at Vienna University. After the
professor diagnosed "a kind of scarlet fever," the boy was kept in bed
for eleven days. Over the next week the lumps increased in size but not
in number. At that time the nobility in Vienna were afraid of pock marks
and all kinds of skin rashes. Indeed, Prince Kaunitz, who became
chancellor in 1753, had a pathological fear of smallpox. Anyhow, on 4
November Wolfgang was well enough to be taken for a drive to
Karlskirche. The Emperor Charles VI had dedicated this church to St.
Charles Borromeo after the cessation of the plague in 1713. In
appreciation of his professional services, Leopold arranged a concert in
Dr. Bernhard's home on 5 November. Subsequently, the professor
invited the Mozart family to his box at the Burgtheater for the opera on
23 November.[1]

Leopold had written a very accurate description of erythema
nodosum, a disorder that was not described in medical textbooks until
1808. Dr. Bernhard is therefore to be forgiven for his mistaken diagnosis
of a kind of scarlet fever.[2]

The rash of scarlet fever consists of raised red flecks, or puncta,
superimposed on a fine flush, or erythema. The rash begins on the face,
and spreads to the neck and upper chest, and then over the trunk and
onto the limbs. Peeling of the skin, or desquamation, appears on about
the fourth or fifth day of the rash, which usually disappears within a
week. The scarlet fever rash is due to an erythrogenic toxin that is
produced by certain strains of beta hemolytic streptococci. The major

hazards of scarlet fever are the initial toxemia, and in some cases, the later complications of acute nephritis on the eighteenth to twenty-first day, and rheumatic fever during the second or third week of the illness. There were 565 deaths from scarlet fever in Vienna in 1822.[3]

Dr. Bernhard's mistaken diagnosis of scarlet fever led Dr. J. Barraud to postulate that Mozart developed post-scarlatina nephritis, the disease that eventually caused his death from renal failure.[4] Mozart's erythema nodosum was first diagnosed by Dr. Hans Holz.[5] In view of subsequent events, the likely cause was streptococcal infection rather than tuberculosis as has been proposed by one author.[6]

Erythema nodosum is an interesting vasculitic syndrome characterized by recurrent crops of painful, red lumps in the region of the skin of the legs, or occasionally the arms. The lumps vary in size from 0.5 to 2.0 cm in diameter and usually resolve within three weeks without leaving a scar. Erythema nodosum may complicate a variety of infections—streptococcal, tuberculosis, leprosy, fungal infections, yersinia, psittacosis, and catscratch disease. Drug allergies are sometimes responsible, or it may be related to a systemic disorder such as sarcoidosis, ulcerative colitis, Crohn's disease, or Behcet's disease. In idiopathic cases, no cause can be found.

Erythema nodosum was first described by Robert Willan, the founder of British dermatology.[7] Willan's first line of treatment for this condition was to prescribe Calomel or a milder purgative. Later, he administered considerable doses of Peruvian bark, either alone or combined with vitriolic acid or wine. In 1783, Willan was appointed physician to the newly established public dispensary in Cary Street, which served the poor in the vicinity of Clare-Market, Drury-Lane, Chancery-Lane, Templebar, Strand, Holborn, Fleet Street and Market, Ludgate, and Black and White Friars.

On his travels Leopold always carried a first-aid kit with him which included bandages, ointments, purgatives, foot-bath salts, tamarind water, violet juice, and of course, his two favorite powders. Margrave powder, formulated by the German chemist Andreas Sigismund Marggraf (1709–82), contained magnesium carbonate, peony and iris roots, mistletoe, crushed coral, and gold. Pulvis epilepticus niger contained the powder of desiccated earth worms, which in the eighteenth century was reckoned to be a specific remedy for epilepsy. The powder derived its black color from the presence of charcoal, and it was used for a variety of other complaints. Its other constituents included deer's antlers, myrrh, coral, frog's heads, and placenta.[8]

Wolfgang was again ailing when the Mozart family were bystanders at a banquet in the Vienna Hofburg on 19 November. This malady may have been a recurrence of tonsillitis. The month of December 1762 was an eventful one for the Mozart family. When Leopold heard the news that Ursula and Francesca Hagenauer had contracted smallpox in Salzburg, he postponed his family's return home so as to avoid catching this dreaded disease. Leopold had kept good health, apart from an occasional twinge of gout, until 19 December when he developed a dental abscess. His face was so swollen that he looked like the trumpeting angel. Another fear arose when Maria Theresa's eleventh child, Archduchess Joanna, who had led Woferl by the hand during the audience at Schönbrunn, died of typhus in December 1762. The Mozart family traveled home in their own carriage, arriving in Salzburg on the evening of 5 January 1763. Woferl was immediately ill with fever and rheumatism in his legs, so that he was unable to stand. Leopold later wrote that this was similar to the boy's illness in Munich in November 1766, and he appears to have recovered after a week or so in bed. The likely diagnosis is rheumatic fever.[9]

Rheumatism and gout are mentioned in the writings of Hippocrates, but the French physician G. de Baillou (1538-1616) was the first to clearly distinguish the two conditions. The pioneers in establishing a causal relationship between acute rheumatism and the subsequent development of mitral valve disease were David Pitcairn of St. Bartholomew's Hospital in 1788, Edward Jenner in 1789, and William C. Wells of St. Thomas's Hospital in 1812. Following the discovery of the stethoscope in 1819 by the Breton physician René Laennec, the way was open for further observations on the nature of rheumatic heart disease by Jean B. Bouillaud of Paris in 1837.

The rheumatic fever syndrome is characterized by fever, polyarthritis, pancarditis, chorea, subcutaneous nodules, and erythema marginatum. Rheumatic fever becomes manifest between one and four weeks after a throat infection with group A beta hemolytic streptococci and has a tendency to recur. Ten to 15 percent of all twelve-year-old children in England were affected by rheumatic fever in 1927, and it is the most common precursor of heart disease in adults under fifty years of age.[10] The peak incidence occurs between the ages of five and fifteen; it is rare before the age of four or after the age of fifty. Recurrent attacks of rheumatic fever can now be prevented by the prophylactic administration of penicillin.

The prognosis of rheumatic fever depends on whether or not there is involvement of the heart by the rheumatic process. If there is not, then the prognosis is excellent. The mortality in Vienna in 1826 was just under 2 percent when thirteen deaths were recorded among 678 cases of rheumatic fever.[11] However, at least two-thirds of all cases of rheumatic fever in childhood develop permanent valve damage.[12] Modern advances in cardiac surgery have permitted seriously damaged heart valves to be repaired or replaced with artificial ones. Penicillin is highly effective in the treatment of streptococcal throat infections, and since its introduction in 1944, the incidence of rheumatic fever has declined dramatically.[13] Fleming, Florey, and Chain were jointly awarded a Nobel Prize in 1945 for their work in developing penicillin.

Thomas Sydenham, the father of English clinical medicine, first recognized St. Vitus' Dance as a rheumatic manifestation in 1686. Sydenham's chorea occurs in about 19 percent of cases of rheumatic fever. (Mozart showed no evidence of it.) It is an affection of the brain characterized by bizarre involuntary movements, incoordination of voluntary movements, and a variable degree of muscular weakness and mental disturbance. Chorea most commonly occurs in female children between five and fifteen years of age, or sometimes in young adults, especially pregnant women. In Germany between the fourteenth and seventeenth centuries, men and women afflicted with St. Vitus' Dance used to wander in troops from town to town, and dance to the sound of musical instruments in the streets and churches. They were encouraged to continue dancing to the point of exhaustion, in the hope of being cured of their malady.[14] In South America during the eighteenth century, the tribes in Patagonia chose boys afflicted with epilepsy and St. Vitus' Dance to be trained as sorcerers. They wore female apparel, and later assumed the power of curing diseases by means of incantations accompanied by the noise of rattles and drums.[15]

Interior of the Rotunda in Ranelagh Gardens, London
Engraving by J. Chereau, Paris, 1760, after Bernardo Bellotto, called Canaletto. Photograph by Mario Cotela. Ranelagh Gardens was an amusement park on the banks of the Thames at Chelsea. It opened in 1742. Mozart gave a harpsichord and organ recital there on 29 June 1764, for a benefit concert. (Courtesy Mario Cotela.)

3

THE GRAND TOUR ILLNESSES,
1763–1766

Following the successful visits to Munich and Vienna, Leopold Mozart became increasingly interested in further travel, which he saw as the logical extension of his childrens' education. He became convinced that it was his obligation to thank God for the miracle of His creation by proclaiming his two prodigies to the world. Then, too, travel offered potential fame and fortune, as well as a release from the boredom of life in Salzburg. Leopold was very ambitious and was keen to place his son in good stead for an appointment later as a Kapellmeister.

It would be wrong for us to assume that Leopold deliberately jeopardized his family's health. On the contrary, he gave priority to avoiding fatigue and always planned a few days rest between engagements to keep the children well. However, he did underestimate the potential hazards of such journeys, for the state of medical knowledge in the eighteenth century was very crude, as we will see. The four tours between 1762 and 1771 were to occupy seven years of Wolfgang's life, no doubt contributing to the early maturation of his musical genius. He was paraded and exhibited around the courts of Austria and Europe, but during these travels, he was exposed to the numerous endemic and epidemic diseases of the times. Travelers were at particular risk of contracting an endemic disease, since they often lacked the immunity of the local population. These journeys were usually undertaken in uncomfortable carriages or draughty river boats, amidst all extremes of weather. The inns and concert halls were often appallingly deficient in terms of facilities for heating, ventilation, and hygiene.

On 9 June 1763, the Mozart family set out in their own carriage on the Grand Tour of Europe; they did not return home until 29 November

1766. Their route included visits to Wasserburg, Munich (ten days), Augsburg (fourteen days), Ulm, Ludwigsburg, Bruchsal, Schwetzingen, Heidelberg, Frankfurt (21 days), and Mainz (14 days). They arrived at Coblenz at midday on 17 September, and two days later Woferl developed catarrh. The children gave a concert on 21 September, and by the following evening the boy was suffering with a head cold, so that they rested at the Three Imperial Crowns Inn for five more days, during atrociously wet weather.

The Mozart family traveled on to Brussels by way of Bonn, Cologne, and Louvain. In Brussels they stayed more than a month and lodged at the Hotel de L'Angleterre. They finally reached Paris on 18 November, by way of Mons, Bonavis, and Gournay. A terrible shock awaited them in the French capital.

In Paris, the Mozarts were invited to stay with the Bavarian ambassador, Count van Eyck, in the Hotel Beauvais.[1] The Countess van Eyck was especially captivated by Woferl and gave him a pocket calendar printed in Liège. The countess, the daughter of Count Arco, the lord chamberlain in Salzburg, was particularly kind to the Mozarts. After remaining indoors for the last few days of January 1764, she was suddenly taken ill with coughing blood (hemoptysis) and died six days later, on 6 February. All of the Mozart family, especially Woferl, were heartbroken and frightfully upset. Such a short illness in a previously robust woman would suggest that her death was due to a serious acute lung infection such as bronchopneumonia.

On the morning of 16 February, Wolfgang awakened with a sore throat. He was ill with a high fever and had difficulty breathing so that he was in danger of choking (angina lacunaris). Nannerl was also afflicted, but her illness was less severe and she was not feverish. After four days in bed Wolfgang felt much better and was allowed up; he was well again by 22 February. Leopold consulted Dr. Herrnschwand, a German physician to the Swiss Guards, who made two visits. Leopold also administered a small dose of Vienna laxative water.

These symptoms are in keeping with a severe attack of follicular tonsillitis, and the difficulty in breathing suggests that his tonsils were quite enlarged and swollen, so that he may even have developed quinsy (peritonsillar abscess).[2] In the pre-antibiotic era such enlarged tonsils were likely to harbor pockets of pus, creating a tendency to develop recurrent or chronic tonsillitis. Such patients presented the risk of developing local complications or systemic manifestations as a result of toxic absorption (blood poisoning—bacteremia or septicemia). The nasty local complications of tonsillitis included cervical adenitis, peritonsillar or parapharyngeal abscess, otitis media (middle ear infection), sinusitis, rhinitis, tracheitis, laryngitis, mastoiditis, meningitis, and bronchopneumonia. A tonsillectomy was indicated in patients with chronic or recurrent tonsillitis, in order to prevent such complications.

Quinsy was described by Hippocrates, while the Roman physician, Aulus Cornelius Celcus, gave an excellent description of tonsillectomy in his treatise written in Latin in the first century. Dr. Philip Syng Physick devised the forerunner of the modern guillotine operation for tonsillectomy in Pennsylvania.

Follicular tonsillitis is associated with the presence of tonsillar exudate and is commonly due to infection with the streptococcus pyogenes. The high prevalence of streptococcal infection in the eighteenth century was related not only to the pathogenicity of this organism, but also to its wide distribution in nature. About 10 percent of adults were carriers; nasal carriers were more contagious than throat carriers, since they were likely to disseminate droplet infection when they sneezed. The carrier rate in children was much higher. However, other bacteria or viruses can also be responsible for exudative tonsillitis. Since the advent of penicillin, both the incidence of the serious complications of tonsillitis and the need for tonsillectomy have declined.

After a financially rewarding five months in Paris, Leopold decided to go to the English capital. They were all violently seasick during a fearful channel crossing in a privately hired boat and arrived in London on 23 April 1764.

Wolfgangerl was unable to play at a benefit concert on 20 May because of illness. It may have been a recurrence of tonsillitis, and he was indisposed for ten days. On 29 June Wolfgang played at a concert for the benefit of the Lying-in Hospital, Surrey. This concert was given in the Rotunda of Ranelagh Gardens on the Thames at Chelsea. The foundation-stone of this hospital was laid in 1765. The boy was hailed as the most extraordinary prodigy and the most amazing genius that ever appeared.

Leopold became ill on the evening of Sunday, 8 July 1764, while attending a concert at Mylord Thanet's in Grosvenor Square. Sackville Tufton (1733-86), who had become the eighth earl of Thanet in 1753, was devoted to the arts. Leopold suffered with fever and chills, and he began sweating profusely. He buttoned up his cloth coat over his silk waistcoat and was carried home in a hired sedan-chair. For six days he attempted to cure himself by taking his favorite household remedies, but when the fever persisted he consulted a physician. Leopold was diagnosed as having a severe inflammation of the throat. He was treated with enemas, laxatives, and venesections (blood-lettings), methods of treatment which at that time were invoked to drive out fever. By 3 August his fever had indeed subsided, but after such drastic shock therapy it is little wonder that he felt weak and exhausted. He was encouraged to eat more to gain strength, but his loss of appetite persisted. The physician told Leopold that he had contracted the kind of "cold" that sometimes develops into "consumption." In her reminiscences of 1792 Nannerl referred to it as a dangerous throat ailment.

In London at that time it was customary for debilitated patients to be sent to the country or the continent for convalescence. Chelsea then was a delightful garden-village situated just two miles from London. So it was that the Mozart family moved into the house of Dr. Randal in Fivefields-Row (now 180 Ebury Street). They stayed for seven weeks, by which time Leopold had fully recovered.

The cause of Leopold's serious illness is not obvious, but a few possibilities come to mind. The English doctors may have been correct, for it could have been tuberculosis. In 1655, the term *consumption* was nonspecific, referring to a progressive wasting disease of the body. However, by 1680 the term was more specifically applied to describe the presence of phthisis (pulmonary consumption).[3] Leopold was an astute observer and was well versed in Latin medical terminology. He diagnosed "Febrem Lentam," which translates simply as an obstinate or persistent fever. The earliest manifestations of active pulmonary tuberculosis are often constitutional symptoms such as fatigue, weight loss, fever, and night sweats. If the body's defense mechanisms manage to overcome the infection before caseation, necrosis, and cavitation have occurred, then the characteristic symptoms of chronic cough and hemoptysis may not develop. The German physician Robert Koch (1843-1910) first isolated and cultured the tubercle bacillus in his Berlin laboratory in 1882. Tuberculous ulceration of the throat is uncommon, and it develops secondary to an active focus in the lungs or elsewhere in the body. Primary tuberculosis of the tonsils was occasionally acquired by the ingestion of contaminated milk. Other possible diagnoses of Leopold's illness include glandular fever (first described in 1889 by E. Pfeiffer), or the nonfulminant form of diphtheria, or even scarlet fever (not all patients develop the rash).

During Leopold's convalescence at Chelsea, Woferl was busily engaged composing his symphonies in E-flat (K. 16) and in D (K.19). The strong influence of Johann Christian Bach is evident in these first orchestral works. The children were commanded to keep very quiet and were not allowed to play the clavier. Nannerl had to copy out the music as she sat at her brother's side. On one occasion he said to her: "Remind me to give the horn something worthwhile to do!"[4]

During the month of June, Daines Barrington visited the Mozarts and took the opportunity to evaluate Wolfgang's genius at some length. He read his paper to the Royal Society of Medicine in London on 15 February 1770.[5] Barrington, who was a lawyer, magistrate, and writer, attested to the boy's incredible gifts with regard to sight reading, thorough knowledge of the principles of composition, mastery of modulation, and powers of extemporary composition. He was also astounded by the child's amazing execution on the harpsichord with little fingers that could hardly reach a fifth. Barrington also recounted

two instances of normal childish behavior. While playing the harpsichord, a favorite cat came into the room, whereupon Wolfgang left
the instrument to play with the cat; nor could he be induced to return to
the clavier for some considerable time. He would also sometimes run
around the room with a stick between his legs by way of a horse.

On 19 July 1765, the manuscript of "God Is Our Refuge" (K. 20) was
presented to the British Museum, where it is now preserved, together
with the three engraved volumes of sonatas (K. 6-15) and the Paris group
portrait by Delafosse after Carmontelle.[6]

After a fifteen-month stay, the Mozarts left London on 24 July 1765.
They attended the Canterbury horse races and reached Calais on 1
August, after a 3½-hour channel crossing. Leopold had special prayers
offered for a smooth passage; on this occasion there was no seasickness,
so that they were able to enjoy their lunch at Calais.

Leopold had originally intended to travel on to Italy, but a Dutch
envoy persuaded him to visit the princess of Weilburg in the Hague.
However, the Mozarts were delayed for a month in Lille by an illness
first contracted by Wolfgang and then afflicting his father. Soon after
their arrival in early August, Woferl came down with a very bad cold
which persisted a few weeks. This may have been a further bout of
tonsillitis, complicated by sinusitis or quinsy. Before the child had
recovered it was Leopold's turn. He suffered severe bouts of vomiting as
well as attacks of dizziness and vertigo. These symptoms suggest an
acute inflammation of the inner ear. Such acute labyrinthitis may have
been secondary to tonsillitis complicated by sinusitis or middle ear
infection.[7] Leopold initially treated himself with purgatives and
footbaths, and then later consulted a Dr. Merlin.

Much later, when Leopold Mozart was again troubled with dizziness in
September 1781, Wolfgang recommended two remedies that were then
prevalent in Vienna:

—get some cart-grease, wrap it in a bit of paper and wear it on your chest. Take
the bone of a leg of veal and wrap it up in paper with a kreuzer's worth of
leopard's bane and carry it in your pocket. I am sure that this will cure you.[8]

Vertigo is characterized by a consciousness of disordered orientation of
the body in space, usually with a sense of rotation, either of the person or
surroundings. During a bad attack it is not possible to stand upright or
walk. There are often associated jerky oscillatory eye movements
(nystagmus) and visceral disturbances such as pallor, sweating, vomiting, or even diarrhea.

The Mozart family crossed the border into Holland on 4 September
1765. They enjoyed the change of scenery and were impressed with the
meticulous cleanliness of the Dutch people. From Rotterdam they

traveled by barge to the Hague where they arrived on the evening of 10 September.

Two days later Maria Anna (Nannerl) appeared to have caught a cold. Initially, it did not seem very troublesome, and she did not take to her bed. However, a change for the worse came on 26 September, when she developed fever and chills. Leopold put her to bed and called in a Dr. Haymann, who had been recommended by several foreign envoys. The doctor bled her on 28 September with some improvement of her pulse, but the fever persisted. Her condition deteriorated, so that Dr. Haymann gave up all hope. Nannerl was aware of her critical condition, and her parents discussed with her the possibility of her dying. She received Holy Communion and was annointed on 21 October. Leopold prepared her to resign herself to God's will, convincing her of the vanity of this world and the happy death of children, who would go straight to heaven where they would enjoy perfect happiness forever. Meanwhile, Wolfgang was intent with his music in the next room.

At 5:00 P.M. on 21 October, Leopold arranged a consultation with the retired Professor Thomas Schwenke and his successor Dr. Cornelius Velsen. Leopold was very impressed with Dr. Schwenke, who had been recommended by the princess of Weilburg and who had formerly been physician to the court and professor emeritus of anatomy. Leopold, grateful for his knowledge of Latin, followed the consultation in detail. Indeed, he contradicted Dr. Haymann when he inaccurately described Nannerl's symptoms, such as presence or absence of pain. Dr. Schwenke took Nannerl's hand and felt her pulse. He then put on his glasses and examined her eyes, tongue, and face. There was talk of a skin rash and pocks on the lung (pneumonia). Throughout the consultation, Nannerl was delirious and recounted her travel impressions in German, French, and English. Some of her utterances caused laughter despite the seriousness of the situation. Through the medicines Dr. Schwenke prescribed, Nannerl slowly began to improve. By 8 November she was able to get out of bed and attempt to walk; her recovery was complete by 12 December.

Wolfgang was even more severely afflicted with this illness and first showed signs of it on 15 November. Leopold had at first treated him with black and margrave powders. On 23 November, Dr. Schwenke was very concerned, and a week later the child's condition was critical. From 1 December he was in a coma and delirious. Over the next two months he became so emaciated that he was hardly recognizable. Leopold had to take great care of his mouth. His tongue had to be constantly moistened because it was dirty and looked like dry wood. On three occasions the skin of his lips became hard and black, and was shed. However, Wolfgang also recovered, and by the middle of January his health was so much better that the canceled September concert was announced for 22

January. Throughout both illnesses, the Mozart parents remained in their turn at their sick child's bedside in six-hour shifts. They found strength in prayer and arranged for several masses to be offered.

The prolonged fever, severe toxemia, slow pulse, delirium, skin rash, pneumonia, hemorrhagic exfoliation of the oral mucous membrane, and prolonged convalescence which Wolfgang and Nannerl experienced all compound to make a diagnosis of endemic typhoid fever almost certain.[9] Alternative diagnoses of typhus fever[10] or streptococcal infection seem much less likely.[11]

The typhoid bacillus was first identified in 1880 by Carl Joseph Eberth (1835-1926). Typhoid fever is confined to the human species, and there is no animal host. The ultimate source of infection is a patient with the disease or a typhoid carrier. Some cases continue to excrete bacilli in their feces or urine for six to twelve months, or longer. In Mozart's time, these convalescent cases and carriers continued to provide a source of infection in endemic areas. A contaminated food handler is particularly dangerous. One of the best known carriers was a female cook named "Typhoid Mary," who between 1900 and 1907 in the United States infected at least twenty-six persons, one of whom died. The incidence of typhoid fever in a community was related to the standard of hygiene, particularly to the efficiency of sewage disposal. For example, in England and Wales during the decade of 1871-80, the average annual death rate from typhoid fever, per million living, was 332. By 1941-50, the rate had fallen to 2. The rise of modern hygiene in Europe began in mid-eighteenth century.[12]

Wolfgang composed his Symphony in B-flat (K. 22) at the Hague, while convalescing from typhoid fever. The family was invited to the six days of festivities to celebrate the eighteenth birthday of Prince William V of Orange in March. Wolfgang was commissioned by the court to compose six sonatas for clavier and violin, which were engraved as Opus 4 (K. 26-31) and dedicated to Princess Caroline. The Mozarts returned to Paris and Versailles via Antwerp and Brussels. After a month in Lyons, they traveled to Switzerland, where they saw the aftermath of the Civil War in Geneva. They proceeded to Bavaria via Zurich, Ulm, and Augsburg, and arrived in Munich on 8 November 1766.

On the day after their arrival, Wolfgang played before the Elector Maximilian III Joseph. That night the child was restless in bed and awakened ill with fever and rheumatism. Woferl could not stand on his feet or move his toes or knees. He was very hot and feverish, and could not sleep for four nights. Leopold wrote that this illness was similar to the one the child had suffered in Salzburg in January 1763. The boy was kept indoors until 21 November and performed again before the elector on the following day. The planned trip to Regensburg was canceled on account of this illness, which appears to have been a second attack of rheumatic fever.[13] Both of Mozart's bouts appear to have been mild, however, so that it would appear unlikely that his heart was seriously affected (although manifest evidence of rheumatic heart disease may be delayed for several years after an attack of rheumatic fever).

The Mozart family arrived home in Salzburg on Sunday, 30 November 1766, after an absence of nearly forty-two months. What excitement they must have felt in showing their spoils to the people of Salzburg. These included nine gold pocket watches, twelve gold snuff boxes, and numerous gold rings set with precious stones. Nannerl had received earrings, necklaces, knives with gold blades, bottle holders, writing tackle, toothpick boxes, various gold objects, and writing tablets. The estimated value of these gewgaws was 12,000 florins. The most valuable item was a gold snuff box from King Louis XV of France, filled with 50 louis d'or (500 florins). The king had offered a proviso that, should Mozart ever want to sell it, it was to be returned to him in exchange for 100 louis d'or.

These financial gains were associated with Mozart's increasing mastery of harpsichord playing and maturation into a composer of astonishing ability. The courts of Europe had been swept off their feet by the Wunderlings, whose novelty, charm, beauty, and sheer brilliance had overcome all class barriers.

4

THE SMALLPOX EPIDEMIC
IN 1767

Leopold was determined that his eleven-year-old son would write an Italian opera, but he could see no such opportunity in Salzburg. The chances seemed good in Vienna, however, especially as Maria Theresa's ninth daughter, the Archduchess Maria Josepha, was to be married to King Ferdinand of Naples in the autumn of 1767. To honor that occasion splendid festivities including operas, plays, balls, and fireworks were scheduled. Accordingly, the Mozart family set out a second time for Vienna on 11 September, traveling in their own carriage with a servant. The next day they stopped for lunch at the Benedictine Abbey at Lambach. After a stopover at Linz, they lunched at Melk and then saw the famous Abbey, where Wolfgang played the organ. The Abbey had undergone an extensive reconstruction into its present form under the Abbot Berthold Dietmayr between 1700 and 1740. After a stopover at St. Pölten, they traveled via Purkersdorf to Vienna where they arrived on 15 September. The family lodged on the second floor of a goldsmith's house in the Weihburggasse. While waiting for an audience with the young Emperor Joseph II, they attended Johann Adolf Hasse's new opera *Partenope* at the Burgtheater; they also met Michael Haydn's fiancée Maria Magdalena Lipp and her family.

A smallpox epidemic was raging in Vienna at that time, and panic set in when Leopold discovered that the goldsmith's three children had contracted the disease. The elder son came down with it at the time of their arrival, and no doubt Wolfgang had been playing with the two smaller children. Leopold sought urgent advice, possibly from Maria Theresa's personal physician, Dr. Alexandre-Louis Laugier, who advised him to flee the city. Accordingly, Leopold took Wolfgang with all speed to Brünn on 23 October, leaving his servant with his wife and Nannerl. Leopold did not know that his son had already been infected, for the incubation period is usually twelve days (nine to fifteen days). Leopold chose Brünn because of two Salzburg connections there: Archbishop Sigismund's brother, Count Franz Anton Schrattenbach, and the daughter of Count Arco, who had married Count Alois Podstatsky-Liechtenstein. The latter count's brother was dean of the cathedral in Olmütz (Olomouc). On 25 October, the Mozart family was reunited at Brünn, and they then traveled to Olmütz, arriving the next day. They found accommodation in the Zum Schwarzen Adler Inn, a miserable damp room which they had to heat with a noisy, smoky stove.

No sooner had they arrived at Olmütz than Wolfgang became ill with smallpox. He was running a fever and complaining of sore eyes. Leopold, feeling an irregular pulse, administered black and margrave powders. The child's condition deteriorated, so that by 28 October he was delirious. After Mass on that day, Leopold approached the dean of Olmütz Cathedral for help. This aristocratic priest reassured him. Having no personal fear of smallpox, he insisted that the family move into the Deanery and forthwith dispatched his steward to prepare two rooms for them. In addition, the dean sent word to his own personal physician and asked him to visit Wolfgang forthwith at the inn. Later that afternoon, Leopold rugged Wolfgang up snugly and drove him to the Cathedral Deanery.

Dr. Joseph Wolff, an astute physician, rendered exemplary care. Wolfgang's eyesight was impaired for nine days; in order to protect his eyes from further injury, he was forbidden to read or write for several weeks. Mozart was most fortunate not to have suffered permanent blindness, which used to result from corneal ulceration, complicated by secondary bacterial infection. Indeed, in some parts of the subcontinent of India and in Algeria, smallpox was held to be responsible for a quarter of all cases of blindness. Wolfgang was laid up with the disease until 10 November. No sooner had he recovered than Nannerl came down with it, although her attack was less severe. Nannerl later wrote that her formerly handsome brother became permanently disfigured by the smallpox. Unfortunately, the eruption is characteristically more severe on the face and lower parts of the arms and legs; the armpits and groin may be entirely spared. Wolfgang thanked Dr. Wolff for his kind attention by composing for him the song "An Die Freude" (K. 53), to words by J. P. Uz.

During Wolfgang's convalescence from smallpox, he was visited daily by Johann Leopold Hay, the bishop's secretary. Hay taught him all sorts of card tricks and games, while later he also learned fencing. Later, in 1780, Hay was appointed bishop of Königgrätz, and he became famous as one of the most tolerant, enlightened, wise, and kind ecclesiastical princes of his age.

On 23 December 1767, the Mozarts left Olmütz. They arrived at Brünn on Christmas Eve where they took lodgings with Count Franz Anton Schrattenbach, who later became governor of Moravia. They remained two weeks with the count and were cordially treated by the nobility. On 30 November, a concert was arranged, and on this occasion the Mozart children were accompanied by the musicians of Brünn, much to everyone's admiration. The prior of Sternberg, Aurelius Augustinius, who attended that concert, attested that Wolfgang showed his dislike of the trumpets, because they were incapable of keeping in time with each other. The Mozarts departed from Brünn in their carriage in a snowstorm on 9 January 1768, and after a stopover at Poysdorf, they arrived in Vienna the next day where they would remain for a year. They took lodgings in the Red Sabre House, at what is now Wipplingerstrasse 19, at the corner of Färbergasse. Mozart would again take lodgings there on 23 July 1782, twelve days before his marriage.

The Mozarts were received at court on the afternoon of 19 January for three hours. The Emperor Joseph II himself led them into the audience which was attended by the Empress Maria Theresa, her son-in-law Prince Albert of Saxony, and all the archduchesses. The empress was most cordial and chatted informally to mother Mozart about her children's smallpox and the Grand Tour, while Joseph II spoke to Leopold and the children about music and other matters, at times causing Nannerl to blush. The emperor half proposed that Mozart should write an opera, so that a contract was eventually signed with the leaseholder of the court theater, Giuseppe Affligio. A fee of 100 ducats was agreed on, and Wolfgang quickly set to work on *La Finta Semplice* (K. 51), an opera buffa in three acts, with libretto by Marlo Coltellini after the original written by Carlo Goldoni. By July 1768, the introductory sinfonia and the twenty-six arias spanning 558 pages were complete. A mini-rehearsal of the work was held in the home of Baron Gottfried van Swieten, who would later supervise Mozart's funeral. However, Affligio blocked the production of the opera, and both Leopold and Wolfgang suffered frustrations and disappointments after a series of postponements. Even a written petition to the emperor by Leopold on 21 September was of no avail, and the twelve-year-old boy's opera was not to be produced in Vienna. Affligio was a terrible rogue and scoundrel, and in 1779 he was condemned to life servitude in the galleys for forging bills of exchange in Florence.

It was little wonder that the Emperor Joseph II shuddered at the mention of smallpox. His beloved wife, Isabella of Parma, the Bourbon granddaughter of Louis XV, had contracted that disease in November 1763 while in her second pregnancy. His daughter Marie Antoinette, and his sister, the Archduchess Marie Christine, were also afflicted, but they survived. On the third day of her illness Isabella gave premature birth to a stillborn daughter, and five days later she died in the arms of her husband. Earlier that year, Joseph's sister, the fourteen-year-old Archduchess Johanna, had died with typhus.

The Empress Maria Theresa also had poignant reasons to sympathize with Mozart's mother about the recent illnesses of her prodigies. The empress's uncle Joseph I had died suddenly of smallpox in 1711, during the War of the Spanish Succession. Maria Theresa's father had intended her to marry Clement of Lorraine, but the youth died of smallpox on the eve of his first visit to Vienna. She subsequently married Clement's brother, Francis (1708-65). Nor was Joseph II's unfortunate second wife, Maria Josepha of Bavaria, to be spared from the ravaging path of destruction. Maria Theresa was present when smallpox became manifest in Josepha, and she stayed to kiss and comfort her daughter-in-law. Within a week the empress herself came down with a severe attack of smallpox which brought her close to death. At the height of Maria Theresa's crisis, her daughter-in-law Josepha died. The strong empress rallied and survived. She attended a Grand Mass of Thanksgiving in St. Stephen's Cathedral. Prince Albert of Saxony, who had come from Pressburg to visit his mother-in-law, also contracted smallpox, though in milder form.

The splendid celebration and rejoicing resumed in September, when the formal betrothal of the Archduchess Maria Josepha to King Ferdinand of Naples was announced. Unfortunately, Josepha accompanied her mother to the crypt to pay their last respects to Joseph's deceased wife. The sarcophagus had not been finally sealed, and in October the young royal bride-to-be contracted smallpox. Maria Theresa, herself nursed her daughter, but Josepha died on the eleventh day of her illness, on 15 October.

The Archduchess Elizabeth, who was renowned for her beauty, contracted smallpox from her sister. Although she survived, she was dreadfully disfigured by the scars of this disease, so that she never married.

The dreaded smallpox or variola is a highly contagious viral disease characterized by fever, toxemia, and a characteristic skin eruption. There are two forms, variola major and minor. There is documentation of smallpox in the ancient world, and three Egyptian mummies from the eighteenth to the twentieth dynasties show evidence of a generalized pustular eruption, consistent with the disease. It was described by the noted physician Galen of Pergamon in the second century, while reliable accounts of smallpox were written, among others, by Ko Hung in China in 340 and by Rhazes of Baghdad in 910. The disease spread from Asia to Europe and North Africa in the Middle Ages, becoming prevalent in the sixteenth century.[1] Smallpox was introduced into the West Indies by African slaves and from there into Mexico and South America. During the epidemics in England in the eighteenth century, over 90 percent of the cases occurred in children under ten years of age, and at that time variola was responsible for one-third of all deaths in children. In 1752, a serious epidemic occurred in the United States, when over 30 percent of the inhabitants of Boston, Massachusetts, were affected, with a mortality rate of over 30 percent. Five epidemics of smallpox occurred in Australia between 1789 and 1917.[2] The disease was so feared by the aborigines that a special song "Nguitkurra" was chanted in the hope of protection.[3]

The skin lesions of smallpox occur in single crops and initially appear as macules. Over a period of ten days they evolve into papules, then vesicles, and finally pustules. The stage of pustule formation corresponds to secondary bacterial infection, usually by streptococci or staphylococci, and blood cultures are positive for these organisms at this stage. This secondary bacterial infection is an important cause of death. In fatal cases pneumonia is common, while septicemia (blood poisoning), kidney abscesses, and endocarditis (infection of the heart valves) occur in some cases. It is the healing of the skin pustules that causes the depressed scars and pitting, with consequent disfigurement.

Smallpox is spread to contacts of infectious patients through droplet infection from respiratory discharges, through direct skin to skin contact, and through infectious clothing and bed linen used by patients. The virus can be disseminated by aerial convection currents within buildings. In endemic areas it was associated with overcrowding, poverty, ignorance, and lack of hygiene.

The elector of Saxony Frederick Christian had died of smallpox on 7 December 1763. The Mozart family were present in the Royal Gallery of the chapel at Versailles on Christmas Day, when King Louis broke the sad news to the dauphine of her brother's death. Leopold had been encouraged to have his children inoculated against smallpox in Paris, where it was the fashion. However, he refused, saying: "I leave the matter to the grace of God. It depends on His grace whether He wishes to keep this marvel of nature in the world in which He has placed it, or to take it to Himself."[4] Prior to the epidemic in Vienna, Dr. Gerhard van Swieten had also been opposed to inoculation, but he soon changed his mind when the empress nearly died of the disease. He applied to Sir William Pringle, physician to George III, who sent a skilled practitioner to Vienna to perform inoculations. Maria Theresa's younger children were variolated, and free inoculations were offered to the children of the poor. Even so 2,330 deaths from smallpox occurred in Vienna in 1806.

Infection with smallpox leads to life-long immunity for the disease. During the tenth century in China, the first method of immunization was developed. Smallpox scabs were pulverized into a powder, which was administered by nasal insufflation, as a secret rite. Variolation was developed in India during the sixteenth century, and the practice spread to southwestern Asia and Egypt. Pustular material from a case was inoculated into the skin by puncture. Following an incubation period of eight days, there developed a febrile illness with a general, usually nonpustular skin eruption on the ninth day. The technique was introduced into England in 1721, soon after Lady Mary Wortley Montagu (1689-1762) had studied it at Constantinople. Variolation then became recognized on the continent, and in 1738 it was used successfully in Charleston, South Carolina, with material that had been allowed to dry. Unfortunately, some people were highly susceptible to variolation and 1 to 2 percent of inoculated subjects died with smallpox. The advocates of variolation, of course, argued that this was a significant advance, since the mortality of naturally acquired smallpox was 10 to 30 percent.

Such was the state of affairs when the English country practitioner Edward Jenner came onto the scene. When apprenticed to a country surgeon, Jenner heard of the belief that infection with cow pox conferred immunity against smallpox. Cow pox was a naturally occurring disease of the udders of cows. On 14 May 1796, Jenner vaccinated a boy named James Phipps with lymph taken from the cow pox vesicles on the finger of a dairymaid, Sarah Nelmes. Phipps developed a typical cow pox pustule, familiar to those who have been vaccinated. On 1 July, Jenner inoculated the boy with smallpox vesicular fluid, and he did not develop the disease. Jenner subsequently proceeded to inoculate other persons with cow pox matter taken from infected cows. Such was the birth of smallpox vaccination.[5] Jenner's studies were published in 1798. Variolation was outlawed in England in 1840. Although modern smallpox vaccines have been found to be effective and safe, vaccination should be performed neither during the first six months of pregnancy, nor in patients with eczema or leukemia, nor in those undergoing immunosuppressive therapy.

In 1959, the World Health Organization adopted a resolution calling for the global eradication of smallpox. Undeterred by the immense difficulties of such a task, they realized their ambition in December 1979, when it was officially certified that smallpox had been eradicated from the world. The remarkable success of this campaign must surely be heralded as one of the greatest achievements in the history of medicine.[6]

5

EIGHTEENTH-CENTURY MEDICINE

During the eighteenth and nineteenth centuries, Vienna achieved fame as a leading center not only in music, but also in medicine. In about the middle of the nineteenth century, Vienna again became the leading European center for medical teaching, with the rise of the new Vienna School of Medicine under such distinguished authorities as Christian Albert Theodor Billroth (Surgery), Ferdinand von Hebra (Dermatology), Josef Hyrtl (Anatomy), Carl Koller (Local Anesthesia), Karl von Rokitansky (Pathology), Josef Skoda (Medicine), Ignaz Philipp Semmelweis (Puerperal Fever), Anton Weichselbaum (Bacteriology), and, of course, Sigmund Freud and Alfred Adler (Psychiatry). However, since Mozart became personally acquainted with some of its members, it is appropriate for us now to discuss the Old Vienna School of Medicine.

THE OLD VIENNA SCHOOL OF MEDICINE

The noted Dutch physician Gerhard van Swieten (1700-72) studied medicine in his native Leyden and at Lyons, where he became the outstanding pupil of Boerhaave, a disciple of Thomas Sydenham. Van Swieten achieved fame through his lectures in anatomy and pathology. In 1744, he was summoned to Brussels to attend Maria Theresa's beloved sister, Princess Marianne, who had fallen seriously ill shortly before being confined. Despite every attempt to save her life, she died two months after having given birth to a stillborn infant.

In response to the enthusiastic admiration of Count Kaunitz, Maria Theresa invited Gerhard van Swieten to Vienna. He went there in 1745 and was appointed personal physician to the empress and director of the

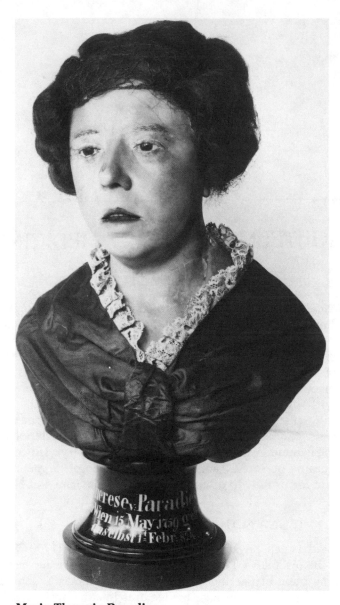

Maria Theresia Paradies
Wax bust. The blind Austrian pianist, composer, and singer was treated with temporary success by Dr. Franz Anton Mesmer. Mozart composed a piano concerto for her, presumably the one in B flat, K. 456. She is said to have played over sixty concertos from memory. (Courtesy of the Historischen Museen der Stadt, Vienna.)

court library. Van Swieten founded the Old Vienna School of Medicine, which soon attracted pupils from all over Europe. Dr. Anton de Haen of the Hague was appointed his assistant and did much to popularize the use of the thermometer in medicine. De Haen also introduced a methodology for the diagnosis of puzzling cases and gave learned autopsy demonstrations. A new anatomy school was built, and a high standard of medical teaching was developed.

The third member of the School, Dr. Leopold Auenbrugger, wrote an historical Inventum Novum in 1761, which clearly outlined the technique of percussing the chest with the fingers, in order to diagnose diseases of the thorax.[1] Dr. Auenbrugger was also musically gifted, and he wrote a libretto of Antonio Salieri's German Singspiel "Der Rauchfangkehrer" ("The chimney sweep").[2] Auenbrugger's two daughters, Caterina and Marianna, were also musically gifted; in 1780, they were honored by Joseph Haydn with his dedication of six piano sonatas, Opus 30.[3]

Dr. Gerhard van Swieten went on to write his famous "Commentary on the Aphorisms of Boerhaave" which was published in Paris in 1759. His son Gottfried became one of Mozart's most important patrons, and introduced Wolfgang to several of the works of Bach and Handel.

The Old Vienna School of Medicine reached further fame through Maximilian Stoll and was institutionalized by the Emperor Joseph II with the inauguration of the Allgemeine Krankenhaus (the Vienna General Hospital), and the Josephinium for military surgery. By the time it opened in 1784 under Stoll, Vienna had set a model for all of Europe of a hospital devoted not only to teaching, but also to the care of the underprivileged.

The outstanding pioneer in the field of communal hygiene was Dr. Johann Peter Frank, who became head of the General Hospital and professor in the university. Between 1779 and 1817, Frank published the six volumes of his *Complete System of Medical Policy* in which he wrote at length about the state's responsibility in safeguarding all aspects of the health of its subjects by regulations and legislation.

THE JACQUIN FAMILY

Dr. Gerhard van Swieten won the loyalty and trust of Maria Theresa and was appointed chief censor. The Dutch physician was given free reign not only in the reform of the medical faculty of Vienna University, but also in the realm of general secular education. Van Swieten instigated the appointment of the famous Leyden botanist, Baron Nikolaus Joseph von Jacquin to the Chair of Chemistry. Under the patronage of Emperor Francis I, von Jacquin designed and was appointed curator of the Botanical Gardens in the Renweg. He was succeeded in this post by his younger son, Joseph Franz. The Jacquins were a musical family, and the baron's other two children, Gottfried and Franziska, became pupils and close personal friends of Mozart.

AN OPERATIVE DEATH IN VIENNA

When Prince Archbishop Colloredo journeyed to Vienna in the summer of 1773, Leopold Mozart and his illustrious son could not resist the temptation to follow. They arrived in the Austrian capital on 16 July, and the next day they took supper with Dr. Franz Anton Mesmer, who played a glass harmonica for them which he had recently purchased for 50 ducats. On 4 August they lunched with Mesmer's friend, Dr. Leopold Auenbrugger.

The hazards of surgery during the eighteenth century are well illustrated by the case of the Salzburg physician, Franz Joseph Niderl von Aichegg, whom the Mozarts visited on 6 September. He had come to Vienna for an operation which was performed four days later. The poor man died during the operation. His death may have been due to shock or cardiac arrest related to inadequate anesthesia, or inhalation of gastric (stomach) contents, causing respiratory arrest, or massive hemorrhage. Robert Liston was the first surgeon in England to employ ether anesthesia, while chloroform was discovered in the 1830s and introduced as an anesthetic agent by the Scottish obstetrician and gynecologist, James Young Simpson.

DR. FRANZ ANTON MESMER

Franz Anton Mesmer (1734-1815), a gamekeeper's son, was born in the Swabian district to the northeast of Lake Constance. His name has been perpetuated by posterity through the terms *mesmeric, mesmerism,* and *mesmerize.* He initially studied theology at the University of Ingolstadt and later went to Vienna where he studied medicine and natural science under Gerhard van Swieten and Anton de Haen. Mesmer's graduation thesis, "On the Influence of the Planets upon the Human Body," was read in 1766. He believed that this influence could be exerted on patients by use of a magnet. This in turn led to his idea that this same power could be exercised by the human hand, a power he called animal magnetism. Dr. Mesmer married a very wealthy widow, ten years his senior. They lived in a magnificent mansion in the Landstrasse suburb, entertaining in the grand style. Franz was also passionately fond of music, playing the cello, clavier, and musical glasses (glass harmonica).

In the spirit of the Enlightenment, there was pari passu with the decline of the ancien regime a burgeoning forward of the middle class who patronized the arts in competition with the aristocracy. The dawning of the great age of Central European instrumental music brought with it a change in opera toward the middle class. The heroic, mythological, and historical opera seria of the Baroque era was replaced by opera buffa, or opera comique, and singspiel. The Mesmers were enthusiastic patrons of music in Vienna.

Mozart composed his one-act German singspiel "Bastien und Bastienne" (K.50) during the late summer of 1768. The libretto by W. Weiskern was based on Rousseau's *Le Devin du Village,* and the singspiel was performed in the home of Dr. Mesmer in September or October of that year. The doctor was later to be given an honorable mention in Act 1 of *Così Fan Tutte* (K. 588). Not to be confused with Dr. Mesmer was his cousin, Joseph Mesmer, who was head of the school of St. Stephen's. The Mozarts distinguished him in their letters as "little Mesmer." Mozart and his father attended a concert in Mesmer's garden at midday on 18 August 1773, and on that occasion the Divertimento (K. 205) may have been performed.

Dr. Mesmer soon established a successful medical practice in Vienna, after having gained experience in assisting the court astronomer, Maximilian Hell, in his magnetotherapeutic treatments. Mesmer became celebrated when he cured his wife's companion, Fräulein Gesterlin, of an hysterical condition.[4] However, Mesmer's most famous patient was Maria Theresia von Paradies (1759-1824), the Austrian composer, pianist, organist, and singer. She was the daughter of the imperial court secretary, Josef von Paradies, and had been blind since the age of four. After several famous surgeons had attempted to cure her without success, she was brought to Mesmer as a patient. He took her into his own house and treated her with temporary success during 1778. The story of her recovery of sight is full of touching episodes such as the occasion when, on first seeing a dog, she remarked that its features were more agreeable to her than those of a man. However, the fame and success of Mesmer's unorthodox treatments drew opposition and hostility from the medical confraternity in Vienna, who brought pressure to bear on Maria Theresia's parents to have their daughter removed from his evil influence. Initially, they were reluctant to force the issue since their daughter was unwilling to leave, and they had witnessed an improvement in her sight. However, when it was rumored that their daughter might lose the disability pension that had been granted by her godmother, the Empress Maria Theresa, Josef von Paradies and his wife decided to extricate their daughter, who was forcefully removed from Mesmer's house in a violent scene. The young virtuosa's blindness recurred, and she never recovered despite further treatments.[5] An official court inquiry pronounced Mesmer a charlatan, and he was compelled to leave Vienna within twenty-four hours (the precise date is unknown).

During the late summer of 1783, Maria Theresia von Paradies departed from Vienna with her mother and her librettist Johann Riedinger on a Grand Concert Tour of Europe. Toward the end of September, they visited the "Mozart Dwelling House" in Salzburg. Maria Theresia requested a new concerto from Mozart, who at that time was visiting his family there. It is thought that Mozart obliged with the Piano Concerto in B-flat (K. 456) which he completed on 30 September 1784 at "Figaro House."[6]

Mesmer fled to Paris and soon established a lucrative practice there. He maintained that he could increase the flow of "magnetic fluid" to or from a patient, even at some distance hence. He further developed his thesis in a book, in which he expounded his twenty-seven famous propositions on animal magnetism.[7] For group therapy he invented "Mesmer's Baquet," a kind of trough filled with mirrors and iron rods, around which the patients would gather with linked hands to the accompaniment of an orchestra playing soft airs. Mesmer dressed in a coat of lilac silk, employed attractive young male assistants, and played the harmonica with great skill so as to touch the emotions. He used three techniques to transmit his magnetic power to the patient: the fixed gaze, a touch with his iron wand, or his famous "passes," in which he would stroke the patient's body with his hands in a ritualistic fashion. Dr. Mesmer was the pioneer of hypnotism, and he exercised a remarkable personal influence over the imagination of his patients. His most dramatic successes occurred in hysterical subjects, who are usually highly suggestible, and in whom he readily induced a somnambulistic trance. His methods caused much discussion in scientific circles. Indeed, a Royal Committee of inquiry was set up by the French Academy of Sciences to investigate him in 1784. The committee concluded that a magnetic fluid did not exist and that the effects attributed to animal magnetism during public treatments had their foundation in the imagination of excitable subjects, aided by the excitement and stimulation of physical touching.[8] An independent committee convened by the Royal Society of Medicine reached similar conclusions. During public treatments, the eerie crises were manifest by emotional outbursts of crying and laughing, together with such spectacular indications as hiccoughs, convulsions, sweating, expectorations, and evacuations. As an adjuvant to his magnetic treatments, Mesmer sometimes used baths, blood-lettings, and purgatives such as cream of tartar.

After the French Revolution in 1789, Mesmer fled to England under an assumed name. He published a new exposition in Germany, but it was coldly received, as a result of which he retired to Switzerland. Mesmer died in obscurity at Meersburg on 15 March 1815.

Later, in 1842, the term *Hypnotism* was coined by the British surgeon James Braid. At La Salpêtrière Hospital in Paris, the father of neurology, Jean-Martin Charcot, made extensive use of hypnosis in his pioneering studies into the elucidation of the nature of hysteria.[9] Hypnotism was later utilized and evaluated further by Ambroise August Liébault of Nancy and Sigmund Freud.

THE TREATMENT OF FEVERS

The efficacy of bed rest had been appreciated since medieval times, while analgesic draughts of opiates were prescribed for the symptomatic relief of pains, backaches, abdominal cramps, coughs, and severe headaches. Alcohol was often given liberally, either as wine diluted with water or as beer. Sweating was encouraged by both physical means and the prescription of diaphoretics. The first method included the taking of hot baths or the application to the skin of hot flannel cloths. The diaphoretics included various draughts, teas, tamarind water, violet juice, and juleps containing sage, mint, snake root, sarsparilla, or salt. The spontaneous occurrence of vomiting and diarrhea was considered a healthy sign, and if absent the effects were promoted by prescribing emetics and purgatives. Loss of appetite and nausea were also treated in this way, in the belief of counteracting the weakness and hypotonicity of the muscles of the stomach and intestines. Commonly used emetics included the root of ipecacuanha and various antimony preparations. Sometimes even stomach washouts were performed with saline or tartar emetic. The wide variety of purgatives included cream of tartar, aloes, rhubarb powder, senna, jalap, magnesium salts, and sodium sulphate. If the laxative failed to act, the bowel was evacuated with an enema administered through a clyster pipe.

Various blistering schedules were used with the aim of expelling noxious fever-producing humors from the body. The blisters were produced by the application to the skin of an adhesive dressing, which contained an intensely irritating powder or ointment made from mustard flour or cantharides. The blister was then repeatedly punctured so as to promote a free serous discharge.

It was appreciated that pyrexias were higher during the evenings than in the mornings and that hyperpyrexic states associated with a temperature in excess of 42 °C (107.6 °F) probably indicated a fatal termination. Physical methods of reducing the temperature were sometimes used, such as mopping the burning forehead with a cold compress, or using cold air draughts, or repeatedly douching the naked body with 5 gallon buckets of cold salted water.

During convalescence, a nourishing diet consisting of boiled eggs, fresh meat, milk, and bread was encouraged. Various tonics and bitters were prescribed, while fortified wines and roast meats were favored. Peruvian bark, which contained quinine, was a most popular tonic; for example, it was sometimes prescribed as a drachm taken hourly for six hours with port wine.

BLOOD-LETTINGS

The full antiphlogistic regimen of purging, dieting, and blood-lettings for the treatment of "inflammatory fevers" had its origin in the classical teachings of Hippocrates. However, various modifications were developed, especially in the management of the "low nervous fevers."

The sucking of impurities from the blood by leeching had been advocated by Arabic physicians in the thirteenth century for a variety of skin conditions, and the practice of leeching was introduced into France by Dr. Francois Joseph Victor Broussais (1772-1838). At the height of its popularity, over 40 million leeches were imported into France each year. During the summer of 1789, Constanze Mozart, who was in her fifth pregnancy, became ill with what sounds like a varicose ulcer in the region of her ankle. She was attended by Dr. Thomas Franz Closset, who applied leeches on 17 July, with apparent improvement of her condition.

Cupping, a method of blood-letting that was less cumbersome than venesection, was especially favored for the treatment of women. Heated cups were applied over sites of scarifications, and the blood was drawn by the vacuum created within the cup. The site of the application was varied according to the nature of the complaint. In 1811, Lorenzo da Ponte sustained fractured ribs and collar bone in a wagon accident. He was treated at Philadelphia by a Dr. Philip S. Physick with twelve cuppings on his two sides.[10]

Periodic venesections were encouraged to promote the body's health, by releasing an excessive buildup of corrupted humours and fluids. Complicated charts were drawn up to advise the physician as to the most opportune time to perform such blood-lettings. Such variables as the signs of the zodiac, the dates of eclipse of the sun and moon, and the prevalent dictates of astronomy and astrology were apt to be taken into consideration. Such periodic blood-lettings would seldom have caused any harm, although any subjective feeling of well-being would have been due to placebo effect, emanating from within the subject's imagination.

Venesections were best known for their therapeutic use in the management of febrile illnesses. Qualified physicians did not always themselves perform the blood-lettings; they were sometimes delegated to a surgeon, or a barber-surgeon, or a barber or bath-attendant. The vein was distended into prominence by the application of a tourniquet; in difficult cases, hot towels were also applied. Blood was commonly taken from the basilic vein above the elbow, but the site was varied according to the complaint. Nose bleeds were favored for the treatment of mental disorders, whereas the sublingual veins under the tongue were used in some cases of throat inflammation. Sometimes the physician considered it important to study such physical characteristics of the blood as color, consistency, taste, smell, temperature, clotting, and caking. Toward this end, the blood was sometimes collected into a series of special beakers or dishes. Occasionally, the blood was even strained through a cloth, so as to isolate any impurities.[11]

There is no doubt that venesections contributed to the deaths of countless numbers of people. The British physiologist, Marshall Hall (1790-1857), who was one of the first to denounce the prevalent practice of blood-letting, described the lancet as "a minute instrument of mighty mischief."[12] We will see how venesections contributed to the deaths of Mozart and his mother. In the 1980s, venesections are still used in the treatment of hemochromatosis and polycythemia.[13]

INFANT FEEDING

During the eighteenth century, newborn infants were sometimes subjected to quite extraordinary practices. For example, soon after birth, the baby would be given sips of wine or spiritous liquors, or a dab of butter and sugar, or a little oil, or panada or caudle, or even a little roast pig to cure it of all the mother's longings! It was commonly believed that infants should be stuffed until they spewed.

In Salzburg at that time, breast feeding was unpopular, and it was a common practice to feed the infants with pap. According to the method of Van Helmont, pap was made as follows: bread was lightly boiled in beer or wine, and then meal and sugar were added so as to produce a mucilaginous consistency. This basic stock could be diluted with water to produce a drink. Pap was administered in specially made feeding bottles, boats, or spoons made from silver or pewter. The use of a polished cow's horn, fitted with an artificial nipple, was also popular. The opponents of milk feeding argued that milk curdled in the stomach and was contaminated with the vices and evil inclinations of the mother or wet nurse. Dr. Gerhard van Swieten argued against this ridiculous hypothesis and was a strong protagonist of breast feeding by the mother. However, for reasons of custom, pride, and indolence, it was then fashionable in Paris and London for mothers to hand their babies over to wet nurses to be breast fed. The mother was then free to socialize, play cards at night, and enjoy other diversions. In London, during the 1760s an average of 2,800 orphans and infant poor were admitted to the workhouses each year, but alas 2,690 of them died. An act of Parliament in 1767 obliged the parish officers of London and Westminster to send their infant poor to be nursed in the country, a measure that brought about a dramatic reduction of the annual deaths to 450.[14]

Leopold Mozart wrote a vivid account of his observations on the tragic consequences of wet-nursing in Paris:

There is an extreme love of comfort, which has caused this nation to turn a deaf ear to the voice of nature. Hence everyone in Paris sends new-born children to be reared in the country. Persons of both high and low rank do this and pay a bagatelle for it. But you see the wretched consequences of this practice. For you will hardly find any other city with so many miserable and mutilated persons. You have only to spend a minute in church or walk along a few streets to meet some blind or lame or limping or half-putrefied beggar, or to find someone lying on the street who had his hand eaten away as a child by the pigs, or someone else who in childhood fell into a fire and had half an arm burnt off while the foster-father and his family were working in the fields. And there are numbers of such people, whom disgust makes me refrain from looking at when I pass them.[15]

Many of the wet nursing institutions gained ill repute from excesses of alcoholism, prostitution, and venereal disease. By the beginning of the nineteenth century, all writers recognized maternal nursing as the best method of nourishment for infants. It was, of course, realized that not all mothers could breast feed their babies, and there was much discussion as to whether such infants should be wet nursed or be fed with animal's milk. With regard to the latter, cow's milk was most popular, but there were advocates for the milk of asses or goats.

In 1775, the administrators of the hospital at Aix became concerned that all their artificially fed foundlings were dying at 4½ months of age. The Faculty of Medicine of Paris appointed Dr. Le Roy to look into the problem. He reported that the infants' deaths were due to lack of the vital principle in milk, and counseled that the infants be fed from the udders of lactating goats. The cribs were arranged on the floor of a large room in two ranks. The bleating goats would enter the nursery and seek out their adopted infant; the goat would then push back the covering with its horns, straddle the crib, and give suck to the infant. Large numbers of healthy foundlings were subsequently reared at Aix by this method.

In 1786, the Italian physician M. Baldini advocated that the best animal milk could be obtained from a black cow with firm, solid flesh, bright eyes, and a swift step. In the nineteenth century, all writers attempted to depopularize the almost universal use of pap as the sole means of rearing infants.

INFANT MORTALITY

Only two of Anna Maria's seven children survived their infancy; Mozart and Constanze fared no better: only two of their six children lived beyond six months. In London and its suburbs, for the period from 1762 to 1771, there were 16,283 births per year but, alas, 7,987 (or 49 percent) of children under two years died, while the mortality of children under five years was an horrific 62 percent (10,145 children).[16] The leading killer diseases during the first year of life were infantile diarrhea, pneumonia, and tuberculosis. Famines following poor harvests contributed to the high mortality in Europe in the 1740s and 1770s, and the life expectancy in Germany during the eighteenth century was barely thirty-five years.[17]

Severe epidemics of infantile diarrhea, carrying a high mortality, were previously common in the summer months and in the autumn. Such epidemics were especially prevalent in overcrowded nurseries and were related to contamination of drinking water, milk, or feeding utensils. The presence of horse-dung in the city streets may have encouraged germ carrying by flies. While a broad spectrum of enteropathic microorganisms are responsible for these attacks of infantile gastroenteritis, the rota virus and other enteroviruses are commonly the origin. The bacterial enteropathogens include the bacillary dysenteries, *escherichia coli*, bovine tuberculosis, cholera, salmonella, and campylobacter. Occasionally, such parasites as giardia lamblia, ascariasis, and strongyloides are responsible. Premature and younger infants under six months of age are particularly vulnerable to this disorder.

EIGHTEENTH-CENTURY DENTISTRY

During the eighteenth century, dentistry was still the province of anyone who decided to do it, be he surgeon or barber-surgeon or apothecary or self-ordained tooth-puller. There were, of course, no anesthetics, but alcohol, opiates, and some crude drugs were used to lessen the pain. Dental caries was linked with indigestion, though it was realized that sweet and viscous foods such as dried figs and preserves made with honey were likely to promote it. Regular cleansing of the teeth was deemed to be important. The forerunner of the toothbrush was various thin pieces of wood, somewhat broad at the ends. Preference was given to small cypress twigs, or the wood of aloes or pine or rosemary or juniper or similar kinds of wood which were rather bitter and styptic. Mouth rinses were popular, and vinous decoctions of sage and cinnamon or mastich or gallia or moschata or cubeb or juniper seeds or root of cyprus or rosemary leaves were popular. Also in vogue were various powdered or liquid dentifrices.[18]

The Mozart Family Portrait

Oil painting by Johann Nepomuk della Croce, Salzburg, winter 1780-1781. The deceased mother's portrait hangs on the wall in the background. Bequeathed by F.X.W. Mozart in 1844. (Courtesy of the International Foundation Mozarteum, Salzburg.)

6

THE ILLNESSES, 1770–1783

During the period from December 1769 to March 1773, Mozart and his father undertook three journeys to Italy. In December 1774, they traveled to Munich to produce *La Finta Giardiniera* for the carnival. After having spent two of his least troubled years in Salzburg, Mozart and his mother set out for Paris in September 1777; they traveled to the French capital via Munich, Augsburg, and Mannheim. After his mother's unexpected death in Paris in July 1778, and in the wake of his personality clash with Friedrich Melchior Grimm, as well as his rejection by Aloysia Weber, Mozart obeyed his father and returned home to Salzburg in January 1779, so as to take up his appointment there and pay off his debts. Following the successful production of *Idomeneo* in Munich in January 1781, Mozart resigned from the Salzburg Court and became a virtuoso performer and freelance composer in Vienna.

Eighteenth-century music was dominated by Italian opera, and Mozart's three visits to Italy were to set the crown on his musical education. Leopold Mozart and Wolfgang, together with a servant, set out for Italy on the morning of 13 December 1769, and they arrived at Rovereto on Christmas Day. When the prodigy arrived at the Church of San Marco to play the organ, it took a quarter of an hour for him to be assisted to the choir through the warm and enthusiastic crowd.

They enjoyed the carnival at Verona, and Mozart gave a stunning performance at his first concert in Italy on 5 January. Among other items he sight-read a trio by Luigi Boccherini. Mozart's presence in Verona inspired Antonio Meschini and Zaccaria Betti to compose poems in his honor. Signor Locatelli showed the Mozarts the Roman amphitheater and other sights.

The Mozarts left Verona on 10 January 1770 after a day's packing, traveling amidst freezing cold weather to Mantua, where they attended a revival of Hasse's opera *Demetrio*. Wolfgang had a cold (corhyza) and was suffering with frost-bite.[1] Thus, Leopold described the skin about his nose and mouth as appearing reddish-brown like copper, and the boy looking as though he had come through a battle campaign. A very kind and warm-hearted Signora Sartoretti gave Wolfgang a soothing ointment for his frost-cracked hands. She also composed a poem to him and gave him a gift of money. Wolfgang recovered well within a few days, for on 16 January he gave another brilliant performance at a concert held in the six-weeks-old Teatro Scientifico (now the Accademia Vergiliana).

Six weeks later, the journey to Florence from Milan was made amidst violent winds and rain, but father and son arrived safely on the evening of 30 March, alighting at the Eagle Inn. The next day they kept indoors and Wolfgang stayed in bed until lunch, as he had caught a slight cold. Leopold made him take tea and violet juice, and was pleased when he perspired a little. Wolfgang was to have played at Lord Cowper's on 30 March, but he had to be excused; in his place Thomas Linley, Jr., (1756-1778), a prodigy violinist and pupil of Nardini played a violin concerto. On 3 April the Mozarts were reunited with their friend, the Florentine castrato Giovanni Manzuoli (1720-1782), who had given Wolfgang singing lessons in London. On that day they also called on Signora Morelli, a poetess with the nomme de plume Corilla Olimpica. She introduced Wolfgang to Thomas Linley. The two prodigies immediately struck up a warm friendship, and on the following afternoon they played duets for two violins at the Eagle Inn. On April 5 the two played together at the home of Gavard, the finance administrator. On the morning of the Mozarts' departure from Florence, "Tommasino" brought a poem "On the Departure of Signor W. A. Mozart from Florence," which he had commissioned Corilla Olimpica to write. Like so many other travelers, the Mozarts were captivated by Florence, and its environs, and Leopold wrote to his wife that it was the sort of place in which one should live and die. They would have stayed longer but wishing to witness the Holy Week ceremonies in Rome they departed Florence on 6 April at noon. Tommasino had spent the morning with Wolfgang and accompanied their carriage as far as the City Gate. The two prodigies parted in tears in what must have been a most moving farewell. Michael Kelly (1762-1826) later wrote about how upset Wolfgang was when he heard of the accidental drowning of Thomas Linley while holidaying at Grimsthorpe Castle in August 1778.

Two alternative coach trips were available between Rome and Naples. The Procaccio took four and a half days but had the advantage of numbers, as several carriages traveled together. Although the scenery was interesting, the standards of many stopover inns were appalling.

The alternative was the express mail coach which completed the journey in twenty-six hours. But this road was open to attack by bandits, and a merchant had been killed within the previous fortnight. During their visit to the Augustinian monastery, the Mozarts had met the provincial general of the order, Padre Vasquez, and accepted an invitation to accompany some friars to Naples. Accordingly, they left Rome at 10:00 on 8 May, together with three other *sedie*, or two-seated carriages. There was the added advantage that they lunched and stopped over at monasteries. They traveled by way of Marino on Lake Albano, Terracina, and Sessa to Capua, where they witnessed a young nun making her solemn profession and taking her veil. After joining in the festivities, they slept until 10:00 and arrived at Naples on the evening of 14 May.

The Mozarts enjoyed the warmer climate and great abundance of fruit in southern Italy. After arising at 9:00 or 10:00, they would go out visiting and then take lunch at a restaurant. Afternoons were given over to composition, and supper on ordinary days would consist of half a chicken or a small slice of roast meat, while on fast days a little fish would suffice.

With puberty approaching, Wolfgang's limbs were growing and his voice was deepening; much to his annoyance he was unable to sing his own compositions for soprano. Two new costumes were tailored. Wolfgang's was of apple-green shot moiré lined with rose taffeta, whereas Leopold chose dark red shot moiré lined with sky-blue taffeta, both trimmed with silver buttons.

The return journey to Rome was made in the mail coach express on 25 June. They managed only two hours' sleep and ate four cold roast chickens and a piece of bread. Danger lurked on the last leg of the journey when the poor shaft horse of their *sedia*, who was being continuously lashed, reared in soft sand and fell. During the sudden lunge of the carriage, Leopold protected Wolfgang with one arm but gashed his right shin bone on the falling dash-board. The nasty gash measured a finger in width; Leopold dressed it with white ointment and lint that his wife had packed. After the twenty-seven hour journey, they arrived in Rome at 8:00 P.M. on 26 June. How they enjoyed the cooked rice and two lightly boiled eggs that Signora Uslenghi prepared for them! Wolfgang was so tired that he fell asleep on the chair in the bedroom. Nor did he remember having been undressed when he awakened refreshed the next morning. Signora Uslenghi was very fond of Wolfgang and gave him the *Arabian Nights* in Italian, which he found very amusing to read.

The fourteen-year-old Wolfgang and his father, intent to escape the oppressive heat of the late Roman summer, left the Eternal City on 10 July and traveled to Bologna, where they lodged at St. Mark's Inn.

Leopold's gashed right shin was to give rise to nasty complications, related to immobility. Although the initial pain and swelling had largely subsided after a few days' rest in bed, in Bologna he developed a recurrence of pain and a swelling of his right leg and foot, so that he was largely confined to bed again. This second bout of edema is in keeping with a deep vein thrombosis of his right calf. With so serious a condition, he was fortunate not to have suffered a pulmonary thromboembolism. This dreaded disorder occurs when a fragment of blood clot dislodges and travels via a large vein to the heart, where, if large enough, it may obstruct the pulmonary artery and cause sudden death. By 3 August the swelling of Leopold's right foot was much improved, but he then suffered an attack of acute gouty arthritis of the toes of his left foot. His immobility may have caused hyperuricemia which precipitated an attack of gout. By the end of August, both of his feet were much better, but the right one still swelled a little toward the end of the day. For his part Wolfgang was becoming excited about his opera *Mitridate, Re di Ponto.*

The Mozarts departed from Bologna on 13 October and traveled via Parma and Piacenza to Milan, where they arrived on 18 October. During this journey Leopold was very troubled by rheumatic pains in his right arm which may have been due to gout. A two-room apartment in the vicinity of the theater had been rented for them, and their bed was "about nine feet wide." Wolfgang had already composed some of the recitatives in Bologna. He then seriously set about composing the overture, twenty-two arias, duet, and concluding quartet. He wrote to his mother and sister, describing how his fingers ached from writing, and he asked them to pray that his opera would be a success. The mornings were given over to composing; after lunch they usually took a fifteen-minute walk to Count Firmian's residence. The count's secretary, Leopold Troger, was a friend of the Mozarts and they spent a weekend with him in the country just outside Milan.

In April in Rome Wolfgang had been troubled with toothache, and during the middle of November, he suffered a few days with a dental abscess, which caused slight swelling of one side of his face. Fortunately, he recovered without any need for active intervention, and the premiere of his three-act opera seria *Mitridate* on 26 December was a tremendous success. It lasted six hours, and many of the arias were encored. After visits to Turin, Venice, and Padua, the Mozarts arrived home on 28 March 1771.

During their stay in Verona, the Mozarts had first heard of a commission from Vienna. The governor of Lombardy and third son of Maria Theresa, Archduke Ferdinand, was to marry the princess of Modena in Milan Cathedral on 15 October 1771. Twenty thousand pounds of wax candles were to illuminate the festivities, which included a concert and banquet on the evening of the marriage, an opera seria, *Ruggiero* by Hasse with libretto by Metastasio on 16 October, and a *festa teatrale* on the following day. The fifteen-year-old Wolfgang was chosen to compose the music for *Ascanio in Alba* with text by Signor Abbate Giuseppe Parini, a rhetorician of Milan University. Father and son departed from Salzburg on 13 August and traveled their now familiar route in the same *sedia*. Amidst hot and dusty weather they arrived in Milan on 21 August. They met and had a long chat with the Princess Maria Beatrice D'Este, who during her nuptual preparations, suffered a transient attack of diarrhea.

Leopold was very bowel conscious. Since his attack of vertigo in Lille, he had been prone to recurrent bouts of dizziness. He wrongly attributed the condition to constipation, so that he regularly took laxatives in the form of Hansl Spielmann pills. In a letter to his wife dated 21 September 1771, Leopold, after having alluded to an outbreak in Salzburg of insanity and dysentery, went on to say, "that is why I wrote to you about the pills, for I want my arse to cure my head."[2] (The word "arse" was in colloquial use in eighteenth-century Austria.) Laxative abuse can damage the nerve plexus of the bowel and give rise to a disorder known as cathartic colon.[3] Meanwhile, Wolfgang was brushing up on his sign language for communication with a deaf and dumb boy. The atmosphere was very conducive to composing, for in the room opposite theirs was an oboist, while they had a violinist upstairs and downstairs, and a singing master gave lessons in the room next door. The libretto arrived on 29 August. Two days later they visited Hasse, who was composing his last opera. Hasse was fond of Wolfgang, and in a letter to the Abbate Ortes wrote the criticism that Leopold "idolizes his son a little too much, and thus does all he can to spoil him."[4] In a letter to his sister dated 13 September, Wolfgang wrote: "but writing is indeed most tiresome, because I have a very heavy cold and a bad cough."[5] This illness would appear to have been an upper-respiratory-tract infection (U.R.T.I.), complicated by tracheobronchitis.

After his return home, Wolfgang was not idle, and by 30 December he had completed his Symphony in A (K. 114). Soon after, Wolfgang was laid up with a serious illness. Nannerl, in a letter to Joseph Sonnleithner on 2 July 1819, wrote of a portrait of her brother in her possession which had been painted when he came back from the Italian journey: "He was then just 16 years old, but as he had just got up from a serious illness, the picture looks sickly and very yellow."[6] Otto Deutsch concluded that this portrait was perhaps the miniature on ivory said to have been painted by Martin Knoller in Milan in 1773. It could therefore be concluded that the serious illness was associated with jaundice. The differential diagnosis includes yellow fever, which was endemic in Italy at that time, and virus hepatitis. However, yellow fever has only a three- to six-day incubation period. If, as seems likely, this illness was contracted in Italy during the autumn, the more likely diagnosis is type A virus hepatitis, with an incubation period of fifteen to fifty days.[7]

During the weeks after his recovery from hepatitis, Wolfgang composed a symphony in G (K. 124), three *divertimenti* (K. 136-8), five songs (K. 147-51), a litany (K. 125), and two trio sonatas (K. 144, 145) for the cathedral.

Wolfgang had been commissioned to compose an opera for the 1775 carnival in Munich. On 6 December 1774, father and son boarded their coach and traveled via Frabertsham and Wasserburg to Munich, where they arrived on the following afternoon. Leopold found that covering their foot-bags with hay was effective in protecting their feet from the cold. Wolfgang developed a toothache on 16 December and could only take soup for two days. He remained indoors for six days as he developed swelling of the inside and outside of his right cheek as well as his right eye. It is probable that he had suffered a dental abscess; he does not appear to have been ill enough to have contracted acute maxillary sinusitis which can produce similar symptoms.[8] Fortunately, he recovered well without serious sequelae. Nannerl arrived in Munich nine days before the first performance of *La Finta Giardiniera*, which was given at the Assembly Rooms in the Prannerstrasse. The premiere on 13 January was attended by the Elector Maximilian III Joseph and was generally applauded.

Mozart's four and a half months in Mannheim were among the happiest and most eventful in his life. The period did not begin auspiciously, however. On 20 February 1778, he became ill with "catarrh, a cold in the head, headache, sore throat, pain in my eyes and earache."[9] He remained indoors for three days and took antispasmodics, black powders, and elderberry tea to make him sweat. This illness has the features of an upper respiratory tract infection, possibly complicated by sinusitis and otitis media. Little did Mozart then realize that he was soon to lose his mother.

Maria Anna Mozart, now in her fifty-seventh year, was a cheerful, robust woman who had kept good health. During the very cold weather in Augsburg on 23 October 1777, she was troubled with abdominal pain, and four days later, at Nördlingen, she came down with a bad cold. She developed a tendency to recurrent cough, and on 18 December, at Mannheim, she again suffered a "heavy cold." Soon after their arrival in Paris, on 23 March 1778, Grimm's mistress, Louise D'Épinay found the Mozarts satisfactory rooms in a fine street at Rue du Groschenet. Since Maria Anna spoke no French, she looked forward to the regular visits from the Heinas and Anton Raaff. On 1 May, she was feeling much better after three weeks of toothache, sore throat, and earache, for which she had been taking black and digestive powders. On 10 June, Maria

Anna lunched with Francois Heina, the husband of the music publisher Gertrude Heina. After lunch, she strolled through the Luxembourg gardens and viewed the fine collection of paintings at the palace. Leopold exhorted his wife to have her annual "blood-letting" before the summer was too far advanced. A little less than "two platefuls" of her blood were venesected on 11 June, and for a few days she appeared to feel better.

Her fatal illness began on about 16 or 17 June, with diarrhea. At first no one was unduly concerned and attributed this condition to polluted water. (Wolfgang had adopted the practice of adding a little wine and ice to his drinking water in order to avoid diarrhea.) However on 19 June, her headaches were so troublesome that she took to her bed for what would be the last time. On the next day she was troubled with shivers and fever which were treated with antispasmodic powder. She refused to see a French doctor, and on 23 June she was stricken with deafness and hoarseness. An elderly German doctor came to see her the next day and prescribed rhubarb powder in wine. It was obvious that she would not recover, and three days before her death, a German priest was called. He heard her last confession, administered the "Blessed Eucharist" and annointed her with the sacrament of Extreme Unction, (the sacrament of the sick). When Wolfgang in desperation informed Grimm of the situation, he sent his physician but all to no avail. There was no cure available for the "internal inflammation." Maria Anna was in a state of delirium during her last three days, until she lapsed into a coma, five hours before her death. She died at 10:21 P.M. on 3 July 1778. Present were Wolfgang, François Heina, and her nurse. The cause of her death is not entirely clear. Although the death certificate stated "heart disease," the symptoms of her illness are certainly compatible with epidemic louse-borne typhus fever, which seems most likely.[10] Twenty percent of such patients would die between the ninth and eighteenth day of the illness. Alternative diagnoses such as tuberculosis or typhoid fever are also possible. The next day Maria Anna's body was interred in the cemetery of Saint-Eustache. This burial ground has since been abandoned, but there is a commemorative tablet to her in the church of Saint-Eustache.

Even as early as 1750, medical authorities in England knew that patients with typhus tolerated purging and bleeding poorly.[11] The word "typhus" is derived from the Greek, typhos, meaning smoky or hazy. Hippocrates used the term to depict a confused state of intellect with a tendency to stupor, but it was not actually applied to typhus fever until 1760, when Sauvages selected it to descibe the mental state of patients suffering from this disease.

The classic epidemic louse-borne typhus fever is caused by infection with rickettsia prowazeki, named after the American Dr. Howard T.

Ricketts and the Austrian Dr. S. von Prowazek, both of whom died of typhus during their studies of its cause. The disease is transmitted by the human body louse, which lives in clothing, and lays its eggs in the seams of the undergarments. The louse takes several blood meals a day from its host, and it becomes infected when it imbibes blood from a typhus case. The infected louse then sheds rickettsiae in its feces, and so the cycle goes on. The lice quickly abandon a corpse, preferring normal body temperature, so that they tend to leave a febrile host. The incubation period is usually ten to fourteen days. Typhus tends to flourish under those conditions of human misery which predispose to the thriving of louse infestation, such as overcrowding, lack of fuel, inadequate facilities for bathing, and the continuous wearing of the same garments for months at a time. Epidemics ordinarily reached their peak in late winter and tapered off in the spring. The mortality rates during epidemics ranged from 10 to 40 percent, and adults were more vulnerable than children. Epidemics of typhus can be readily controlled by delousing procedures, which were revolutionized with the first synthesis of DDT in Germany in 1874.

Typhus fever has had a decisive influence on many battle campaigns throughout history. Notable epidemics occurred during the Thirty Years War, the Napoleonic Wars, and the First World War. During the Siege of Granada in 1489, there were 17,000 deaths from typhus in the Spanish Army, almost six times the number killed in combat. In 1528, the French Army was at the point of decisive victory over the forces of Charles V, during the Siege of Naples, when 30,000 of their army were rapidly stricken with typhus. As a result, the remnants of the French Army were forced to withdraw. Typhus ravaged the Soviet Union between 1918 and 1922, producing 30 million cases, 3 million of whom died.

In the autumn of 1780, Mozart was commissioned to compose for the Munich carnival season an opera seria *Idomeneo, Re di Creta*, based on a libretto chosen by the court. The twenty-five-year-old composer responded by writing his first operatic masterpiece. The preliminary music was composed in Salzburg in collaboration with his librettist Abbate Varesco, the court chaplain. Having been granted six weeks leave of absence, he traveled to Munich in the mail coach on 5 November 1780. He arrived the next day after a bumpy, hard ride complaining of a sore tail; he lodged at Herr Fiat's in the house known as the "Sonneck" on the Burggasse 6. Leopold acted as an intermediary between his son and Varesco. The ensuing correspondence is invaluable in giving a detailed account of Wolfgang's method of dealing with his opera texts and modifying them in response to the shortcomings of the singers.

On 22 November, the composer was ill with a bad cold and productive cough. Although he had applied Leopold's remedies of early nights and foot-baths, and had stayed indoors for two days, on 1 December, during the first orchestral rehearsal of the opera, his symptoms worsened slightly and he took fig syrup and almond oil. At that time, laxatives were invoked as a panacea for many illnesses in the belief that they would expel the offending evil toxins from the bowel. The symptoms of this illness suggest upper respiratory tract infection, complicated by bronchitis.

The preparations for the opera were interrupted by the death of Maria Theresa on 29 November, with the ensuing six weeks of mourning. Mozart had to send home for his black suit, which was in need of repair. The Elector Karl Theodor attended the third rehearsal on 23 December and made his famous remark "who would think anything so great could be hidden in so small a head."[12]

The premiere of *Idomeneo* (K. 366) was given at the Residenz-Theater (now known as Cuvilliés Theater), Munich, on 29 January 1781 to universal acclamation.

Mozart resigned from the Salzburg court on 10 May 1781. Later that evening, he became ill at the opera and had to leave during the first act. He felt feverish and was trembling in every limb, so that he staggered along the street like a drunkard. The composer took tamarind water and remained in bed the next day. This illness may have been a viral infection.

The horn player Joseph Leutgeb secured a loan from Leopold Mozart in order to open a cheese business in Vienna. Mozart liked to frolic with Leutgeb and composed the Horn Concerto in E-flat (K. 417) for him. On the autograph he wrote: "Wolfgang Amadé Mozart has taken pity on Leutgeb, ass, ox, and fool, at Vienna 27 May 1783."

At this time Wolfgang suffered yet another minor illness, which "left me a cold as a remembrance."[13] It sounds like another upper respiratory tract infection. Jahn wrote that at this time Mozart contracted cholera during an epidemic, but this is not likely for there is no mention of such a serious illness in the composer's letters to his father dated 3, 5, and 21 May 1783.[14]

Constanze retained her good health during her first pregnancy, and she came into labor at 1:30 A.M. on 17 June 1783. Mozart sent for her mother and the midwife at 4:00 A.M., and a baby boy was delivered at 6:30. Constanze confirmed to the Novellos that the Minuet and Trio of the String Quartet in D Minor (K. 421) were composed immediately after their son's birth.

The baby was christened Raimund Leopold in the Amhof church, in honor of the godfather, Baron Wetzlar's eldest son. When Wolfgang and Constanze visited Salzburg during the summer of 1783, they left their baby son in the care of a foster mother in the Neustift suburb of Vienna. Unknown to them, Raimund died on 19 August, aged two months. The death certificate stated "Gedärmfrais," which translates as intestinal cramp. Almost certainly, this was infantile gastroenteritis, which, as we have seen, was the leading cause of infant mortality at that time.

In their letter to Leopold Mozart dated 6 December 1783, Wolfgang and Constanze requested a further prescription of eczema ointment from the chemist Tomaselli. It would appear that Constanze suffered from varicose eczema during their visit to Salzburg and that this ointment was most effective. Varicose eczema tends to recur during pregnancy.

During the Mozarts' visit to Salzburg in the summer of 1783, Michael Haydn is said to have been under pressure to complete six chamber duets for his prince. However, Haydn fell seriously ill after having completed only four. When Mozart heard of his predicament, he kindly dashed off a pair of duets for him in just two days. Such was the origin of the duets for violin and viola in G (K. 423) and B (K. 424). Mozart composed them at Haydn's bedside during his daily visits.[15]

7

THE ILLNESSES, 1784–1790

During the first three years of this period, the triumphant Mozart conquered the city of Vienna as undisputed master of the clavier, made a considerable income from concerts, and composed twelve of his greatest piano concertos and *Figaro*. Alas, he also contracted the serious illness which may have eventually caused his death. After the successful production of *Don Giovanni* in Prague, his fortunes declined and he was plagued by frequent ill health, depression, poverty, frustrations, and disappointments.

While attending Paisiello's opera *Il Re Teodoro in Venezia* at the Burgtheater on 23 August, Mozart became ill with chills and drenching sweats. He wrote to his father:

Four days running at the very same hour I had a fearful attack of colic, which ended each time in violent vomiting. I have therefore to be extremely careful. My doctor is Sigmund Barisani, who since his arrival in Vienna has been almost daily at my Rooms. People here praise him very highly. He is very clever too and you will find that in a short time he will make his way.

Mozart's letter detailing this illness is missing, but fortunately for historians Leopold relayed the above information to Nannerl in a letter dated 14 September 1784. In that letter Leopold also wrote: ''So not only my son, but a number of other people caught rheumatic fever, which became septic when not taken in hand at once.''[1] Apparently, Dr. Barisani had informed Wolfgang that he was treating several other similar cases in Vienna at that time. No other details of this illness are known, but presumably Mozart was well enough to attend the christening in St. Peter's Church of his son Karl Thomas who was born on 21 September. Eight days later his family moved from Trattnerhof[2] to a fine apartment on the Schulerstrasse.[3] At any rate, Mozart was in high spirits on 31 October when some of his female pupils performed at a small domestic concert given on his name-day. During his convalescence from this illness, he completed the Piano Concerto in B-flat (K. 456) on 30 September, the Piano Sonata in C Minor (K. 457) on 14 October, and the String Quartet in B-flat (K. 458) on 9 November.

Let us now turn to a discussion of the nature of this serious febrile illness which was contracted during an epidemic and which resulted in symptoms of recurrent colic and vomiting in association with multiple joint pains. The three common causes of such abdominal pain are biliary colic, renal colic, and intestinal colic. There is no evidence of biliary colic, but several authors have diagnosed renal colic due to stone or infection such as pyonephrosis or pyelonephritis.[4] It is to be emphasized, however, that such conditions would not have been contracted during an epidemic. Furthermore, such diagnoses would not account for the joint symptoms.

The fact that several patients in Vienna at that time were suffering from this illness would suggest that an infection was responsible. Now we have seen that Mozart was prone earlier in his life to recurrent streptococcal infections, and that he tended to react to such infections by developing immune-complex disease. Thus, for example, in childhood Mozart developed erythema nodosum in October 1762, while he contracted rheumatic fever in December 1762 and again in November 1766. It has been proposed that Mozart suffered a third attack of rheumatic fever following streptococcal infection in August 1784.[5] Such a diagnosis is tenable because occasional cases of rheumatic fever present with acute abdominal pain, and it also accounts for the joint symptoms. However, we should remember that the term *Revmatisches fieber* as used in 1784 was nonspecific and simply referred to any febrile illness that was associated with pain or swelling of the joints.[6] The way to the accurate bedside diagnosis of rheumatic fever was not open until after 1819 when Laennec discovered the stethoscope.

There is an alternative diagnosis which is in keeping with the known symptoms and which also takes into account Mozart's subsequent development of chronic renal failure. Strong evidence for chronic renal failure will be presented in the next chapter. It is proposed that in August 1784 Mozart developed Schönlein-Henoch Syndrome after another streptococcal infection, and furthermore that immune complexes were deposited in his kidneys so as to cause chronic glomerularnephritis.[7] The case for such a diagnosis would be stronger if there was evidence of an exanthem and an abnormality of the urinary deposit, but there is no such record. Further arguments in support of the Schönlein-Henoch

Syndrome (SHS) diagnosis will be presented during the discussion of Mozart's later illnesses. The syndrome is described in the following section.

SCHÖNLEIN-HENOCH SYNDROME

This syndrome is a hypersensitivity vasculitis in which immune complexes are deposited in the small blood vessels of the skin, joints, gastrointestinal tract, kidneys, and occasionally other internal organs such as the brain or lungs. Such deposition of immune complexes tends to produce inflammatory changes and sometimes bleeding into these organs. The syndrome was named after two German doctors, Lucas Schönlein (1793-1864) and Eduard Henoch (1820-1910). In 1837, Schönlein named the combination of joint symptoms and skin purpura, while Henoch reported the abdominal symptoms in 1874 and emphasized the association of nephritis in 1899. Henoch stressed the serious nature of the nephritic complications and reported cases that progressed to anasarca and death.[8] The majority of case reports in the medical Literature prior to 1948 were in children. However, since 1970, it has been recognized that the syndrome is not uncommon in adults.

Although in many cases a specific cause cannot be identified, in one series two-thirds of patients had preceding symptoms of an upper respiratory tract infection, and evidence of streptococcal infection was present in about one-third of patients.[9] Since the advent of penicillin, such post-streptococcal cases have become less common. Other infections which may be responsible for the syndrome include the staphylococcus, hepatitis B virus, influenza, cytomegalo virus, malaria, and mycobacteria. Sometimes drug reactions are responsible, while various food allergies (milk, eggs, wheat, rice, fish, nuts, beans, and others) have been incriminated. The syndrome has also been associated with insect bites, smallpox vaccinations, influenza vaccination, TAB inoculation, and exposure to cold.

The skin is involved by a specific exanthem which is usually purpuric, but the purpura may be confined to the dependent parts of the body and produce no symptoms of itch or sting. Occasionally, there is absence of purpura, and in some cases gross swelling of the skin due to edema develops.

Joint manifestations by way of pain, limitation of movement, or swelling occur in about two-thirds of cases. The knees and ankles are most frequently involved, while the hips, wrists, and elbows are less commonly affected. Joint symptoms usually subside in two to seven days, and chronic arthritis does not develop.

The gastrointestinal tract is involved in about one-half of adult cases of the syndrome. The manifest symptoms are intestinal colic, vomiting, nausea, diarrhea, and gastrointestinal bleeding. Abdominal pain is the most common symptom in such cases, whereas the bleeding may be occult or overt.

The incidence of renal involvement in adult cases of SHS is as high as 61 percent; an many as 29 percent of adult cases of SHS nephropathy die usually because of renal failure.[10] Such patients with renal involvement usually have blood in their urine (hematuria), which may be gross or microscopic. Males outnumber females by two to one. Attacks may be continuous or recurrent, over weeks, months, or years, with complete recovery in between. Followup studies have shown that about 10 percent of cases of SHS nephropathy go on to develop chronic renal failure.[11] Immune complexes have been detected in the blood of such patients by various methods and have been shown to contain IgA (immunoglobulin A). Many patients with SHS nephropathy have a primary underlying immune disorder called Berger's syndrome or IgA disease.[12]

Mozart composed two songs for tenor, male choir, and organ (K. 483, 484), which were to be sung at the opening of the "New-crowned Hope" Lodge on 14 January 1786. However, he sent a written apology that he was unable to attend:

It is an hour since I came home—afflicted with acute headache and cramp in the stomach. I went on hoping for improvement but unfortunately am experiencing the reverse so that I realize fully that I am not destined to attend our first ceremony today and so I beg you dear brother to apologize for me on the spot.[13]

It would appear that Mozart was ill again in April 1787 and attended a second time by his childhood friend Dr. Sigmund Barisani, who by this time was the senior physician at the General Hospital. Barisani made an entry to this effect in Mozart's album on 14 April:

Do not forget thy friend, whose happiness
And pride it is to know he served thee twice
To save thee for the world's delight. This boast
Is yet surpassed by joy and pride to know
Thou art his friend, as he is ever thine.[14]

The details of this illness are unknown, but it is reasonable to conclude that it was a recurrence of the serious illness of August 1784. There is one further clue. Dr. Barisani knew of Mozart's habit of composing well into the night. Being concerned about the harmful consequences of this practice, he advised his friend not to be stooped over at the clavier for hours on end, but rather to take turns at composing while standing.[15] The good doctor also encouraged Mozart's participation in games that he enjoyed, such as billiards and bowls.[16] From that time Mozart would take a morning gallop on his horse.[17] Perhaps during this illness he complained of pain aggravated by bending and was concerned about his posture. Such symptoms could have been related to swelling of the kidneys owing to a recurrence of Schönlein-Henoch nephritis. Sir William Osler pointed out the lifelong liability to recurrence in some patients, while in a more recent series of adult cases of SHS, 26 percent of the patients developed recurrent attacks.[18] Furthermore, the serial decline of renal function during recurrent attacks has been documented.[19]

Mozart's only entry in his thematic catalogue during the month of April 1787 was his sublime String Quintet in C (K. 515), entered on the nineteenth. However, his illness was not without its lighter moments, and when the Jacquin family paid him a visit on 24 April, he presented a double canon (K. 228) to Joseph Franz von Jacquin (1766-1839).

Leopold Mozart was also unwell at that time. During his latter years, he had maintained relatively good health, apart from gout and arthritis. In reply to Nannerl's anxious inquiry, Leopold responded in his letter dated 24 February 1787:

An old man must not expect anything like perfect health; he is always failing, and loses strength just as a young man gains it. One must just patch oneself up as long as one can. We may hope for a little improvement from the better weather now. You will of course find me very much thinner, but, after all, that is of no consequence.[20]

His condition soon deteriorated with the development of edema of his feet and a sickening pulsating sensation in his upper abdomen. Nannerl came to stay with him from the middle of March until the beginning of May, and he appeared to gain benefit from a *serum lactis* medicine. In his last letter to Nannerl, dated 11 May, Leopold wrote: "I am about the same, move my bowels, and have an appetite. My feet are somewhat less swollen but I still feel a pulsating sensation below the stomach and have to await the effects of the plaster."[21]

Leopold Mozart was consoled by the daily visits of his friend, the court councillor of war, Franz D'Yppold (Ipold). On 29 May another friend, Theobald Marchand, in Munich, promised to send a medicine prescription with Father Joseph Bullinger:

At bedtime take a tablespoon full, mixed with half a tablespoon of fresh water. Cover yourself with a warm blanket, as you will break out into a light sweat. After you have remained in bed for two hours, you may change into a dry shirt, and have a cup of tea, coffee, or chocolate. At about 4 p m a mild enema should be taken every two days, and a light laxative every six days. Continue this treatment for only eight days and let me know its effect, so that I can advise you whether to continue or not.[22]

Leopold never received this prescription, however. He died suddenly on 28 May 1787, aged sixty-seven years, and he was buried that same day. Leopold's old friend Dr. Silvester Barisani diagnosed "congestion of the spleen," while the *Salzburger Intelligenzblatt* stated he died of "consumption."[23] Leopold Mozart's symptoms suggest a diagnosis of severe congestive heart failure: the pulsating sensation below his stomach may have been due to pulsation of his liver, which occurs in cases of severe heart failure on the right side associated with tricuspid valve incompetence. It is possible that his congestive heart failure was due to constrictive pericarditis, which resulted from an earlier bout of tuberculosis in 1764. Hyperthyroidism seems less likely since there was no mention of a goiter. A sudden cardiac death due to coronary thrombosis has also been proposed.[24] Leopold's well-tended grave is in St. Sebastian's cemetery at Salzburg.

There is no record of further medical problems until 1790, which was the most dismal year in Mozart's life: the composer was then troubled with persistent depression and frequent illness. The symptoms are mentioned in his letters to Michael Puchberg. On 8 April 1790 Mozart wrote: "I would have gone to see you myself in order to have a chat with you, but my head is covered with bandages due to rheumatic pains, which make me feel my situation still more keenly."[25] At the beginning of May he wrote: "I am very sorry that I cannot go out and have a talk with you myself but my toothache and headache are still too painful and altogether I still feel very unwell."[26]

Later in that month Mozart completed the second Prussian Quartet in B-flat (K. 589). In June he stayed at Baden with Constanze, who was again ill and taking the baths there, and he also composed his last String Quartet in F (K. 590). During July Mozart completed his orchestration of Handel's "Alexander's Feast" (K. 591) and "Ode for St Cecilia's Day" (K. 592), for van Swieten's Society of Noblemen. However, he was soon ill again, and on 14 August he wrote to Puchberg:

Whereas I felt tolerably well yesterday, I am absolutely wretched today. I could not sleep all night for pain. I must have got overheated yesterday from walking so much and then without knowing it have caught a chill. Picture to yourself my condition—ill and consumed by worries and anxieties. Such a state quite definitely prevents me from recovering.[27]

Such symptons viewed in isolation are too vague to permit accurate diagnosis. In view of Mozart's past medical history, they would be compatible with tonsillitis, complicated by cervical lymphadenitis and sinusitis, and also another dental abscess. However, such symptoms are also compatible with recurrent Schönlein-Henoch Syndrome. Recurrent arthralgias of a few days' duration, in association with vague symptoms of fever, headache, malaise, and fatigue, are common in this condition.[28]

Even so, recent research on Mozart's skull raises the possibility, that his headaches during the spring of 1790, may have been due to an extradural hematoma following a head injury. While there is no documented history of such an injury, admittedly the records are incomplete. However such a diagnosis does not account well for Mozart's other symptoms at that time.

8

THE LAST YEAR, 1791

During his last year, encouraged by the upturn in his financial situation, Mozart showed remarkable resilience in his ability to overcome his mental and physical sufferings. He was able to unleash his final astonishing outburst of creativity, composing six of his greatest masterpieces.

Mozart was continuously ill during the last six months of his life. His depression worsened, and he became preoccupied with thoughts of death. There also developed paranoid features in his personality, associated with a possessive jealousy and emotional lability. Mozart also became tormented by mental delusions.

In July a tall, gaunt stranger in a grey cloak visited Mozart's apartment on the Rauhensteingasse to commission a Requiem Mass for an anonymous patron. A few days later the stranger returned and paid half the commission. After the stranger's departure, Mozart is said to have fallen into a profound reverie; then, suddenly calling for ink and paper, he began to write. The stranger reappeared on the day that Mozart set out for Prague; he was in fact Anton Leitgeb, the son of the mayor of Vienna. The anonymous patron was Count Walsegg-Stuppach, who was the landlord of Michael Puchberg. The count's wife had died on 14 February 1791, and he wanted to pass off the work as his own.[1]

From that time Mozart became obsessed with the idea that he had been poisoned and that he had been commissioned to write his own Requiem. One day, about six months before his death, while walking in the Prater Gardens, he said to Constanze: "I know I must die. Someone has given me acqua toffana and has calculated the precise time of my death—for which they have ordered a Requiem, it is for myself that I am writing this."[2]

During the composition of *Die Zauberflöte* Mozart suffered recurrent violent headaches and blackouts. Holmes wrote: "He sunk over his composition into frequent swoons, in which he remained for several minutes, before consciousness returned."[3] And Jahn wrote: "Even before the completion of the Zauberflöte he had become subject to fainting fits which exhausted his strength and increased his depression."[4]

On about 25 August Mozart, with Constanze and Franz Xaver Süssmayr, set out for Prague in order to produce a festive opera seria, *La Clemenza di Tito*, which had been commissioned by the Bohemian Estates for the coronation in that city of Emperor Leopold II on 6 September. During the three-day journey Mozart worked furiously, and at night he transcribed his day-time sketches made in the carriage. A "coronation journal" published in Prague referred to Mozart's illness in that city at that time.[5] Nissen reported a slight irritability of his nerves, as well as an anxiety and preoccupation with morbid thoughts of death. Mozart's friend, Franz Xaver Niemetschek, was present and wrote a more detailed account in his biography:

In Prague Mozart fell ill and dosed himself ceaselessly; his colour was pale and his countenance sad, although his merry sense of humour often bubbled into jesting in the company of his friends. At the moment of departure from the circle of his friends he was so sad that he wept tears. A foreboding sense of his approaching death seemed to have produced this melancholy mood—for at this time he already had the seed of the disease which was so soon to carry him off![6]

Two weeks after his return to Vienna, Mozart conducted the premiere of *Die Zauberflöte* at the no longer extant Freihaus Theater on 30 September. Constanze was ill again, and a week later she took her baby, Franz Xaver Wolfgang, to Baden, accompanied by her sister Sophie. On 15 October Mozart and his son Karl drove to Baden to collect them. According to Nissen, Constanze was alarmed to see the deterioration of her husband's health, and she noted his worsening pallor, enervation, and weight loss. She took away the score of the *Requiem*, with which he was preoccupied, called in Dr. Franz Closset, and attempted to cheer him up by promoting visits from his friends. Mozart recovered for a time and resumed work on the *Requiem*. He conducted his Little Masonic Cantata (K. 623) at the inauguration of the New Temple of the New-crowned Hope Lodge, at his last public appearance.

In summary then, Mozart's chronic ill health during the last six months of his life became manifest with symptoms of depression, personality change, paranoid delusions, headaches, blackouts, anemia, and weight loss. Such symptoms are readily accounted for by a diagnosis of chronic renal failure.[7] It is proposed that the cause of such chronic renal failure was a chronic glomerularnephritis, first contracted as a complication of Schönlein-Henoch Syndrome in August 1784 and further exacerbated during recurrences in April 1787 and again in the spring-summer of 1790. We will now discuss the syndrome of chronic renal failure.

Patients with chronic nephritis show a gradual decline in kidney function, which in the earlier stages is asymptomatic. This presymptomatic phase can last several years, and it can be diagnosed only by laboratory tests such as the detection of protein in the urine, impaired creatinine clearance, elevated blood urea, or renal biopsy. Commonly, there develops an elevation of blood pressure and hemorrhages in the retina of the eye, which may be detected by the attending physician. It is to be emphasized that during Mozart's lifetime there was no knowledge of nephritis or hypertension. Richard Bright did not write his classic paper on the significance of protein in the urine in the diagnosis of renal disease until 1836;[8] while the invention of the sphygmomanometer, to measure blood pressure, was made by Ritter von Basch in 1876.[9] Mozart's blood pressure was therefore never recorded, and his urine was never tested for protein. Eventually, however, unless the patient with chronic nephritis dies from an unrelated cause, symptoms of chronic renal failure or uremia do develop. The symptoms of uremia are often initially insidious and protean, and may first become manifest in some organ other than the kidney such as the brain—bilious headache, blackouts, convulsions, visual impairment, lassitude, depression, and a variety of mental symptoms including delusions and insanity; the cardiovascular system—hypertension, heart failure; the gastrointestinal tract—vomiting, diarrhea, abdominal pain, weight loss; or such metabolic features as anemia or acidosis. There may also be kidney symptoms—excessive thirst associated with the passage of large volumes of dilute urine.[10]

In Mozart's case it was the brain. Such neuropsychiatric symptoms as depression, personality change, and mental delusions in a young man have been well documented in cerebral vascular disease.[11] Uremic blackouts are sometimes due to sudden rises of blood pressure or hypertensive encephalopathy. Several other authors have also diagnosed chronic renal failure as the cause of Mozart's chronic ill health during his last year, but they have been less expansive in dealing with his mental symptoms.[12] These authors have incriminated a variety of other causes of chronic renal failure such as post-streptococcal nephritis, chronic pyelonephritis, calculous disease—pyonephrosis, and end-stage kidney disease. Further evidence for a diagnosis of Schönlein-Henoch nephropathy will be presented in the discussion of the cause of Mozart's fatal illness and death.

The question of a space-occupying lesion in Mozart's brain also needs to be considered at this stage. The association of blackouts, fainting fits, personality change, mental symptoms, and headache certainly raises the possibility of a space-occupying lesion, such as a frontal lobe tumor. However, in between his fits and episodes of exhaustion, Mozart continued to work and compose with a clear mind. Sometimes the gradual blunting of alertness, of memory, and of power of attention, owing to raised intracranial pressure, may be delayed, but it eventually develops in all cases. Even during his fatal illness, Mozart remained conscious until two hours before his death. Furthermore, Vincent Novello recorded that Constanze had mentioned the composer's complaint of great pain in his loins about six months before he died; this tends to favor the kidneys as the primary site of his trouble.[13] An intracranial abscess also needs to be considered, but there is no clue to a predisposing site of infection, and the course seems too prolonged. The possibility of bacterial endocarditis and mycotic aneurysm will be considered in relation to the cause of Mozart's death.

The important new discovery, that Mozart may have suffered with a chronic extradural hematoma following a head injury, needs also to be considered here. It seems probable that such a lesion would have been aggravated by chronic renal failure and hypertension. In that event, the hematoma may have contributed to Mozart's headaches and blackouts.

More recently, it has been proposed that Mozart's kidney ailment may have been due to some kind of congenital anomaly such as polycystic kidneys.[14] This theory has been advanced because of the well-documented association between external ear malformations and congenital renal tract anomalies. However, there is substantial evidence against this hypothesis.[15] First, there is no significant documented association between Mozart Ear and polycystic kidneys.[16] Second, the majority of case reports of concurrent anomalies of external ear and renal tract have also included deafness, earlobe pits, cervical fistulae, or various other anomalies: we have seen that Mozart's hearing was not impaired, nor did he show evidence of any of the above defects.[17] Finally, if this theory is true, then Franz Xaver Wolfgang Mozart must also have inherited a kidney disorder. There is no record of renal symptoms, and an autopsy established gastric cancer as the cause of his death.[18] (Franz Xaver Wolfgang's death certificate is reproduced in the Appendix.)

The history of recurrent blackouts led one author to the erroneous diagnosis of epilepsy.[19] Mozart did not show evidence of a seizure disorder. We will see that he suffered a convulsion two hours before his death; however, that was clearly a preterminal event, consistent with a cerebral hemorrhage (see p. 204). Similarly, Mozart's history of depression, obsessiveness, and euphoria might lead one to a consideration of the controversial behavioral symptoms ascribed to temporal lobe epilepsy.[20] However, Mozart showed no evidence of aggressive behavior, and we will see that his vulnerable personality and cyclothymic disorder readily account for such symptoms.

PART II

Lifestyle

The Loretto Kindl
The Child Jesus of Loreto
Mozart and his family were very devoted to this small ivory statuette. The Kindl's blessing is still administered today by the Capuchin nuns in the convent of St. Maria Loretto in Salzburg. (Courtesy of the International Foundation Mozarteum, Salzburg.)

9

RELIGIOUS BELIEFS AND ATTITUDES

Mozart was baptized into the Catholic Church at 10:30 A.M. on 28 January 1756 in Salzburg Cathedral. His parents gradually introduced him to the rudiments of the Catholic faith, and he took the name Sigismundus at his Confirmation.[1] Wolfgang attended Mass regularly, recited the rosary, and observed the church laws of fasting and abstinence from meat during Lent. He was taught that death was not to be feared since it opened the door to the ultimate end of man in the beatific vision. In due course he received the sacraments of Penance and Holy Communion.

The ecclesiastical principality of Salzburg was founded by St. Boniface in 739. One of its most important rulers was Wolf Dietrich von Raitenau, who was consecrated as archbishop in 1587. He laid the foundation stone of the cathedral in 1610 and was responsible for many of the fine buildings including Altenau Palace (now Mirabell), the Residenz, the Capuchin Monastery, the Augustinian Monastery in Mülln, and his own mausoleum in St. Sebastian's graveyard. Wolf Dietrich died a prisoner in the Hohensalzburg fortress in 1617. The pilgrimage church at Maria Plain was consecrated in 1674, and the Glockenspiel chimes were installed in 1702. In 1771, the population of Salzburg was 16,123. Leopold Mozart and his son served under the last prince archbishops of Salzburg.

The Enlightenment (Aufklärung) reached this city in the 1740s. Through the advances of enlightened reason and science, man was to find virtue and happiness. At the Benedictine University from 1744, Thomistic philosophy was gradually replaced by the Leibniz-Wolffian School, with its aim of finding a synthesis of reason, religion, metaphysics, and theology. The Enlightenment saw certain aspects of organized religion as a barrier to progress. The seeds were sown for the gradual collapse of the ancien régime with its two grand classes of humanity rigidly divided into the plebs and patricii, and the gradual rise of the middle class.

On the Grand Tour Leopold Mozart, in his letters to Lorenz Hagenauer, made several comments on variations in contemporary liturgical practice. In Schwetzingen[2] he referred to the scarcity of Holy Water stoups, crucifixes, fast-dishes, and holy pictures in hotel rooms, while in Brussels he described the limited use of rosary beads in the churches, and the failure of the faithful to strike their breasts at the moment of elevation of the consecrated host.[3] During March 1765, Mozart's mother became godmother in London to Charlotte Hummel at an Anglican ceremony.[4]

Mozart was enthusiastically received in Bologna in March 1770. The highlights of his five days there included his attendance at the glittering reception in honor of Count Joseph Kaunitz, and his two visits to Padre Martini. Leopold and his son also visited the church of Corpus Domini to see the incorrupt body of St. Catherine Vigri, a patroness of artists, who had been a Poor Clare nun and whose body has been seated in an upright position since 1475.[5] On 10 April 1770, Mozart and his father, during their stopover at Viterbo, visited the Monastero Clarisse St. Rosa, where in the Reliquary they saw the incorrupt body of St. Rose (1235-52). As a remembrance they took away a relic and fever antidote. Since 1921, each year on her feast day, 4 September, St. Rose's incorrupt heart has been carried in annual procession.[6]

Throughout his life Mozart retained a remarkable child-like trust in God. Indeed, his reliance on divine providence was so unqualified that his words sometimes sound almost fatalistic.[7] Consider, for example, the letter to his mother from Bologna on 29 September 1770:

I am sincerely sorry to hear of the long illness which poor Jungfrau Martha has to bear with patience, and I hope that with God's help she will recover. But, if she does not, we must not be unduly distressed, for God's will is always best and He certainly knows best whether it is better for us to be in this world or in the next. She should console herself, however, with the thought that after the rain she may enjoy the sunshine.[8]

Mozart was the fourth composer to receive a papal knighthood. In response to the enthusiastic exhortations of his secretary of state, Cardinal Pallavicini, the 248th pontiff of the Roman Catholic Church, Pope Clement XIV conferred on Wolfgang the title of Knight of the Golden Order during a private audience at his temporary residence, the Palazzo Santa Maria Maggiore on 8 July 1770. The fourteen-year-old cavalier wore the golden cross of the order on a red sash, together with sword and spurs. In the brief, the Pope referred to his excellence since early youth "in the sweetest sounding of the harpsichord." The other three composers who had previously received this knighthood were Orlando di Lasso, Christoph Gluck, and Carl Ditters von Dittersdorf. Pope Pius VI dubbed Abbé Georg Joseph Vogler a Knight of the Order of the Golden Spur in 1775.

Mozart's simple faith and trust in God are well reflected in the letter to his father from Augsburg on 25 October 1777:

Papa must not worry, for God is ever before my eyes. I realise His omnipotence and I fear His anger; but I also recognise His love, His compassion and His tenderness towards His creatures. He will never forsake His own. If it is according to His will, so let it be according to mine. Thus all will be well and I must needs be happy and contented.[9]

Three and a half months later, in his letter from Mannheim on 7 February 1778, Mozart clearly stated his ambitions to his father and justified his reluctance to take on many piano pupils:

I am a composer and was born to be a Kapellmeister, and I neither can nor ought to bury the talent for composition with which God in His goodness has so richly endowed me (I may say so without conceit, for I feel it now more than ever); and this I should be doing were I to take many pupils, for it is a most unsettling métier and I would rather, if I may speak plainly, neglect the clavier than composition, for in my case the clavier with me is only a side-line, though, thank God, a very good one.[10]

Another touching example of his simple faith and trust in God is associated with Mozart's Paris Symphony in D (K. 297). The rehearsal of this symphony for the Concert Spirituel went so badly that Mozart was unable to sleep from worry. With confidence he "prayed to God that it might go well . . . all to His greater honour and glory," and in return he promised to say a rosary. After the triumphant performance of his symphony on 18 June 1778, Mozart went off to the Palais Royal, where he had a large ice cream; he then said a rosary as he had vowed to, and he went home to mother.[11]

Mozart apparently retained considerable composure during the last fortnight of his mother's life. A few hours after her death, he wrote two heart-rending letters to Salzburg; one was to his father and sister forewarning them of an impending disaster, and the other was to his friend Father Joseph Bullinger, outlining the details of her death and pleading with him to break the sad news gently. He received tremendous consolation from his religion, as he expressed to his father in his letter of 9 July 1778:

In those distressing moments there were three things that consoled me—my entire and steadfast submission to the will of God, and the sight of her very easy and beautiful death which made me feel that in a moment she had become so happy; for how much happier is she now than we are! Indeed I wished at that moment to depart with her. From this wish and longing proceeded finally my third source of consolation—the thought that she is not lost to us forever—that we shall see her again—that we shall live together far more happily and blissfully than ever in this world. We do not yet know when it will be—but that does not disturb me; when God wills it, I am ready.[12]

A little later he continued:

It will be a great help to restoring my tranquillity to hear that my dear father and sister are submitting wholly and with calmness and fortitude to the will of God—are trusting Him with their whole heart in the firm belief that He orders all things for the best. My dearest father! Do not give way! Dearest sister! Be firm! You do not yet know your brother's good heart—for he has not yet been able to prove it. My two loved ones! Take care of your health. Remember that you have a son, a brother, who is doing his utmost to make you happy—knowing well that one day you will not refuse to grant him his desire and his happiness—which certainly does him honour, and that you also will do everything in your power to make him happy. Oh, then we shall live together as peacefully, honourably and contentedly as is possible in this world—and in the end, when God wills it, we shall all meet again in heaven—for which purpose we were destined and created.[13]

During the Grand Tour, the Mozart family had arrived in Geneva on 20 August 1766. Grimm's mistress, Madame D'Épinay, had given them an introduction to François-Marie Arouet Voltaire (1694-1778), who at that time was living at the Château de Ferney. The Mozarts had intended to visit him from Geneva, but apparently Voltaire was too ill to receive them. On the day of his mother's death, the twenty-two-year-old Mozart voiced his vehement condemnation of the famous writer and philosopher of the Enlightenment: "Now I have a piece of news for you which you may have heard already, namely, that that godless arch-rascal Voltaire has pegged out like a dog, like a beast! That is his reward!"[14]

During the fortnight after his marriage, Mozart wrote two letters to his father in which he attempted to justify his precipitate decision. In his letter on 17 August 1782 he wrote:

Indeed for a considerable time before we were married we had always attended Mass and gone to confession and received communion together; and I found that I never prayed so fervently or confessed and received communion so devoutly as by her side; and she felt the same. In short, we are made for each other; and God who orders all things and consequently has ordained this also, will not forsake us.[15]

According to prevalent Catholic custom at that time, all members of the Mozart family were particularly devoted to the Mother Mary and the Child Jesus, under various titles. Their two favorite pilgrimage churches were the one at Maria Plain and the Capuchin Church of St. Maria Loretto in Salzburg. During times of illness or particular need, it was their custom to have special prayers and masses offered to God through the intercession of the Virgin Mary. Leopold Mozart was from his university days a member of the Greater Marian Congregation at Salzburg.[16] During Mozart's quinsy in Paris in February 1764 and his typhoid fever at the Hague in November the following year, Leopold asked Lorenz Hagenauer to arrange for special masses to be offered. Leopold's wife sought a similar favor from Mannheim in December 1777.

Mozart was also devoted to the Virgin Mary. In his letter from Paris on 9 July 1778, he asked his father to arrange for holy masses to be offered at Maria Plain and the Loretto church for his intentions. Mozart's "Coronation Mass" (K. 317) was written in 1779 for Salzburg Cathedral, but he composed his Mass in F (K. 192) for Maria Plain in 1774. The small oil painting of the Virgin and Child at Maria Plain had miraculously escaped intended destruction by the Swedes at Regen in 1632, and it was brought to Salzburg twenty years later. The present-day Basilica, designed by Giovanni Antonio Dario, soon established itself as the leading pilgrimage shrine in that area.

Soon after his return to Vienna from Salzburg, in the postscript of the letter to his father, dated 10 December 1783, Mozart asked Leopold to send a couple of images of the infant Jesus of Loretto. From the middle of the seventeenth century, the small ivory statuette of the Child Jesus with ornate crown, scepter, and cross had become a popular object of devotion in the convent of St. Maria Loretto at Paris—Lodron-Strasse 6. Among the pious practices was a ceremony to cure headache sufferers through head contact with the statue. Little dolls, based on a wax copy of the statue, are still manufactured by the Capuchin nuns at Salzburg.[17]

The magnificent basilica at Loreto in Italy enshrines the house of the Holy Family, which was moved there from the Holy Land, probably by the Crusaders toward the end of the thirteenth century. The dome of the basilica was completed in 1499. Mozart and his father visited the Loreto shrine when they were en route from Rome to Bologna on 21 July 1770. They took away six little bells, candles, and other trifles as a remembrance.[18] Nannerl also spoke of this visit in her letter to Schlichtegroll in April 1792.[19] Leopold and Wolfgang intended to visit Genazzano to see the miraculous image of Our Lady of Good Counsel, but such a plan was frustrated by Leopold's nasty carriage accident.[20] In his letter to Nannerl from Rome on 25 April 1770, Mozart mentioned having attended vespers and mass in the church of San Lorenzo on the feast of Our Lady of Good Counsel.[21] Devotion to the saints was also popular in Salzburg. A picture of St. Johannes von Nepomuk was found in the Mozart household, while Nannerl had a special devotion to St. Crescentia.[22]

Unfortunately, through loss of family correspondence, there are gaps in our knowledge of Mozart's religious feelings during his latter years. However, we do know that he continued to attend Mass regularly, and that he maintained his trust in God and his belief in life after death in a better place.

When Mozart heard of his father's serious illness during the spring of 1787, he wrote expressing his concern and sorrow. It is to be remembered that at about this time, Mozart himself suffered a recurrence of serious illness. He attempted to console his father:

As death, when we come to consider it closely, is the true goal of our existence, I have formed during the last few years such close relations with this best and truest friend of mankind, that his image is not only no longer terrifying to me, but is indeed very soothing and consoling! And I thank my God for graciously granting me the opportunity (you know what I mean) of learning that death is the key which unlocks the door to our true happiness. I never lie down at night without reflecting that—young as I am—I may not live to see another day. Yet no one of all my acquaintances could say that in company I am morose or disgruntled. For this blessing I daily thank my Creator and wish with all my heart that each one of my fellow-creatures could enjoy it.[23]

This famous passage from Moses Mendelssohn's *Phaedon* was inspired by the death of his friend Count August Clemens Hatzfeld, a canon of the cathedral. Mozart had met the count in 1786 at Maria Hilff. An amateur violinist, he had played the violin part for the adaptation of *Idomeneo* at Prince Auersperg's Palace in the spring of that year.

Five months later, Mozart's childhood friend, Dr. Sigmund Barisani, died unexpectedly at age twenty-nine. Wolfgang wrote the following under his friend's entry in his album:

Today, September 3 of this same year, I was so unfortunate as to lose by death this noble-natured man, my dearest, best friend, and the saviour of my life. It is well with him! But with me—us—and all who knew him—it can never be well again, until we are so happy as to meet him in another world never to part again.[24]

It was at Baden on 18 June 1791 that Mozart entered his sublime motet "Ave Verum Corpus" (K. 618) for four voices, organ, and strings. The motet was probably composed for Stoll for performance on the feast day of Corpus Christi, which fell on 23 June. The Ave Verum is listed in the traditional Manual of Prayers of the Catholic Church, and the prayer is recited by the faithful after reception of the body of Christ in Holy Communion. The forty-six bars of this masterpiece are overflowing with fervor and beauty. On Sunday, 26 June, Mozart took part in the Corpus Christi procession from the Piarists' church in the Josefstadt suburb of Vienna. The composer had become friendly with the Piarists and was to visit them again in October, as he was keen for his son Carl to be educated in a Catholic school. In his last preserved letter to Constanze, dated 14 October 1791, Mozart wrote:

Karl was absolutely delighted at being taken to the opera [*Zauberflöte*]. He is looking splendid. As far as health is concerned, he could not be in a better place, but everything else there is wretched, alas! All they can do is to turn out a good peasant into the world. But enough of this. As his serious studies (God help them!) do not begin until Monday, I have arranged to keep him until after lunch on Sunday. I told them that you would like to see him. So tomorrow, Saturday, I shall drive out with Karl to see you. You can then keep him, or I shall take him back to Heeger's after lunch. Think it over. A month can hardly do him much harm. In the meantime the arrangement with the Piarists, which is now under discussion, may come to something.[25]

The Piarists were a small religious order whose seminary in the Josefstadt suburb had been dissolved by the Emperor Joseph in 1782 but was to be reopened in 1791. Mozart had lunch with the Piarists after Mass on 9 October 1791, and he voiced his intention to the rector of placing Carl with them.

The members of the clergy among Mozart's friends included Abbé Joseph Bullinger, Father Dominicus Hagenauer, Abbé Maximilian Stadler, and also Bishop Joseph Hurdalek, who was the rector of the seminary at Prague from 1785 to 1790.[26] In his moving letter to Bullinger soon after his mother's death, Mozart wrote about friendship and wealth. Admittedly, such sentiments may have been colored by his debts and his clash with Grimm at that time:

You know well that the best and truest of all friends are the poor. The wealthy do not know what friendship means, especially those who are born to riches; and even those whom fate enriches often become spoilt by their good fortune. But when a man is placed in favourable circumstances not by blind fate but by reasonable good fortune and merit, that is, a man who during his early and less prosperous days never lost courage, remained faithful to his religion and his God, was an honest man and a good Christian and knew how to value his true friends—in short, one who really deserved better luck—from such a man no ingratitude need be feared![27]

The history of the magnificent great C Minor Mass (K. 427), which is performed each year in St. Peter's church during the Salzburg summer festival, is also of interest at this point. When Constanze fell ill during their courtship in 1782, Wolfgang made a vow that should he bring her to Salzburg as his wife, he would compose a grand Mass in thanksgiving. In the letter to his father, dated 4 January 1783, he stated that the score was half completed. He resumed work on it after their arrival, but there was insufficient time for him to complete the Agnus Dei. The Mass for double chorus and full orchestra was performed during the Sunday Mass in St. Peter's church on 26 October 1783: Constanze sang the soprano part as her husband had promised. According to Johann Rochlitz, Mozart, while in Leipzig in 1789, stated that he was deeply moved by his religious beliefs when composing meaningful parts of a Mass.[28]

Mozart was not blind to any flaws in the church, however. He was openly critical of the human imperfections of the clergy and the injustices within the church. He sometimes complained about such church laws as fasting and abstinence from meat during Lent.

My chief fault is that—judging by appearances—I do not always act as I should. It is not true that I boasted of eating meat on all fast-days; but I did say that I did not scruple to do so or consider it a sin, for I take fasting to mean abstaining, that is, eating less than usual. I attend mass every Sunday and every Holy Day and, if I can manage it, on weekdays also, and that you know, my father.[29]

In the next chapter we will see that Mozart's religious beliefs profoundly affected his moral behavior. His Catholicism has been further discussed by a number of scholars.[30]

It is unfortunate that we seldom hear many of Mozart's religious works today. In this category, it is of interest to consider eight compositions that were dedicated to Our Lady, the mother of Jesus. These were three Regina Coeli (K. 108, 127, 276), the Offertory (K. 277), the Gradual (K. 273), the two Loretan Litanies (K. 109, 195), and also the Magnificat (K. 193).

MOZART'S FREEMASONRY

The origins of Freemasonry can be traced back to the historic foundation in London of the Grand Lodge of England in 1717. From that lodge the craft developed rapidly all over the continent, especially in the Germanic countries. Maria Theresa's husband, Francis I, had been initiated at the Hague in 1731. Pope Clement XII issued the Papal Bull of 1738 which condemned Freemasonry. Although a devout Catholic, Maria Theresa abrogated the publication of this Bull in Vienna; however, she suppressed the Order in 1764. The craft continued to exist in secret, but after her death, it was openly protected by Joseph II, so that the movement continued to flourish in Vienna until the concerned emperor issued a hand billet on 11 December 1785 in which he commanded that the number of Vienna lodges be restricted to not more than three. Such was the background to the founding of the New-crowned Hope Lodge. Later, Freemasonry was forbidden in Austria from 1795 to 1918.

Mozart was admitted to the Beneficence Lodge in Vienna as an apprentice on 14 December 1784. Three weeks later he attended the True Concord Lodge, and under Master Ignaz von Born he was promoted to the second grade of fellow-craft degree, on 7 January. By the following year, he had been promoted to the third grade as a master.[31] His reasons for entry are unknown, but presumably he was attracted to the high ideals of the craft. He also joined for reasons of companionship, friendship, and material advancement. Mozart had come under a strong Masonic influence among his friends, patrons, and publishers.[32] Furthermore, since Mozart held no court appointment, and consequently received no commissions to write music for the church, he would have been attracted to compose music for the craft, especially as there were no preestablished requirements to comply with.

The True Concord Lodge was founded in Vienna in 1781. The craft drew to its ranks intellectuals and leading figures from all walks of life, and by 1785 True Concord's membership numbered 200.[33] Although Joseph II was not a Mason, he was in sympathy with their cause. In the antireligious spirit of the Enlightenment, his regime cracked down and directed itself against religious orders, the celibacy of the clergy, devotion to the saints, and such popular expressions of piety as pilgrimages and veneration of relics. Since Catholicism was the official religion of the state in Austria, many of the Viennese Freemasons were also Catholics. Leopold Mozart joined the craft on 6 April 1785, but because of his limited stay in Vienna, the usual formalities were dispensed with, and he was hastily promoted to the third degree of master Mason on 22 April. Apparently, Leopold continued to attend secret meetings in Salzburg.[34]

It is unknown why Wolfgang induced his father to join a Viennese lodge. Since 1783 there had been a lodge "Zur Fürsicht" in Salzburg, which Leopold could have joined but did not. In addition, there were supposed to have been two so-called Illuminanten lodges in Salzburg, until their suppression by the elector in 1784.[35] In his letter to Nannerl dated 14 October 1785, Leopold commented on these lodges:

I learned via Herrn Rahm and letters from Marchand that not even a hundredth part of the circulating rumors about the story of the Illuminanten in Munich, is true. That there was an investigation, and that some have been exiled, or have left voluntarily, is true; the remaining ones who made a frank statement to the Elector about their activities, have remained, even the head of the lodge, Dr. Bader. The most interesting fact is that a list of about 70 members of the Bavarian lodge is circulating here, among them mostly clerics of rank, such as Count Spauer, the Canonicus of Salzburg. As I was told by Herrn Rahm, the real freemasons, including the Elector himself who is a member, are actually incensed about these more radical members, because of whom these romanticisms brought about a more stringent investigation.[36]

Joseph Haydn was initiated as an apprentice at the Concord Lodge on 11 February 1785, but he never attended another meeting. Hence, in 1786, his name was struck off the register of members.[37]

Mozart regularly attended Masonic lodges for the remainder of his life. He visited the Truth and Unity Lodge in Prague several times in the early spring of 1791, and during his last attendance on 10 September, his cantata "Die Maurerfreude" (K. 471) was performed in his honor. It was on that occasion that he promised an even finer tribute to the Masonic spirit—Die Zauberflöte.[38]

10

THE ETERNAL FEMININE

As a prodigy, Mozart was forever being pampered and fussed over by women. While a fifteen-year-old Cavaliere, he used Nannerl as a confidante in his puppy love affairs with Maria Anna Barisani and Barbara von Mölk, and there were many such innocent flirtations. Despite his "entire lacking in any pretensions as to physiognomy and bodily appearance," it would appear that there were several women who did find him attractive.[1] However, it seems unlikely that he was sexually promiscuous during his teens and early twenties. He clearly stated his reasons in the letter to his father (dated 15 December 1781):

The voice of nature speaks as loud in me as in others, louder, perhaps, than in many a big strong lout of a fellow. I simply cannot live as most young men do in these days. In the first place, I have too much religion; in the second place, I have too great a love of my neighbour and too high a feeling of honour to seduce an innocent girl; and, in the third place, I have too much horror and disgust, too much dread and fear of diseases and too much care for my health to fool about with whores. So I can swear that I have never had relations of that sort with any woman.[2]

Early in October 1777, Mozart had been horrified to see the syphilitic ulceration that had eroded away the nose of Joseph Myslivechek in Munich. This produced a lasting impression and dread of venereal disease. Furthermore, in his letter from Prague to his friend Baron Gottfried von Jacquin (dated 4 November 1787), Mozart wrote:

Well, dearest friend, how are you? I trust that you are as fit and well as we are. You cannot fail to be happy, dearest friend, for you possess everything that you can wish for at your age and in your position, particularly as you now seem to be entirely giving up your former rather restless way of living. Surely you are becoming every day more convinced of the truth of the little lectures I used to inflict upon you? Surely the pleasure of a transient, capricious infatuation is as far removed as heaven from earth from the blessed happiness of a deep and true affection? Surely in your heart of hearts you often feel grateful to me for my admonitions? You will end up by making me quite conceited. But, jesting apart, you do owe me some thanks after all, if you have become worthy of Fräulein N-(Marianne von Natorp), for I certainly played no insignificant part in your reform or conversion.[3]

However, it would appear that in his later years Mozart was on occasion smitten by certain members of the fair sex, as we will see.

Mozart met his "Bäsle" (little cousin) during his visit to Augsburg in October 1777. He described her as beautiful, sensible, sweet, clever, and merry. Together they played jokes on people, had great fun, and later exchanged portraits. She dressed in the French style to please Wolfgang and looked 5 percent prettier. Leopold Mozart was hostile and critical of his son's behavior and wrote: "In Augsburg too you had your little romance, you amused yourself with my brother's daughter, who now must needs send you her portrait."[4] A week later Mozart defended himself, and in reply wrote: "What you say so cuttingly about my merry intercourse with your brother's daughter, has hurt me very much; but since matters are not as you think, it is not necessary for me to reply."[5]

"Bäsle" accepted Mozart's invitation to join him in Munich after his rejection by Aloysia Weber, and the pair traveled by coach to Salzburg, in January 1779. Their prankish antics were in keeping with Mozart's joker mentality, which he displayed throughout his life, and we must support Einstein, Schurig, Schenk, Ghéon, Abert, Paumgartner and Stanley Sadie who maintain the innocence of their relationship. (The complex psychology of the Bäsle letters will be discussed in Chapter 16.) Maria Anna Thekla never married, but she became the mistress of a village postmaster, and she bore him a daughter named Marianna Viktoria Mozart, who died in 1857.[6] "Bäsle" lived to become an octogenerian, and she died in Bayreuth on 25 January 1841. Such longevity would be unusual in a sexually promiscuous woman exposed to the high prevalence of syphilis and the other venereal diseases of those times.

Mozart's wife was born at Zell, Wiesental, on 5 January 1762, the third of four daughters of the bass singer and music copyist, Fridolin Weber. Constanze was denied a good education, but she possessed a pleasant soprano voice and played the piano well. She was amiable enough and tried hard to please. Mozart described her in a letter to his father on 15 December 1781: "She is not ugly, but at the same time far from beautiful. Her whole beauty consists in two little black eyes and a pretty figure. She has no wit, but she has enough common sense to enable her to fulfill her duties as a wife and mother."[7]

Mozart was a good-natured, lovable fellow who needed a lot of affection. We have seen evidence of his tender moral convictions and objections to the taking of a mistress, so that when he fell in love with Constanze his thoughts soon turned to wedlock. The marriage was precipitated by intrigues, and it is to Constanze's credit that she tore up the document that Mozart had been coerced into signing by her mother and guardian, Johann von Thorwart. That document obliged Mozart to pay Constanze an annual gratuity of 300 gulden, if he had not married her within three years. The twenty-six-year-old groom married his twenty-year-old bride in St. Stephen's Cathedral on 4 August 1782; Mozart's best man was Dr. Wenzel Gilowsky. The couple, the priest, and their friends wept tears of joy after the ceremony, and Baroness von Waldstätten gave them a fine wedding feast. Leopold Mozart disapproved of the marriage, but his blessing arrived the day after the ceremony. Nannerl also considered Constanze unsuited to her brother. However, the young couple were very much in love, and the earlier years of their marriage were happy, exciting, and optimistic. During their nine and a half years of married life, she bore him six children.

No doubt the failure of Leopold Mozart and Nannerl to lovingly accept Constanze into their family was to give rise in large part to Wolfgang's gradual estrangement from them. It must have continued to be a source of mental anguish to them all. Constanze has become the subject of much criticism, being cast by some biographers as insensitive, dim-witted, extravagant, and a neglectful wife who failed to appreciate and inspire her husband's great genius. However, it should be remembered that Constanze encouraged her husband's study and composition of fugues in 1782. Although her intellectual influence on Mozart does not appear to have been important, she does seem to have satisfied his physical and emotional needs within her capability, and her judicious appreciation of his art in no way prejudiced his productive outflow.

We will see that following his father's death Mozart became increasingly dependent on his wife's affection for his well-being, but let us now consider his prima donnas.

Throughout his life Mozart was particularly attracted to the human voice, and of the many sopranos he heard there were four favorites. The first of these was the Neopolitan prima donna, Anna Lucia De Amicis, who was engaged in Milan for Lucio Silla (K. 135) in December 1772. The concert aria "Se Tutti I Mali Miei" (K. 83) may have been written for her in 1770, two years after her marriage to the Florentine physician Francesco Buonsollazzi. Mozart was enchanted with her baby son Giuseppe, whom he met in Milan in January 1773. Burney described De Amicis as the first to sing staccato divisions and the first to reach up to

E-flat in altissimo with a true, clear, and powerful reality of voice. The platonic nature of his friendship with De Amicis has not been challenged.

Mozart was taken up for a time, in 1777, with an attractive young singer, Mlle. Kaiser in Munich, but he fell madly in love with Aloysia Weber when he was aged twenty-two, and her rejection must have hurt him deeply. Two years later in the letter to his father (dated 15 December 1781) he described her thus: "Mme Lange is a false, malicious person and a coquette."[8] Seven months previously Mozart had written: "I was a fool, I admit, about Aloysia Lange, but what does not a man do (when he is in love?). Indeed I loved her truly, and even now I feel that she is not a matter of indifference to me."[9]

Wolfgang does not appear to have borne her any lasting malice, for he continued to assist her in her career. He composed seven concert arias for her between 1778 and 1788 (K. 294, 316, 383, 416, 418, 419, and 538). In July 1829, Aloysia Lange was interviewed by Mary Novello concerning her rejection of the composer. Aloysia said that she could not love him at that time, and was not capable of appreciating his talent and amiable character, but afterwards she much regretted it. There has never been any convincing evidence that their relationship was anything but very proper. Aloysia played Madame Herz in Der Schauspieldirektor (K. 486), and she sang Donna Anna in the Viennese premiere of Don Giovanni (K. 527) in 1788, and Sextus in a concert performance of La Clemenza di Tito (K. 621) in 1795. She married the actor Joseph Lange on 31 October 1780; only one of their seven children, a son, survived to maturity. The jealous Lange apparently held an iron grip on the pursestrings, and they separated in 1795.

Mozart was also very fond of Nancy Ann Selina Storace, whose brother Stephen was one of his most gifted composition pupils and whose father was an Italian double-bass player. Nancy was one of the most celebrated opera buffa sopranos of her time; she earned a very large income and was favoured by the Emperor Joseph II. In 1784, she impulsively married the touring English violinist and composer, John Abraham Fisher, who was more than twice her age. The marriage soon broke up, and the emperor took the unusual step of banishing Fisher from Austria, allegedly on the pretext of Fisher's cruelty to her. Mozart spent many happy hours in the company of the Storaces. Michael Kelly's memoirs described a Quartet Soiree in their home which was attended by Paisiello and the poet Casti—Haydn (first violin), Dittersdorf (second violin), Mozart (viola), and Vanhall (cello). The departure of Nancy's husband from Vienna probably did add some romantic glamor to their relationship, and in response to their deep and sympathetic understanding, the scena and aria "Ch'io Mi Scordi Di Te" (K. 505), to a text by Lorenzo Da Ponte, was dedicated to her. Einstein described it as a declaration of love in music. The autograph is marked "Composto per la Sig^ra Storace dal suo servo ed amico W. A. Mozart, Vienna Li 26 Di Dec^bre 1786."[10] Nancy, who was the first Susanna in *Figaro*, returned to London early in 1787. Although Mozart's plans to go to London never materialized, he maintained a correspondence with her. Unfortunately, their letters have not survived. Nancy never remarried, but following the sudden death of her brother Stephen in 1796, she undertook a successful concert tour of the continent with the tenor John Braham. In 1802, she bore him a son, Spencer, who later changed his name to Meadows and became a minor canon at Canterbury Cathedral. Nancy retired in 1808, separated from Braham eight years later, and died in Dulwich in 1817, at age fifty-one.[11]

The Czech soprano Josepha Duschek was one of Mozart's oldest and most loyal friends. Josepha Hamberger was also a gifted pianist; having become a pupil of the noted composer, pianist, and teacher Franz Xaver Duschek (1731-99), she married him in 1776. Josepha met Mozart in Salzburg, her mother's home town, in August 1777. She was very sympathetic about his unhappiness in that city and offered him a warm open invitation to visit Prague. Mozart composed two concert arias (K. 272, 528) for her. Josepha took part in the Leipzig concert on 8 May 1789, when she sang the arias (K. 505, 528). After Mozart's death, the Duscheks helped Constanze rear their two surviving sons. Josepha was famed for the dramatic expressiveness of her singing.

The aria "Basta, vincesti . . . ah, non lasciami, no" (K. 295a) was composed in Mannheim on 27 February 1778 for the magnificent soprano Dorothea Wendling, who later created the first Ilia in *Idomeneo*. Wolfgang gave the details in a letter to his father dated 28 February 1778: "Yesterday at Wendlings I sketched the aria which I had promised his wife, adding a short recitative. She had chosen the words herself—from 'Didone' "[12] Dorothea's sister-in-law, Elisabeth Wendling, sang the first Elettra in *Idomeneo*, and in 1781 Mozart composed the aria "Ma, che vi fece, O stelle" (K. 368) for her. On 8 March 1781, he composed the aria "Misera, dove son!" (K. 369) for Karl Theodor's mistress, the Countess Baumgarten, with a view to obtaining the elector's favor. For Auguste Wendling at Mannheim he composed two songs (K. 307, 308).

Mozart had arrived at Berlin on the evening of 19 May 1789, and he stayed with the stucco worker Sartory on the Gendarmen-Markt. Upon hearing that *Die Entführung* was being performed that evening, he went straight to the National Theater in his traveling coat. The opera had been running under the title of *Belmonte und Constanze* since 16 October 1788. Mozart stood by the doorway leading to the orchestral pit, so as to listen incognito. The cast included Marianne Hellmuth as Constanze and Henriette Baranius as Blonde. The composer's expression fluctuated according to his satisfaction or displeasure at the rendering of certain passages. Gradually, he became completely absorbed in the production, and without knowing it, he pressed closer and closer to the audience, who started to take notice of this funny little man still dressed in his topcoat. During the oft-repeated words "Nur ein feiger Tropf verzagt" in Pedrillo's aria, the second violin was mistakenly playing D-sharp instead of D. Mozart, no longer able to restrain himself, shouted at the top of his voice: "Damn it all, will you play D!" The composer was soon recognized by some of the musicians, and soon there was a buzz of excitement throughout the theater that "Mozart is here." Some of the cast were so overwhelmed by his presence that they refused to continue the performance; Henriette Baranius was among them. The conductor implored Mozart to plead with the singers to continue, and this he did successfully. It is reputed that backstage Mozart said to Henriette: "What nonsense is this? You sang splendidly—and so that you will do even better next time, I shall go over the part with you."[13]

Henriette Rietz (née Baranius) the stunning mistress of the Prussian king, Frederick William II, was reputed to have possessed a remarkable beauty and grace. Mozart remained in Berlin for nine days, and it was rumored that he had an affair with Henriette, as reported by Jahn. It was said "that Mozart became so deeply involved with her that it cost his friends much trouble to extricate him."[14] Later, on 20 December 1790, Frau Baranius sang Zerlina in a German production of *Don Giovanni* in Berlin.

Mozart greatly admired the voice of the Austrian soprano Catarina Cavalieri (1760-1801) who was Salieri's mistress. She created the role of Constanze in *Die Entführung* (K. 384). In the letter to his father (dated 26 September 1781), Mozart said: "I have sacrificed Constanze's aria a little to the flexible throat of Mlle Cavalieri."[15] She sang the soprano part of *Davidde Penitente* (K. 469) as well as Mlle. Silberklang in *Der Schauspieldirektor*. Cavalieri was intended to sing Bettina in the incompleted *Lo sposo deluso* (K. 430), and she performed Donna Elvira in the Vienna premiere of *Don Giovanni* (K. 527), for which occasion Mozart composed the extra aria "Mi tradi" (K. 540 c) for her. Catarina sang Galatea in Mozart's rescored version of Handel's *Acis and Galatea* (K. 566), and the Countess in the Vienna revival of *Figaro* in 1789. In that most interesting letter to Professor Anton Klein (dated 21 May 1785) in which Mozart voiced his national Germanic pride, the composer said of Cavalieri that "Germany may well be proud of her."[16] She and Salieri attended *Zauberflöte* as Mozart's guests on 13 October 1791.

The Italian soprano Adrqana Ferraresi del Bene (Adriana Gabrielli) had an incredible vocal compass but lacked acting ability. She was Lorenzo Da Ponte's mistress and sang Susanna in the Vienna revival of *Figaro* in 1789, for which occasion Mozart composed two substitute arias (K. 577, 579) for her. The composer referred to one of these arias in the letter to his wife (dated end of August 1789):

The little aria, which I composed for Madame Ferraresi, ought, I think, to be a success, provided she is able to sing it in an artless manner, which, however, I very much doubt. She herself liked it very much. I have just lunched at her house.[17]

Ferraresi was the first Fiordiligi in *Così Fan Tutte* (K. 588). Her intrigues with Da Ponte caused trouble in the camp of the Court Theatre, and following their joint dismissal by Emperor Leopold II, in the second half of 1791, the pair traveled together to Trieste. Da Ponte blamed machinations on the part of Antonio Salieri, Johann Thorwart, Francesco Bussani, and the secret agent of the imperial court, Giuseppe Latenzi. Later, in July 1797, she appeared in the first performance of *Così* in that city.

Louise Villeneuve joined the Italian opera company in Vienna in 1789. Mozart composed three concert arias for her (K. 578, 582, 583). She later created Dorabella in *Così Fan Tutte*.

A cloud of mystery and intrigue surrounds the events in the camp of Schikaneder's Troupe during the summer of 1791. Benedikt Schack and Franz Xaver Gerl were the regular composers for this company, and Gerl played Sarastro in the premiere of *Zauberflöte*. His very pretty and attractive wife, Barbara Gerl (née Reisinger), played Papagena. Mozart had composed the duet "Nun, Liebes Weibchen" (K. 625) for Act 2, Scene 4, of Schikaneder's opera *Der Stein der Weisen* and it was sung by Barbara Gerl and Schikaneder at the Freihaus Theater on 11 September 1790. Jahn stated that contemporaries had affirmed that Barbara Gerl "had completely entangled Mozart in her coils" and that Mozart's infatuation with this woman influenced his decision to accept the commission to write the music of *Zauberflöte*.[18] According to Seyfried, Mozart usually wrote in Gerl's lodgings or in Schikaneder's garden-house. Be that as it may, Franz Xaver Gerl remained on friendly terms with Mozart; indeed, he sang the bass part in the rehearsal of the *Requiem* at the composer's bedside on the day before his death. Mozart's pupil Johann Nepomuk Hummel had this to say:

I declare it to be untrue that Mozart abandoned himself to excesses, except on those rare occasions on which he was induced by Schikaneder, during the summer of 1791, when his wife was at Baden, and the excesses to which he then gave way have been magnified by report, and made the foundation of exaggerated representation of Mozart's thoughtless life.[19]

However, it would appear that Barbara Gerl was the unnamed mistress referred to by Jean-Baptiste-Antoine Suard:

I have said that he loved his wife greatly; she deserved it: she encouraged him in his work and sustained him in his fits of melancholy. Mozart was tenderly attached to her; but that did not prevent him from conceiving a fancy for other

women, and his fancies had such a hold over him that he could not resist them. I
have heard it said that he wrote La Flûte Enchantée only to please a woman of the
theatre with whom he had fallen in love, and who offered him her favours at this
price. It is added that his triumph had very cruel consequences, and that he
contracted from it an incurable disease of which he died shortly after. This fact
seems to me very unlikely; La Flûte Enchantée is not the last of his operas, and
when he composed it, his health was already seriously impaired.[20]

Suard's latter conclusion was very sound, for we will see that Mozart
bore no evidence of syphilis and that during his composition of
Zauberflöte he was in the grip of uremic cerebral vascular disease.

The youngest singer to be placed under Mozart's tutelage was Maria
Anna Gottlieb (1774-1856), both of whose parents were members of the
Vienna Burgtheater Company. Having made her debut at age five, she
created the role of Barbarina in Figaro at age twelve, and she created
Pamina in Zauberflöte at seventeen. In 1792, she began a lengthy career
at the Leopoldstadt Theater, where she gained fame as a singer and
dancer in performances of Singspiel and musical parodies. Gottlieb
appeared at the first Mozart Festival in Salzburg in 1842, and again in the
Jubilee of 1856, when she died on 4 February during the centenary
celebrations.

Mozart's genius consumed him with an unquenchable desire to
compose. However, he disliked teaching, which he found too time-
consuming. Furthermore, he lacked the patience and dedication which
his father, for example, possessed. In his letter from Mannheim to
Leopold (dated 7 February 1778) he justified the delay in his departure
for Paris, and he wrote:

I could not get on at all without pupils, which is a kind of work that is quite
uncongenial to me—and of this I have an excellent example here. I could have
had two pupils. I went three times to each, but finding one of them out, I never
went back. I will gladly give lessons as a favour, particularly when I see that my
pupil has talent, inclination and anxiety to learn; but to be obliged to go to a house
at a certain hour—or to have to wait at home for a pupil—is what I cannot do, no
matter how much money it may bring me in. I find it impossible, so must leave it
to those who can do nothing else but play the clavier.[21]

And so it was that Mozart never came to rival Steffan, Kozeluch, or
Righini as the most successful and fashionable music teacher in Vienna,
although quite often he was forced to take in pupils out of necessity.
Many of them were highly born young ladies who were prompted by the
fashion to gain snob-value by taking lessons from so famous a musician.

There was one pupil, however, whose friendship the composer valued
dearly. She was Franziska von Jacquin, who later married Herr Lagusius
and whose pet name was Signora Diniminimi. In his long letter from

Prague to his friend Baron Gottfried von Jacquin (dated 15 January 1787), Mozart wrote:

I kiss your sister's hands a hundred thousand times and urge her to practise hard on her new pianoforte. But this admonition is really unnecessary, for I must confess that I have never yet had a pupil who was so diligent and who showed so much zeal—and indeed I am looking forward to giving her lessons again according to my small ability.[22]

Mozart had composed for Franziska the "Skittle-Alley Trio" (K. 498) in 1786, and in the letter to her brother (dated ? 29 May 1787) he enclosed the Piano Sonata for Four Hands in C (K. 521), saying: "Please be so good as to give the sonata to your sister with my compliments and tell her to tackle it at once, for it is rather difficult."[23]

Several other compositions were dedicated to various pupils, including the Piano Sonata in C (K. 309) for Rosa Cannabich, and the Sonata for Piano and Violin in C (K. 296) for Therese Pierron Serrarius. The piano variations (K. 352) were written for his first pupil in Vienna, Countess Maria Rumbeke.

Mozart composed the Sonata for Piano in C Minor (K. 457) and the Fantasia for Piano in C Minor (K. 475) for Therese von Trattner. The dedication of two of his finest piano works to her leaves little doubt that Mozart was fond of her. Therese was the second wife of Johann von Trattner, and she was very kind to Mozart during his serious illness in August 1784. He completed the sonata on her name-day, and the dedication contained written instructions for performance. Therese probably performed this sonata at the small concert given by his lady pupils on 31 October 1784. After Mozart's death, Therese refused to hand over the dedication to Constanze; this has led to speculation about an affair.

The six sonatas for piano and violin (K. 296, 376-380) and the Sonata for Two Pianos in D (K. 488) were composed for Josepha Auernhammer. Mozart dedicated his piano concertos in E-flat (K. 449) and in G (K. 453) to Barbara von Ployer; he also composed two piano concertos for celebrity virtuosi—in E-flat (K. 271) for Mlle Jeunehomme and in B-flat (K. 456) for Maria Theresia von Paradies.

Several of Mozart's pupils were attractive young women, and no doubt he was tempted to flirt with some of them. In July 1829, the Novellos visited their banker Joseph Henickstein in Vienna. Henickstein claimed that he knew Mozart well and that he was of the most merry and lively character. He said that the composer did not show the great genius in his conversation, but that he had a moderately good tenor voice, played the violin well and the viola still better. Henickstein said that Mozart had given piano lessons to his sister. The following comments were separately recorded by the Novellos in their travel diary. Vincent wrote: "Mozart would not take pains in giving lessons to any ladies but those he was in love with."[24] Mary Novello wrote: "He, (Henickstein) thought him too gay in his manner, he was always in love with his pupils. They have often gone out together to give a serenade which was then much in fashion."[25]

In the case of Josepha Auernhammer, however, it was the other way around—she made the advances, and he did not reciprocate since he found her unattractive. During his wife's frequent absences at Baden, Mozart at times felt lonely, frustrated, and depressed; it has also been alleged that he indulged in occasional flirtations with maids.

J.E.F. Arnold, of Erfurt, wrote in 1803: "Besides this (excessive work) he was a husband, brought up two children, and had many intrigues with lively actresses and other women, which his wife good-naturedly overlooked."[26] Constanze did not substantiate these accusations either in the Nissen biography or during her interviews with the Novellos. Mozart's sexual provocativeness will be discussed further in chapter 16, and we will then more fully understand how Mozart's immature personality led him into impulsive and irresponsible infatuations.

If Mozart did have adulterous affairs, they were probably associated with guilt and remorse, for he continued to love his wife. In his last letter to Constanze (dated 14 October 1791) he concluded:

I am happiest at home, for I am accustomed to my own hours. This one occasion put me in a very bad humour. Yesterday the whole day was taken up with that trip to Bernstorf (Perchtoldsdorf), so I could not write to you. But that you have not written to me for two days, is really unforgivable. I hope that I shall certainly have a letter from you today, and that tomorrow I shall talk to you and embrace you with all my heart.[27]

MOZARTIAN ECONOMICS

Table of Money Values[1]

Germany and Austria

Taking the South German kreuzer (worth 4 pfennige, slightly more than the English farthing) as the standard, the following equivalent values of silver coins are obtained:

 60 kreuzer (or 16 groschen) = 1 gulden, about 2 shillings. [$3.00]
 90 kreuzer (or 24 groschen) = 1 reichsthaler, about 3 shillings. [$4.50]
120 kreuzer (or 32 groschen) = 1 laubthaler or federthaler, about 4 shillings. [$6.00]

The following gold coins were in common use in Germany and Austria:
1 ducat (used all over Europe) = 4½ gulden, about 9 shillings. [$13.50]
1 max d'or (used chiefly in Bavaria) = 6¼ gulden, about 13 shillings. [$18.75]
1 friedrich d'or (used chiefly in Prussia) = 8 gulden, about 16 shillings. [$24.00]
1 pistole (used all over Europe) = 7½ gulden, about 15 shillings. [$22.50]
1 carolin (used chiefly in Southern Germany) = 9 gulden, about 18 shillings. [$27.00]
1 souverain d'or (used chiefly in Austria) = 13½ gulden, about 27 shillings. [$40.00]

France

 4 liard = 1 sou = about half-penny. [$0.06]
20 sous = 1 livre, about eleven pence. [$1.25]
 1 louis d'or = 24 livres, about twenty shillings. [$30.00]

Mozart
Silverpoint drawing by Doris Stock, Dresden, 16 or 17 April 1789. The drawing was hastily sketched on ivory board, during Mozart's visit to the artist's brother-in-law, the consistorial councillor, Christian Gottfried Korner, a friend of the poet Friedrich von Schiller. This is one of the last portraits of Mozart. (Courtesy of the Deutsche Bucherei, Leipzig.)

Italy

---

1 paolo (a silver coin of Tuscany, worth originally about 56 centesimi, and used as the equivalent of half a lira) = about sixpence. [$0.75]
1 cigliato (or, more commonly, gigliato) = a ducat, about 9 shillings. [$13.50]
1 zecchino (a Venetian gold coin) = about 9 shillings. [$14.00]
1 doppio = probably a doppio zecchino, about 20 shillings. [$30.00]

Holland

---

1 rijder = about 28 shillings. [$42.00]

All admirers of Mozart's music are pained to read of the composer's catastrophic plight at the time of his death, but his debts were magnified ten times by the scandal-mongers, the publication of his importunate letters to Michael Puchberg, and the tendency of early biographers to etch an exaggerated, unremitting, and misguided account of Mozart's poverty during his latter years. Five authors have recently shed new light on this subject, and there is general agreement about Mozart's extravagant lifestyle.[2] However, controversy persists as to the extent of Mozart's gambling; the difficulties are compounded by the incomplete records of his finances.

During the eighteenth century, music patrons were still largely drawn from the ranks of the nobility. Throughout his life, Mozart had been encouraged by his father to cultivate relationships with the upper strata of society. It is understandable that the immature Mozart came to adopt a lifestyle far beyond his means and status. For the first twenty-five years of his life, his father took charge of money matters, and it should come as no surprise that Mozart was unable to manage his financial affairs. In response to censure by his father about his carelessness with money, he had this to say:

So rely absolutely on my brains and my good heart, and you will never regret it. Why, where could I have learnt the value of money, when up to the present I have had so little to handle? All I know is that once when I had twenty ducats, I considered myself wealthy. Necessity alone teaches one to value money.[3]

Let us then attempt to estimate Mozart's income in Vienna. We know from letters to his father that the composer was confident that he could earn 1000 gulden a year from a grand concert and four clavier pupils.[4] In addition, there were the potential gains from publications of his music and the commission of operas, so that he felt justified in relinquishing his court salary of 450 gulden at Salzburg. He charged the high fee of six ducats for twelve lessons as a piano teacher, and his first pupil was

Countess Maria Rumbeke. By the end of January 1782, he had acquired four pupils, from whom he was receiving 18 ducats a month. Although the potential income from clavier teaching was 972 gulden a year, it is to be remembered that his pupils from the nobility were usually absent during the summer months, as well as during the winter carnival.

In the letter to his father dated 11 April 1781, Mozart stated, that had he been free to give private concerts in the homes of the nobility, during the previous three weeks he would have earned at least 450 gulden. It is unknown how much he earned from performing parts of *Idomeneo* at Countess Thun's in May, or from his private concert at the Auernhammer home on 23 November, when he performed K. 365 and K. 448 with his host's daughter Josepha. Nor is there any record of how much he received the previous week for playing before the Archduke Maximilian and the duke of Württemberg. Likewise, it is unknown whether his intention, to produce an Advent Cantata for his own benefit was realized.[5] Mozart advertised his six sonatas for violin (K. 296, 376-80) for subscription, but by July there were only seventeen subscribers. However, Artaria published them in November. Emperor Joseph II generously paid Mozart 225 gulden for winning the piano competition against Muzio Clementi at the Hofburg on 24 December 1781.

This encouraging trend in his financial state continued during 1782 when it would appear likely that he earned as much as 2,000 gulden. In addition to his benefit concert at the Burgtheater on 3 March, he also took part in the first of twelve subscription concerts organized by Philipp Martin on 26 May in the Augarten. Mozart was paid 100 ducats (450 gulden) for the composition and production of *Die Entführung Aus Dem Serail*. In the letter to his father dated 20 July, he stated that the opera had brought in 1,200 gulden in two days. His most popular stage success was performed in Vienna forty-two times during his lifetime, and presumably at least once for the composer's benefit. It is unknown how much he received for the Wind Serenade in C Minor (K. 388) which was probably composed for the fabulously wealthy young Prince Alois Liechtenstein, who was intent on establishing a wind band. During Advent Mozart took part in his pupil's concert and played in the drawing room of Countess Thun.[6]

In March 1783, he was busily involved in performance on four occasions; however, his own academy concert on 23 March was an unprecedented success. The emperor, contrary to his usual practice, remained until the end and sent Mozart 25 ducats, while the receipts were estimated at 1,600 gulden. His three new piano concertos (K. 413-5) were advertised for subscription at 4 ducats, but it was a failure and they were published early in 1785. The loss of income during the four months' journey to Salzburg was in part compensated for by his concert at Linz on 4 November.

There seems little doubt that Mozart earned a very considerable income in excess of 4,000 gulden a year during the next two years, when his popularity as a virtuoso was at its height. During the first six months of 1784, he gave private performances in the homes of the nobility on no less than nineteen occasions. Such appearances were potentially lucrative, returning fees as high as 200 gulden. The oboist Ludwig Lebrun, according to Leopold Mozart, earned 2,500 gulden from three of his concerts. In addition to his benefit concert in the Burgtheater on 1 April, Mozart received 1,056 gulden from 174 subscribers for the three Lenten subscription concerts at Trattner's Hall in March, and also appeared before the emperor at Regina Strinasacchi's concert in April. In addition, he conducted *Die Entführung* for Aloysia Lange's benefit on 25 January.

The receipts from Mozart's benefit concert on 10 March 1785 were 559 gulden, and he made at least seven other appearances at the Burgtheater that year. He received 2,025 gulden for the six lenten Mehlgrube subscription concerts, while Artaria paid him 450 gulden for the six string quartets dedicated to Joseph Haydn.[7] It is unknown how much he received for his composition of two interpolated numbers for Francesco Bianchi's opera *La Villanella Rapita*, which had its premiere at the Burgtheater on 28 November 1785.[8]

Mozart continued to earn a very high income during the next two years. He conducted *Idomeneo* in March 1786 at Prince Johann Auersperg's Palace Theater,[9] and appeared with Josepha Duschek at the Hofburg.[10] He gave his last public benefit concert at the Burgtheater on 7 April 1786, but it is unknown whether his four planned Advent concerts in Trattner's Casino were realized.

Although the reason for Mozart's decline as a virtuoso pianist is unknown, it seems likely that several factors were responsible. Perhaps Count Arco's prophecy was fulfilled in that the fickle Viennese palate had become saturated and had developed an appetite for something new. It seems probable that Mozart was drawn by his inner creative genius to compose operas and chamber music, and that he was forced to slacken his pace by the sheer exhaustion of celebrity concert life. We will explore the possibility of the alleged defamatory consequences of notorious gambling in Chapter 13, but we will see that his cyclothymic depression was largely responsible for his withdrawal from his life as a celebrity.

In any event, Mozart received 675 gulden for the commissions of *Der Schauspieldirektor* and *Le Nozze di Figaro*, and he was presumably well rewarded for the private performance of *Figaro* in June in the Palace Theater at Laxenburg.

Mozart's visit to Prague in January 1787 was fabulously successful, so that he made 1,000 gulden from his public benefit concert and performance of *Figaro*.[11] Ann Storace netted 4,000 gulden from her farewell benefit appearance at the Kärntnertor Theater on 23 February 1787, and it is likely that Mozart accompanied her with the Scena and Rondo, K. 505. It is also probable that he performed that year in the public benefit concerts of his friends Friedrich Ramm and Ludwig Karl Fischer.

Mozart arranged for his inheritance of 1,000 gulden to be paid to his advantage in Viennese florins.[12] Little remained of the gewgaws worth 12,000 gulden from the Grand Tour. Leopold had presumably pawned most of them to finance the three Italian journeys.

Mozart would surely have earned at least a further thousand gulden during the autumn in Prague from his production and benefit performance of *Don Giovanni* and the revival of *Figaro*.[13] Mozart abandoned his plan to visit London during the Carnival of 1788 because of his father's indignant refusal to look after his children, and his appointment on 6 December as Imperial Kammermusicus on a salary of 800 florins.

Although Mozart's income declined during 1788-90, he was by no means reduced to that gloomy state of destitution which nineteenth-century biographers would have us believe. He attempted to arrange subscription concerts in Trattner's Casino and probably gave the first one in the second week of June 1788, but there is no record.[14] Indeed, the paucity of reliable data on Viennese concert life during these years calls for caution about any definitive statement about Mozart's popularity as a pianist then.[15] In any event, he played at a private concert at the Venetian ambassador's residence on 10 February 1788. He may also have performed at Stefano Mandini's benefit concert later that month, when one of his symphonies was played.

Gottfried van Swieten had founded a Society of Noblemen for the Cultivation of Classical Music, Kavaliers-Gesellschaft Klassischer Musik. He was in particular a devotee of Bach and Handel. Private concerts for this group were often held in the theater of Count Johann Esterhazy's Palace. Mozart reorchestrated one of the arias of C.P.E. Bach's Resurrection Cantata. During Lent in 1788, he conducted two private performances, as well as a public one in the Burgtheater. Later that year in Advent, he conducted for his own benefit Handel's Pastorale "Acis and Galatea" (K. 566), in Jahn's Hall which seated up to 400 people. Mozart also conducted private performances of Handel's *Messiah* (K. 572) during Lent in 1789, *Alexander's Feast* (K. 591), and *Ode for St. Cecilia's Day* (K. 592) during 1790.

Early in 1788, Mozart advertised his String Quintets (K. 406, 515, 516) for sale by subscription at 4 ducats, but the response was slow. As a result, he postponed their publication until the following January. He received 225 gulden for the Vienna premiere of *Don Giovanni* on 7 May 1788. It is to be remembered that his sinecure appointment as chamber musician entailed few obligations other than the composition of dances for the court balls. On one of the receipts he noted: "Too much for what I do, too little for what I could do."[16] The fees paid by composition pupils were a modest few hundred gulden.

Mozart borrowed 100 gulden from Franz Hofdemel to help finance the journey to Berlin. On 13 April 1789, he gave a private concert to a packed house in the large music room of the Hôtel de Pologne in Dresden. The next evening he played his Piano Concerto in D (K. 537) before the elector,[17] who rewarded him the next day with an expensive snuff box containing 100 ducats, after his trial of skill on the organ and pianoforte with Johann Wilhelm Hässler.[18] Mozart also played in many noble and private houses at Dresden with boundless success.[19] However, his public benefit concert with Josepha Duschek, at the Hall of the Gewandhaus, Leipzig, on 12 May was a disappointment: "The applause was magnificent, but the profits were wretchedly meagre."[20]

His traveling companion, Prince Karl Lichnowsky, borrowed 100 gulden from Mozart and parted company with him at Leipzig in the middle of May. Mozart's mission was at last accomplished on 26 May when he played before the king and queen at the Berlin Royal Palace. Although he gave no concert in Berlin, he is reputed to have received a gold snuff box containing 100 Friedrichs d'or (700 gulden) from King Frederick William II for the String Quartet in D (K. 575). According to Rochlitz, the king of Prussia, despite the intrigues of Duport and Reichardt, offered Mozart the post of Kapellmeister, with a salary of $3,000. However, he refused out of loyalty to his Emperor Joseph II.[21] Constanze Nissen confirmed this story to the Novellos in 1829, but she stated that Mozart was offered a salary of 1,600 zechins a year (equivalent to 8,000 gulden).[22] Otto Jahn believed this story, despite his fruitless search of the Archives in the Berlin Royal Library for some trace of documentary evidence, though later biographers were unconvinced.[23] The story seems more credible in the light of the recent, more realistic revaluation of Mozart's income at that time.

The glittering success of Mozart's concert life during 1781-86, and the production of *Figaro* were very much dependent on the personal involvement and support of the emperor, and no doubt Mozart was attracted to the atmosphere of informality, egalitarianism, and intellectual licence in Joseph's court. However, a series of setbacks in the Empire, which included the Bavarian Succession in 1784, the French Revolution, and the disastrous war with Turkey (1788-91), led to civil unrest and a hostile backlash from the nobility, which necessitated a dramatic revision of Joseph's enlightened policies. Furthermore, the emperor's frequent ill health throughout 1789, and the decline in the Austrian economy, with its consequent credit shortage and rising interest rates, would have had significant impact on Mozart's monetary difficulties.[24]

Nor was the Vienna opera to escape the financial pinch. German singspiel had been cultivated since October 1785, but the venture was abandoned after the performance of *Die Entführung* on 4 February 1788, and the Kärntnertor Theater remained closed for over three years.[25] In January 1789, when the Emperor Joseph II learned that the Italian opera company was in debt to the tune of 80,000 gulden, he understandably was of a mind to disband the enterprise. However, Lorenzo Da Ponte elaborated a brilliant subscription scheme and persuaded the emperor to allow the company to continue. *Figaro* was revived at the Burgtheater on 29 August, and Mozart composed two new soprano numbers for Adriana Ferrarese del Bene, who sang Susanna.[26] Mozart supervised the rehearsals, but Joseph Weigl conducted the performance. Later that year Mozart composed three further insertion arias for two other Italian operas.[27]

Even in that most dismal year of 1790, Mozart earned over 2,000 gulden. He received 900 gulden for the commission of *Così Fan Tutte*, whose premiere he conducted on 26 January. The opera was very well received, but owing to Joseph II's death on 20 February, further performances were postponed until June. *Così* was given ten times that year but not again during the composer's lifetime. On 9 April, Mozart took part in a private concert at Count Hadik's, when K. 563 and 581 were performed. In May he made unsuccessful application to the court for the post of second Kapellmeister, while in July he completed his own orchestration of Handel's *Alexander's Feast* (K. 591) and *Ode for St. Cecilia's Day* (K. 592), which were performed privately at van Swieten's Society of Noblemen. Mozart also orchestrated the duet "Nun, Liebes Weibchen" (K. 625) for inclusion in Schikaneder's opera *Der Stein der Weisen* at the Freihaus Theater in September.

In order to journey to Frankfurt for the coronation of Leopold II on 9 October, Mozart borrowed 1,000 gulden at 5 percent interest from a merchant named Lackenbacher.[28] There is also mention that at this time Mozart pawned a silver platter to meet the expenses of this journey.[29] Two concerts were planned, but only one was given in the Great Municipal Playhouse on 15 October. In the interest of economy, only a small orchestra took part; however, most of the visiting nobility had already departed from Frankfurt, so that the attendance was poor and the profits meager. On 20 October, he played in the concert hall of the Electoral Palace at Mainz (now the Gutenberg Museum) and received 15 carolins (165 gulden) from the elector. Early in November, he took part in a court concert held in honor of King Ferdinand IV of Naples and Sicily in the Imperial Hall of the Electoral Palace in Munich. During the autumn Mozart reluctantly accepted a commission for the works for mechanical organ from Count Joseph Deym.[30] His indignation was expressed to Constanze in his letter from Frankfurt on 3 October:

I have now made up my mind to compose at once the Adagio for the clockmaker and then to slip a few ducats into the hand of my dear little wife. And this I have done; but as it is a kind of composition which I detest, I have unfortunately not been able to finish it. I compose a bit of it every day—but I have to break off now and then, as I get bored. And indeed I would give the whole thing up, if I had not such an important reason to go on with it. But I still hope that I shall be able to force myself gradually to finish it. If it were for a large instrument and the work would sound like an organ piece, then I might get some fun out of it. But, as it is, the work consists solely of little pipes which sound too high-pitched and too childish for my taste.[31]

The tide had now turned, and Mozart returned home to his fine first-floor apartment at Rauhensteingasse 8. Upon his return he found an invitation from Robert May O'Reilly to compose operas for London; in addition, Salomon invited him to visit the English capital during the winter season of 1791-92.[32] Lorenzo Da Ponte was also keen to reform their coalition so as to produce operas for London. However, Mozart was unable to accept such lucrative invitations at that time since Constanze was again pregnant, and he was fully occupied with compositions of the moment. This upturn in his financial situation continued throughout his last year. He received commissions from Johann Tost for String Quintets (K. 593, 614) and from Ignaz Alberti for three songs (K. 596, 597, 598). In March Mozart composed the bass aria (K. 612) and piano variations (K. 613). He had returned to the concert platform to play his last piano concerto in B-flat (K. 595) at Jahn's Hall on 4 March. Mozart may have played the viola part when the Harmonica Quintet (K. 617) was played at Marianne Kirchgessner's concert at the Kärntnertor Theater on 19 August. During the summer of 1791, he negotiated the sale of musical items to Herr Deyerkauf for a discounted fee of 180 gulden.[33]

Mozart received a downpayment of 225 gulden for the commission of the Requiem, and on 2 September he probably conducted a festival performance before the emperor of Don Giovanni in the National Theater, Prague to a crammed house holding more than 1,000 people.[34] Mozart received 900 gulden for the commission of La Clemenza di Tito, in addition to traveling expenses of 225 gulden,[35] while for Die Zauberflöte he may have received benefits or a share in the profits.[36] His income from the Masonic music is unknown.

The total number of Mozart's identifiable works printed during his life was 144.[37] Artaria published forty-nine during the composer's last four years; with this firm Mozart ranked third behind Haydn and Pleyel.[38] During his last eight years, about 195 of his compositions, including reprints, were published in Vienna, giving an average of twenty-five per year. Admittedly, these tallies include small works such as dances, minuets, and songs.

Mozart offered three piano concertos (K. 413-5) to Sieber of Paris for 30 louis d'or (300 gulden).[39] He had previously received 15 louis d'or from this publishing firm for his six violin sonatas (K. 301-6).[40]

We should also recall that Prince von Fürstenberg paid Mozart 143.5 gulden for three symphonies (K. 319, 338, 425) and three piano concertos (K. 451, 459, 488) on 8 November 1786.[41] Eleven sets of piano variations were published in Vienna during 1780-91.[42] According to one source, Artaria paid 25 ducats for every half-dozen variations.[43] By extrapolating these figures, it would appear that Mozart would have earned at least 500 gulden a year from publishers.

How much money then did Mozart earn in Vienna? It has been estimated that between December 1785 and December 1791 he earned 11,000 gulden, or an average of 1,833 gulden a year.[44] However, this figure underestimates the composer's income from private concerts and publications. It has also been suggested that Mozart earned 10,000 gulden a year from his concerts alone during the years 1783-86, but this estimate seems to be inflated.[45] More recently, it has been calculated that his average annual income in Vienna was 3,000 to 4,000 gulden.[46] We support this estimate and would submit that Mozart's average total income during the last eleven years of his life was at least 3,500 gulden a year.

It is of interest for us now to compare Mozart's income with that of his contemporaries. Let us first consider other composers. The salary of the first Kapellmeister at Salzburg was 1,300 gulden, while Christian Cannabich earned 1,800 gulden in 1779; Gluck certainly merited his stipend of 2,000, whereas Niccolò Jommelli (1714-74) of Naples was reputed to have earned 4,000 gulden.[47] Antonio Salieri earned 1,200 florins as court Kapellmeister in 1788, while Leopold Kozeluch received 1,500 florins a year as composer to the Vienna court chapel from 1792. It is apparent that Mozart's income compares very favorably with that of these composers. But we should now turn to the income of the singers and actors at the Burgtheater, with whom he and Constanze had free social intercourse.

Joseph Lange earned 1,400 gulden, Stephanie the Younger 1,600, while the highest paid actor, Schröder, received 2,500. The latter two actors paid rentals of 500 and 700 gulden for their apartments.[48] Opera singers earned even higher incomes. Michael Kelly received 2,000 gulden in addition to lodging, fuel, and candles, Antonia Bernasconi 2,250, and Nancy Storace 4,500.

The disparity between the distribution of wealth is reflected in the Esterházy's annual income of 700,000 gulden![49] The Empress Maria Theresa gave 12,000 gulden as a wedding present to her lady-in-waiting.[50]

The chief surgeon in Vienna was paid 1,200 gulden, a primary school teacher 100, servants as much as 120, cooks 12 to 30, and a maid received just 25 gulden plus keep. It is clear that Mozart's income placed him in the upper-middle-class bracket of Viennese society. Let us now turn to his expenses.

In the late eighteenth century, Vienna had a population of 300,000. It was an expensive city, with an annual inflation rate of 6 percent. There were very few shops in the inner city because retailing was forbidden; as a result, shoemakers, tailors, dressmakers, and various craftsmen worked in their attic homes. Door-to-door selling was carried out by street vendors, who transported their produce from the suburbs or traded in the great markets outside the city walls.

Approximate estimates of the cost of living are to be found in extant guidebooks, whereas more detailed analyses have been published.[51] According to contemporary guidebooks in 1786 and 1792, the annual cost of living for a middle-class gentleman would have been 464 and 550 florins, respectively.[52] The late Carl Bär found the latter source very useful for his painstaking and detailed estimate of Mozart's expenses. The prices paid for food, drink, and tobacco were modest, and the average family spent 1 gulden a day for food, while 50 gulden a year would suffice for heating and lighting. In 1786, for instance, the modest sum of 31 kreutzers would purchase a meal consisting of soup, two meat dishes, vegetables, unlimited bread, and a quarter liter of wine. However, footwear and clothing were expensive in Vienna, which boasted 3,200 tailors.

At the time of his death, Mozart's wardrobe consisted of six cloth coats in the colors of white, blue, red, nankeen, brown, and black, two overcoats, two fur coats, four waistcoats, nine pairs of breeches, two plain hats, three pairs of boots, three pairs of shoes, nine pairs of silk stockings, nine shirts, four white cravats, one nightcap, eighteen pocket handkerchiefs, eight pairs of underpants, two night-dresses, and five pairs of understockings.[53] The estimated costs of silk stockings, good quality suits and coats, and a lady's fine dress were 5, 50, and 100 gulden respectively. It has been estimated that the Mozart family spent about 400 gulden a year on clothing and footwear.[54]

Mozart spent the first hour of his day being dressed. The care of his powdered wig and pigtail was expensive; hairdressers charged 2.5 gulden a month. The additional costs of powder and pomade would have amounted to 40 gulden a year, while domestic wages would have accounted for a further 50 gulden each year.

In the absence of a court appointment, Mozart's financial success was dependent on the monetary support of wealthy benefactors from the nobility, and it is to his credit that he gained the loyal patronage of Baroness Waldstätten and the Barons Raimond Wetzlar and Gottfried van Swieten. Mozart's meticulous dressy standard was costly, and following his marriage in August 1782, he faced the additional expenses of purchase of household furniture and rental for accommodation.

Wolfgang and Constanze occupied six different apartments during their first five years of married life; these moves reflected the increasing affluence of their lifestyle. Mozart's choice of a honeymoon apartment at the "Red Sabre" on the Hohe Brücke was made not only on the grounds of economy, but also out of sentimental memories of his lodging there for a year in 1768. However, five months later they moved to a finer third-floor apartment at the "Little Herberstein House."[55] In February 1783, Mozart was again in debt. His kind landlord Wetzlar paid the expenses of rent and removal to temporary quarters on the Kohlmarkt.[56] At this time, Baroness Waldstätten loaned Mozart money to offset a short-term loan to the publisher in reference to his three piano concertos (K. 413-5). The baroness had not only hosted a magnificent wedding reception, but had also loaned him her Stein pianoforte for his early concerts in Vienna. Constanze and Wolfgang occupied a first-floor apartment on the Judenplatz for eight months,[57] and then in January 1784 moved to fine rooms off the second staircase on the third floor of Trattnerhof, in the inner city at Graben 29. Their landlord discounted their semiannual rent from 75 to 65 gulden.[58] During the height of his affluence, Mozart moved into what was to be his finest first-floor apartment on the Schulerstrasse.[59] It consisted of four rooms, two closets, a kitchen, attic, cellar, and two storage cupboards. The annual rent was 460 gulden, and the Mozarts remained there until April 1787. Constanze had employed a chambermaid and cook as early as the spring of 1784, and it is likely that at least two other servants were employed for this large apartment.

Mozart's considerable gross income from concerts was offset by the cost of hall rent, heating, lighting, advertising, transport of instruments, tuning, and payment of musicians, together with copyist fees for instruments and singers. A government official at Mannheim paid Mozart three louis d'or (30 gulden) for the expenses of copying three of his compositions (K. 80, 174, 179).[60] It is to be noted that Josepha Duschek paid 200 gulden to her orchestra for a single benefit concert, while the musicians were paid 240 gulden for the Vienna premiere of *Don Giovanni*.[61] Mozart later economized with a small orchestra of only five or six violins for his Frankfurt concert in October 1790. G. F. Richter and Mozart contributed to a half yearly rental of 550 gulden for Trattner's Hall, where Mozart gave his Lenten subscription concerts in 1784. The rental fee for the Mehlgrube Hall during Lent 1785 was only 6.75 gulden per performance.

Early in 1785 Mozart had a heavy pedal fitted to his fortepiano; the cost of this instrument has been estimated at 900 gulden. His billiard table with accessories may have cost about 300 gulden.[62]

Mozart occupied six different apartments during the last six years of his life. The total cost of rental and renovations has been precisely estimated to have been 2,000 gulden, or an average of 333 gulden per year. These moves once again reflected his fluctuating fortunes. The upturn in his financial situation during his last year is reflected in his ability to afford 275 gulden a year for his fine apartment at Rauhenstein-gasse 8.[63]

The total expenses of the five travel journeys to Prague, Berlin, and Frankfurt between January 1787 and September 1791 have been esti-mated to be 1,375 gulden, while at least 500 has been allowed for Con-stanze's health cures at Baden. With the inclusion of Mozart's loans of 300 gulden to Franz Gilowsky and 500 gulden to Anton Stadler, Bär has calculated that Mozart's total expenses over the period between December 1785 and December 1791 amounted to 11,000 gulden, or an average of 1,843 gulden per year.[64]

Of course, this estimate does not include the medical costs of Con-stanze's pregnancies, or Mozart's illnesses, or the funeral expenses of their children. Nor does it include the cost of newspapers, books, sheet music, interest on loans, or horse grooming. It should also be remembered that each year Mozart rented a small garden outside the city.[65] He must have spent a significant sum on the purchase of sheet music paper. Most of the scores from his latter years were written on 12-stave paper manufactured in northern Italy.[66] Mozart had to pay 400 gulden a year for Carl's fees at the Perchtoldsdorf boarding school.[67] Mozart's preoccupation with finances is vividly reflected on his autograph sketch for a piano concerto, now in the Mozarteum at Salz-burg: the page is swamped with figures and calculations.[68]

In summary, it is estimated that Mozart's average expenses during his years of married life in Vienna were of the order of 2,000 gulden a year. Nor should we forget that Mozart's Court salary of 800 gulden was subject to a 5 percent tax.[69]

Mozart's Last Residence in the Rauhensteingasse, Vienna
Photograph before destruction by bombing during World War II. The spacious
apartment occupied the first floor. Mozart died here on 5 December 1791.
(Courtesy of the International Foundation Mozarteum, Salzburg.)

12

EXTRAVAGANCE, GENEROSITY, AND DEBTS

An ordinary musician in Mozart's Vienna was paid 200 to 800 florins a year, according to his age, skill, and experience.[1] We have concluded that Mozart earned a very considerable average income of 3,500 gulden, which today is equivalent to 70,000 American dollars, or 140,000 deutsche marks, or 980,000 Austrian schillings.[2] It is clear that Mozart could well afford to live in the upper-middle-class society that was emerging in Vienna at that time.

Michael Kelly has written a colorful account of the merriment and splendor of the extravagant lifestyle in eighteenth-century Vienna. It was, for example, the custom for a gentleman to wear a diamond ring on each little finger and two watches, so as to embellish the expensive embroidery of formal dress apparel with gold, silver, or silk.[3] There is much documentation of Mozart's extravagance, and Nissen mentioned his fondness of expensive watch-chains and fine lace.[4]

In Mannheim Mozart exchanged two of his watches for a fine Parisian timekeeper worth 200 gulden:

Talking of watches, I must tell you that I am bringing with me for myself—a real Parisian one. You know the sort of thing my jewelled watch was—how inferior the little stones were, how clumsy and awkward its shape; but I would not have minded all that, had I not been obliged to spend so much money on having it repaired and regulated; yet in spite of that the watch would one day gain and the next day lose an hour or two. The watch the Elector gave me did just the same and, moreover, the works were even worse and more fragile. I exchanged these two watches and their chains for a Parisian one worth twenty Louis D'or. So now at last I know what the time is—which I never managed to do with my five watches. At present, out of four watches I have at least one on which I can rely.[5]

It would appear that at times the Mozarts entertained lavishly. Although it was seemly only for the carriages of princes to be drawn by six horses, on one occasion Mozart snubbed such traditional custom by purchasing six Polish ponies.[6] In April 1785, Leopold Mozart related that Wolfgang and Aloysia Lange had planned to accompany him back to Munich, to give a concert there, and that each of them had six pairs of shoes made, although nothing came of the trip.[7]

Nannerl acknowledged that her brother was unable to manage his financial affairs. Alfred Einstein laid much of the blame on Constanze, because of her incompetent housewifery and her propensity to share in her husband's Bohemian lifestyle.[8] Yet it is to be remembered that Mozart kept a record of expenses at Figarohaus from March 1784 to February 1785, and that Constanze continued it a while longer. No doubt she was puzzled as to where all the money was going; Mozart tried to appease her with renewed ardor for better financial management. Leopold Mozart praised his son's household economy at table. During and after her second marriage, Constanze showed outstanding talent as a shrewd and capable businesswoman. It is not known how long she remained unaware of the extent of her husband's gambling losses since she understandably chose to gloss over his faults and failings.

The reason for Mozart's extravagance is readily apparent from a study of his personality. From his early childhood he had rubbed shoulders with the aristocracy of the ancien régime; indeed, his father encouraged him to court the favor of the hand that fed him. However, Mozart's narcissistic outlook extended into the financial arena, and his fantasied perception of money was out of touch with reality. Mozart never had to worry about money, for his father had always governed the purse strings. Even though the Grand Tour (1763-66) had cost the Mozarts about 20,000 gulden, the estimated value of the spoils, which had accrued during their absence from Salzburg for nearly 42 months, was 12,000 florins.[9] By way of a fascinating contrast, the Hummels' three-year European tour (1788-91) cost 14,036 gulden.[10]

Mozart's pride and honor obliged him to keep up appearances, but we have seen that he could well afford 400 gulden a year to dress like a prince. In his letter to the Baroness von Waldstätten, dated 28 September 1782, he describes his passion for luxurious clothing:

As for the beautiful red coat, which attracts me enormously, please, please let me know *where it is to be had and how much it costs*—for that I have completely forgotten, as I was so captivated by its splendour that I did not take note of its price. I must have a coat like that, for it is one that will really do justice to certain buttons which I have long been hankering after. I saw them once, when I was choosing some for a suit. They were in Brandau's button factory in the Kohlmarkt, opposite the Milano. They are mother-of-pearl with a few white stones round the edge and a fine yellow stone in the centre. I should like all my things to be of good quality, genuine and beautiful. Why is it, I wonder, that those who cannot afford it, would like to spend a fortune on such articles and those who can, do not do so?[11]

Mozart liked living in a spacious and prosperous apartment where he frequently entertained distinguished visitors. It also provided space and privacy for his creative work. After he disentangled himself from his oppressive financial cares, he obtained a splendid flat on the Rauhensteingasse, during his last year. This fine apartment occupied 145 square meters (1,530 square feet) and included an attached stable for his horse. The living room, music room, study, and billiard room provided him with a quiet relaxing area of 71.21 square meters (752 square feet).[12] This large living area with high ceilings (4 meters or 13 feet) would have been costly to heat during the winter. The Mozarts employed a cook, a chambermaid (Lorl), a servant, and probably a domestic as well.

Jahn conceded that Wolfgang was an imprudent spendthrift who was unable to control his wants and to live within his actual means. Combined with his good-natured softheartedness and spontaneous generosity[13], these qualities inevitably led to financial difficulties. Rochlitz related that Wolfgang not only gave free admission to the chorus singers at Leipzig, but also a generous donation to one of the bass singers, who had especially pleased him. Furthermore, when a poor old piano tuner, stammering with embarrassment, begged for a thaler, Mozart pressed a couple of ducats into his hand and hurried away from the room.[14] On another occasion, Wolfgang was accosted in the street by a beggar, who claimed to be a distant relative. Having no money to give him, Mozart went into the nearest coffee house, wrote a minuet and trio, and sent the beggar with it to his publisher, who paid him what it was considered worth.[15]

Sophie Haibel related how his gullibility made him an easy prey for hangers on: "False friends, secret blood-suckers, and worthless people, who served only to amuse him at table, and intercourse with whom injured his reputation."[16] There seems little doubt that here she was referring to Gilowsky and Stadler. Franz Anton Gilowsky, a cousin of the witness at Mozart's wedding, ran a local letter post in Vienna in 1784.[17] When he fell into debt, Mozart kindly loaned him 300 gulden on 23 August 1786. A property bond for this amount was filed in Mozart's estate.[18] Gilowsky's assets went into liquidation in May 1787. Although his bankruptcy was annulled a year later, he was again declared insolvent in 1790 and 1800.

There are some strange aspects to Mozart's friendship with Anton Stadler, for whom he composed the sublime Quintet and Concerto (K. 581, 622). Stadler was a fellow brother Freemason who played the clarinet and basset horn at Masonic gatherings. He also played in the Prague Orchestra for the festival performance of *Don Giovanni* and *Tito* in September 1791. Not only did Stadler fail to repay a loan of 500 gulden, but also there is a very strong suspicion that he purloined a pawn ticket from Mozart's open cashbox.[19] Yet in 1785 and 1787, Michael Puchberg had distrained Stadler for 1,400 gulden, and again in 1799 his wife for 150 gulden.[20] Unfortunately both the autograph of the Clarinet Concerto and Stadler's letter to Mozart from Prague, dated 7 October 1791, are lost.[21] Could Mozart have been under some obligation to Stadler as a gambling associate? Why did certain members of the *Tonkünstler-Societät* object to his admission? Was it envy, or his dissolute way of living?

Throughout his working life, Mozart was in trouble with creditors. The sojourn to Paris was a financial disaster, and in February 1778 Leopold Mozart was in debt to the tune of 700 gulden.[22] Mozart borrowed 15 louis d'or (150 gulden) from Baron Grimm for the expenses of his mother's terminal illness and funeral. He was later obliged to obey his father's command to return to Salzburg, so as to pay off his debts, which by November 1778 had accrued to 863 gulden.[23]

Even his departure for Salzburg in the midsummer of 1783 was not without incident. He was accosted on the steps of his carriage over a debt of 30 gulden, from which he extricated himself only with some difficulty.[24] Mention has already been made of his repaid loans from Baroness Waldstätten, Hofdemel, and Lackenbacher, and we will be returning to certain crucial events during 1787 in the next chapter. Mozart borrowed 9 gulden from his publisher Hoffmeister in November 1785, pending the publication of his piano quartet, K. 478.[25]

Although the majority of Mozart's loans can be accounted for by periodic cash shortages arising from the irregularity of his income and the extravagance of his lifestyle, three episodes associated with his spending in 1781, 1787, and 1791 require an alternative explanation.

Idomeneo was given its premiere at the Residenz-Theater (now known as Cuvillié's Theater) in Munich on 21 January 1781. Mozart never mentioned his honorarium, but we can assume that he was handsomely rewarded by the Elector Carl Theodor. He probably received at least 450 gulden for it. Mozart's four months in the Bavarian capital were among the happiest in his life, and he was delighted to be back in the merry company of his former Mannheim friends, so that several compositions were forthcoming (K. 341, 349, 351, 361, 368, 369, 370). However, as a result of his folly he had to borrow about 540 gulden from two separate sources. He repaid his father 50 ducats in two installments during the summer.[26]

Mozart's pride and honor obliged him to keep his debts a secret. Three weeks later he wrote: "We must never let people know how we really stand financially."[27] His folly at Munich had also been responsible for his having borrowed 12 louis d'or (120 gulden) from Herr Scherz of

Strasbourg. Mozart had assumed that his father had paid this debt. In December 1783, however, he was surprised and embarrassed to be issued a summons from Scherz, who demanded not only repayment of the debt but also the accrued interest. Mozart refused to pay the interest. He asked his father to go guarantor for a month, until he could pay the principal:

What annoys me most about the whole business is that Herr Scherz will not have a very good opinion of me—a proof that chance, coincidence, circumstances, a misunderstanding and heaven knows what may rob an innocent man of his good name! . . . If he had reminded me during the first year, I should have paid him on the spot with pleasure. I mean to pay it still, but at the moment I am not in a position to do so.[28]

Let us now examine Mozart's fascinating letters to Michael Puchberg. During the last four years of his life, Mozart wrote twenty letters to this wealthy merchant, I & R Warehouse supervisor, and fellow brother Freemason, and only three were unanswered. In response to the first four written during the summer of 1788, Puchberg sent 336 gulden.[29] On 17 June, the Mozart family moved again from the inner city out to a cheaper apartment at the Währingerstrasse 16, facing the garden. Twelve days later his six-month old daughter Theresia died. Mozart owed 200 gulden to his former landlord on the Landstrasse and was being pressed for payment. In the face of these great difficulties and complications, he was forced to raise money on two pawnbroker tickets. He now feared the loss of his honor and credit. Despite these adversities with Puchberg's moral support his most astonishing burst of creative activity was released during that summer (K. 542, 543, 545, 546, 547, 548, 549, 550, 551).

In response to four letters during the latter half of 1789, Puchberg sent another 450 gulden.[30] The composer's monetary difficulties at that time were related to Constanze's illness. He owed 400 gulden to chemists and to Dr. Johann Nepomuk Hunczowsky (1752-98), a physician attached to the Military Hospital at Gumpendorf.

During that dismal year of 1790, Puchberg generously sent 610 gulden, in response to nine letters from the composer.[31] We have seen that in that year Mozart's income was affected by his frequent depression and ill health. He suffered recurrent temporary embarrassments, among them a debt to a haberdasher for 100 gulden. Yet in his letter to Puchberg dated March-April 1790, Mozart realized he was on the threshold of his fortune, and he was confident that he would be appointed assistant Kapellmeister to Salieri. Indeed, he exhorted Puchberg to be silent about his debts, lest his application be jeopardized, but it was all in vain. On 1 October 1790, Mozart pledged all his goods and chattels as security for his loan of 1,000 gulden from the licensed merchant Heinrich Lackenbacher.

Mozart's last three letters to Puchberg were written during April and June of 1791. Mozart borrowed another 55 gulden which amounted to a progressive total of 1,451 gulden. Mozart intended to repay this large debt through a draft from his publisher Hoffmeister, upon the security of future compositions. In his letters from Frankfurt, he exhorted his wife to negotiate the draft through the intermediary of either Anton Stadler or an anonymous third party NN., whom Constanze later distrusted.[32] Indeed, Mozart was prepared to pay the exorbitant interest of 20 percent. In his last letter to Puchberg he said: "I require the loan only for a few days, when you will receive 2000 gulden in my name, from which you can then refund yourself."[33] No such draft was forthcoming. It is tempting to speculate that Mozart's extravagant folly with Schikaneder's troupe during his last summer may have been responsible.

On several occasions Mozart begged Puchberg for even pittances, resorting to despondent pleas devoid of self-respect:

In a week or a fortnight I shall be better off—certainly—but at present I am in want! Can you not help me out with a trifle? The smallest sum would be very welcome just now. You would, for the moment at least, bring peace of mind to your true friend, servant and brother.[34]

The pitiful tone of these letters goes counter to Mozart's pride, but the exaggerated representation of his state can largely be accounted for by his depression. The Puchberg letters are full of sadness. Such a tone strongly suggests an inner psychic masochism which Mozart felt compelled to share under the trusted seal of Masonic brotherhood. Was Puchberg a gambling colleague? It would appear that Mozart repaid a few hundred gulden, and it is very much to Puchberg's credit that he did not come forward for the remainder at the time of Mozart's death. A few years later, when Puchberg himself became insolvent, Constanze repaid him 1,000 florins.[35]

On 20 December 1791, Mozart's widow was personally issued a suspense order, as was the custom, from the I&R Commissary for Suspensions and Inventories. Constanze nominated Dr. Niklas Ramor as trustee and guardian of her two children. The obligatory inventory of assets and liabilities has been faithfully reproduced by O. E. Deutsch.[36]

On the credit side of the ledger, at the time of his death, Mozart was owed 133 florins in salary, while he left 60 florins in cash. The conservative valuation of his goods and chattels was 399 florins, made up of the following: silver 7 (most of it had been pawned), clothing 55, linen 17, household goods 296, and books and music 24. His three most valuable items of furniture were his fortepiano with pedal (80), billiard table and accessories (60), and two divans with six matching canvas-covered chairs (50). His viola was valued at only 4 florins, his rolltop writing desk 8, and his gilt-cased clock 5. Mozart's outstanding loans for 800 florins had to be written off.

Such inadequate credits were offset by outstanding debts of 918 florins. The sources of the bills were as follows: two tailors 296, a decorator 208, two apothecaries 214, two merchants 100, a tradesman 59, a cobbler 32, and a surgeon, Herr Andre Igl, who may have performed the venesections, 9. His honorable friend Michael Puchberg did not rub salt into the wound.

Mozart made no will. His coffers were too depleted to honor the pledge in his marriage contract to provide his surviving widow with an augmented dowry of 1,500 florins. Dr. Ramor made patrimonious provision for 400 florins to be deposited in trust at 4 percent interest for the two surviving sons.

In her application to the court for a pension, Constanze listed four reasons for her state of impoverishment: (1) her husband's lack of opportunity in Vienna; (2) his failure to accept lucrative offers abroad out of loyalty to his emperor; (3) his failure to enroll his dependents in the Society for the Widows and Orphans of Musicians; and (4) his sudden premature death at a time when his future prospects were beginning to brighten. Mozart did in fact make application for membership in the Tonkünstler-Societät on 11 February 1785, the very day his father arrived in Vienna. His application was held in abeyance pending the submission of his birth certificate and the resolution of certain differences within the Society. However, he never submitted his birth certificate.[37] The Tonkünstler-Societät was founded by Salieri's teacher, Florian Gassmann.

Franz Niemetschek summarized the causes of Mozart's poverty in his biography as follows:

It is true that he often earnt considerable sums, but with an insecure and irregular income, added to the frequent accouchments and lengthy illnesses of his wife in an expensive town like Vienna, Mozart in fact very nearly starved . . . as it was impossible to belittle his greatness as an artist, ill-natured people tried to defame his moral character.[38]

Joseph Deiner's memoirs in Vienna, published in 1856, contain one of the earliest biographical references to Mozart's poverty. Deiner recalled having seen Wolfgang and Constanze dancing merrily around the composer's study during the winter of 1790. When Deiner asked Mozart whether he was teaching his wife to dance, the composer laughed and replied: "We're only getting warm, it's freezing in here and we can't afford any wood."[39] After Deiner returned with some of his own firewood, Mozart accepted it and promised to pay generously when he could afford to do so. And so there emerged a misguided portrait of an impoverished, angelic composer who was exploited by creditors and publishers alike.

13

MOZART'S GAMBLING

Leopold Mozart lived frugally during his latter years in Salzburg on his court salary, with supplemental income from teaching and royalties from his Violinschule.[1] He died at sixty-seven leaving an estate valued at 2,000 gulden. Mozart earned four times his father's income and died at the age of thirty-five, leaving debts of about 2,000 gulden. His average income in Vienna of about 3,500 gulden should have more than covered his estimated expenses of 2,000. The explanation most often offered centers on Mozart's gambling proclivities.

The term gambling derives from the Anglo-Saxon words *gamen* (sport), and *gamon* (play), and it combines excitement with the trilogy of chance, strategy, and skill. There has always been a tendency for man to gamble; gambling has been referred to as the universal neurosis of humankind. The tossing into the air of astragali has been traced to prehistoric times.[2] The earliest dice from Iraq and India date from about 3000 B.C. Indeed, dice have been discovered in the ancient tombs and the ruins of Babylon.

The origins of gambling are found in Greek mythology. Legend has it that the goddess of fortune, Tyche, was one day seduced in the woods on Olympus by Zeus. Her daughter invented gambling games and took sadistic pleasure in witnessing the irresponsible chaos which the players suffered. Gambling houses were erected with window lamps to attract clients to these dens of iniquity.

Roman soldiers used dice to cast lots for the robe of the crucified Jesus. The Roman emperors, especially Augustus and Claudius, were passionately fond of dicing games, but such games were restricted to certain festive seasons for the common people.

During the Middle Ages, gambling was sometimes associated with

such indecencies or vices as insobriety, swearing, idleness, thriftless-
ness, cheating, and crime. However, the attempts of kings and bishops to
suppress gambling were unsuccessful.

It is uncertain whether playing cards originated in China during the
seventh to tenth centuries, or in India, or whether they were invented by
primitive peoples. Nor is it certain whether playing cards were
introduced into Europe during the travels to and from China, in the latter
half of the thirteenth century, by Marco Polo and his father, or from
Arabia by the gypsies. There are references to the existence of cards in
Italy from 1299 and in Germany from 1380, while in England, cards
were established by 1465. The term *deck of cards* dates from
Shakespeare's time. Tarot cards were first used in Italy in the fourteenth
century, the original tarot deck consisting of twenty-two picture cards,
with allegorical representations of material forces, virtues, and vices.
The fool card was the precursor of the modern joker. The original tarot
deck was used for simple games and fortune telling. The Venetians were
the first to add fifty-six numerical cards to form the seventy-eight card
tarot deck. Tarocchi, a popular sixteenth-century game, is still played
today in parts of Central Europe. Franz Schubert played a game of
Tarteln und Mariage with Baron Schonstein one evening in October
1824.[3] Tarot cards were also used for education, conjuring, and sleight of
hand tricks. Women could also play cards, which was to become popular
with all classes of society.

Abnormal gambling is characterized by a lack of moderation, or
uncontrolled indulgence in it, and is referred to as compulsive or
pathological gambling.

We have seen that Mozart lived extravagantly, but then he could
comfortably afford expenses of 2,000 gulden a year toward this end.
What about the discrepancy in his ledger? How could he have spent an
additional 15,000 gulden in ten years? Kraemer concludes that Mozart
lost a fortune playing billiards and faro, and that Constanze attempted to
conceal this blemish on her husband's character.[4] After a careful review
of Mozart's finances, Rudolph Angermüller is in sympathy with
Kraemer's view, although he points out the lack of conclusive evidence.[5]
Even though some of Kraemer's estimates of Mozart's income appear to
be greatly inflated, we must agree with his gambling hypothesis. Let us
now further examine the available evidence.

Two episodes of excessive spending in 1781 and 1791 have already
been discussed. Let us now return to certain extraordinary events in
1787. Despite having made 1,000 gulden in Prague during January of
that year, the Mozart family, on 24 April, moved from their finest
apartment on the Schulerstrasse to a cheap flat in the Landstrasse
suburb, where the yearly rent was only 50 gulden. We should also
remember that the landlord was obliged to receive three months' notice

of such a move at that time. Leopold Mozart, in his last letter to his daughter, had this comment: "Your brother is now living in the Land-strasse No. 224. He does not say why he has moved. Not a word. But unfortunately I can guess the reason."[6] Is it not most likely that here Leopold was referring to his son's gambling losses? Leopold kept abreast of his son's activities, and he, more than any other person, had deeper insight into Wolfgang's failings and shortcomings. Yet Mozart's reception of his inheritance of 1,000 florins and his earning of a further 1,000 gulden in Prague during the autumn of 1787 did not extricate him from debt.

Faro was the favored game of high-born gamblers throughout Europe in the late eighteenth and early nineteenth centuries. Many a fortune was lost at the upturn of a card in faro. It also remained popular in America until 1925, when it was overtaken by craps. In faro, the players bet on the order in which certain cards will appear, when taken singly from the top of the pack. The name faro was probably derived from the picture of a Pharaoh on a French pack imported into Britain. The game was forbidden by specific mention in English law as early as 1739. In faro, a case-keeper provides a display of a running record for the players, of which cards have been played and which are still to come. The emblem of the tiger was often on display outside a faro house. Two of the dens favored by the gambling ace Casanova were the Caffé degl' Italiani in London and the Tavern Zum Krebs in Vienna.[7]

The dissolute libertine Giovanni Giacomo Casanova brazenly executed a spectacular escape from the Piombi dungeons under the Doge's Palace in Venice on 31 October 1756. Six years earlier, he had become a Freemason at Lyons, and in 1757 he had introduced the lottery to Paris. Casanova met Count Giuseppe Affligio (under the pseudonym Marcati) in Pesaro, Venice, and Lyons; Affligio was also a professional gambler. From 1785 Casanova spent his twilight years in Bohemia at Dux as librarian to Count Joseph Karl Emanuel Waldstein (not to be confused with Beethoven's patron). A skilled card player and notorious gambler, Casanova was friendly with Lorenzo Da Ponte and, in Prague, with the Masonic general, Count Johann Pachta, an amateur composer.

Overtones of hypomania are reflected in Mozart's letter to his friend Baron Gottfried von Jacquin from Prague, dated 15 January 1787. In that letter Mozart recalls the exciting events following his arrival in Prague on 11 January. After lunch he enjoyed a ninety-minute concert, given by Count Thun's private orchestra. At six o'clock Mozart drove to the ball with Count Joseph Emanuel Canal (1745-1826), a botanist and music lover, who also maintained a private orchestra. Count Pachta is said to have tricked Mozart into composing a dance for him by inviting him for dinner an hour before the appointed time.[8] Casanova is known to have been present in Prague during October 1787.[9]

Mozart and his pregnant wife arrived in Prague on 4 October 1787 for the production of *Don Giovanni;* they were followed four days later by his librettist Da Ponte. Mozart and Constanze initially stayed at the Three Lions Inn, but later moved in with their friends the Duscheks at the Villa Bertramka in the suburb of Smichov. Mozart completed the music of *Don Giovanni* on a stone table in the garden of the villa, amidst the merry chatterings and shouts of his friends, who were amusing themselves at billiards. The professor of classical literature and aesthetics at Prague University, August Gottlieb Meissner, recalled an amusing afternoon at the Duscheks' villa, which was attended by Mozart, Da Ponte, Casanova, Bondini, Guardasoni, and singers from the cast. On that happy occasion, Mozart was beside himself with excitement at the thought of the opera's premiere in a couple of days. He talked in rhymes, played all kinds of tricks, and behaved frivolously, in keeping with cyclothymic hypomania.[10]

The premiere of *Don Giovanni* had originally been planned for 14 October, to honor the recent marriage of the emperor's niece Archduchess Maria Theresia to Prince Anton Clemens of Saxony, but it was not ready. There was further delay when one of the singers became ill. Da Ponte was summoned back to Vienna by Salieri, and he reluctantly left Prague on about 15 October. In the poet's absence, perhaps his infamous friend Casanova offered assistance to Mozart. It is likely that Casanova attended the premiere on 29 October, and he certainly drafted an alternative text for Leporello's escape scene, following the Sextet in the second act.[11] No explanation for this fascinating eventuality has been offered. However, our point is that Mozart would have been unable to resist challenging Casanova to a game of faro, or vice versa, and that his likely defeat by the gambling ace provides a probable explanation for the composer's debts at that time. Such an hypothesis is even more credible when we consider that Mozart showed evidence of hypomanic behavior during both his visits to Prague in 1787. Furthermore, it is to be emphasized that gamblers with cyclothymic disorder are prone to uncontrolled gambling sprees during their upswings in mood following a depressive episode.

Gambling was an accepted recreational norm among all strata of Austrian society during the eighteenth century. It was especially prevalent among the aristocracy, who could better afford such extravagance. A prince would spend as much as 100,000-150,000 florins a year, while a count would expend a mere 20,000 to 80,000.[12] Furthermore, the prompt payment of a gambling debt was a sacred matter of honor. The majority of pathological gamblers begin to show their proclivities in late childhood, and are often preoccupied with it by their teenage years. It is therefore opportune for us to return to Mozart's childhood to seek further information.

It is not difficult for us to understand how Mozart's photographic memory and fascination with figures would have contributed to his attraction to playing cards, and more especially to the unique thrill of gambling at piquet or faro. As noted earlier, Wolfgang was taught all manner of card games and tricks by Johann Leopold Hay during his convalescence from smallpox at Olmütz in the autumn of 1767. It took little time for the child to become proficient in such games, or even as adept in them as his teacher.[13]

Leopold Mozart handpainted the back of playing cards in watercolors and was a keen partaker in the lottery, conducted by the Zesi family in Salzburg.[14] Furthermore, in his letter from Milan on 26 October 1771, Wolfgang stated:

I have no news except that numbers 35, 59, 60, 61, 62 were drawn in the lottery; and so, if we had taken these numbers, we should have won. But as we did not take any tickets, we have neither won nor lost, but we had our laugh at other people who did.[15]

The Mozarts were keen members of the card club at Salzburg, where tarot and piquet were popular. Piquet is the classic two-hand French fifteenth-century card game, with its unique and richly varied format. It retains a French courtly terminology, and combines trick play and melding into an exciting game. It requires intense concentration and facility with mental arithmetic. After the departure of Wolfgang and his mother to Mannheim Leopold and Nannerl consoled themselves with a game of piquet. Piquet was also a favorite card game in Britain, until it was overtaken in popularity by whist and later bridge. The game is now out of fashion, and piquet markers have become antiques.

Musicians work irregular hours and often have to face the boredom of idle hours between performances. In the eighteenth century, card playing was a popular means of whiling away the time. Both Wolfgang and his father were critical of the Salzburg court musicians. In his letter from Schwetzingen in July 1763, Leopold sang his praises of the Mannheim orchestra: "The orchestra is undeniably the best in Germany. It consists altogether of people who are young and of good character, not drunkards, gamblers or dissolute fellows, so that both their behaviour and their playing are admirable."[16] In his letter from Paris in July 1778, Wolfgang also contrasts the musicians at Salzburg and Mannheim, but he omits any reference to gambling![17] Mozart often played cards of an evening at Mannheim.[18]

In Vienna, Mozart had the opportunity to gamble at home, at court, in the coffee houses, at the casinos, in the houses of his friends and gambling associates, or at the lodge. His letters also mention the casinos at Baden and Mainz. Michael Kelly related that one evening at the

Ridotto Rooms in Vienna, he lost 40 zecchinos (180 gulden) at gambling to a gallant English colonel. The following morning Nancy Storace kindly loaned him half this amount to honor his debt.[19] Gambling tables were provided at the Redoutensaal in Vienna during the Court masked balls.

Maria Theresa, before her accession to the Habsburg crown in the autumn of 1740, was known to have been a determined, high-spirited girl, with a passion for dancing and card playing all through the night. Her consort, Francis I, a Freemason, was a noted gambler who could lose 30,000 ducats in a night at cards and still maintain his good humor. Maria Theresa was a much more intent card player, although she played for lower stakes.[20]

The first London coffee house was opened in about 1652, and over the next century these popular establishments flourished in continental Europe. A coffee house opened in Vienna in 1683, and by the early nineteenth century eighty-four had been established in the Austrian capital. They became the meeting places most favored by men. All kinds of hot and cold refreshments were served but not meals. Men used to gather there to read newspapers, or smoke, or play chess or cards. Billiards was also popular, and one of the waiters would also serve as a marquer and chalk up the points of the game. Franz Schubert often played billiards or skittles with his friends, in their favorite coffee houses, such as Bogner's Cafe on the Singerstrasse.[21] Billiards became so popular in Vienna that in 1784 it was decreed that billiard rooms could only be established on the ground floor of a building or premise, presumably for fear of collapse of the floor at a higher level. Hugelmann's café on the Ferdinandsbrücke became famous for its Billiards Academy.

A casino was originally a room near a theater, where people used to retire after the play for music, dancing, or card playing. Later, as in Mozart's time, the casino became a public hall with every facility for entertainment, including a gambling room. (The casino at Monte Carlo was not established until 1879.)

Mozart gave his six Friday Lenten subscription concerts in the town casino "Zur Mehlgrube" (flour market) on the Neuermarkt during 1785.[22] Later that year, a second casino was established at Trattner's Hall on the Graben. He planned to give four subscription concerts at Trattner's Casino during Advent of 1786 and may have first performed his Piano concerto in C (K. 503) there on 5 December 1786. Roulette was founded in the middle of the eighteenth century and became the leading attraction at the casinos a century later.

The word "billiards" derives from the French billard, which is both the name of the game and the cue. During her imprisonment in 1576, Mary Queen of Scots voiced her displeasure when her billiards table was removed, while Cleopatra played billiards in Shakespeare's famous play.[23] The earliest wooden billiard balls were soon replaced by elephant tusk ivory, until John Wesley Hyatt (American printer and coinventor of celluloid) first synthesized plastic balls in 1868. The leather tip and chalk had been introduced in 1806. By the end of the seventeenth century, billiards was an expected diversion in the country estates of gentlemen. A century later, billiard tables were popular in European taverns and casinos, as well as in the Viennese coffee houses.

The French variant, Carom, was favored on the continent. It was played on a cloth-covered table without pockets. Skittles was very popular in Vienna, and in this continental variant of billiards, the game was made more difficult by setting up small cones in the middle of the table. The aim of the player was to upset the cones indirectly with one of the opponent's balls. This game of skittles is not to be confused with the English skittles, or ninepins, a game also played by the Mozarts. The modern English game of billiards with pockets dates from about 1800.

We have seen that Dr. Sigmund Barisani encouraged Mozart's participation in ball games and horse riding, while Constanze also liked to join in. His pupil Freystädtler stated that Mozart often conducted his musical exercises over a game of bowls.[24]

Mozart was passionately fond of billiards; at home he often played alone or with his wife in case of need.[25] Constanze confirmed to Mary Novello that her husband sometimes composed while playing billiards.[26] Nissen mentions Mozart's humming an air from the first Quintet in *Die Zauberflöte* while playing billiards in Prague.[27] The "Skittle-Alley Trio" (K. 498) was composed for the Jacquins on 5 August 1786 over a game of skittles. Thomas Attwood related that Mozart would at any time prefer to play billiards with him to a lesson.[28]

Sophie Haibel in her Memoirs, immediately after having alluded to Mozart's passionate attachment to billiards, made veiled reference to his weakness for gambling: "To keep him from intercourse of an unworthy kind, his wife patiently took part in everything with him."[29]

Mozart wrote to his wife on 7 October 1791, after his return from *Die Zauberflöte*: "Immediately after your departure I played two games of billiards with Herr von Mozart, the fellow that wrote the opera which is running at Schikaneder's theatre; then I sold my nag for fourteen ducats."[30] Was not such a nonchalant description intended to mask his true inner sadness at that time? Mozart was fond of animals, and although admittedly he may have been obliged to sell his horse to pay off a debt incurred by Constanze's health cure at Baden, is it not equally plausible that he did so to offset a gambling loss at billiards? Mozart tended to become depressed during his wife's absences, and gambling provided an outlet. In any event, after having sold his horse, he orchestrated most of the Rondo of his Clarinet Concerto, which is overflowing with a sad personal resignation to his fate.

Mozart was presumably a good amateur player. At any rate he had no difficulty in outplaying Michael Kelly, who wrote: "Many and many a game have I played with him, but always came off second best."[31] Wolfgang's skill in the game would have been enhanced by his keen eyesight and his excellent balance and coordination. Nevertheless, he would of course have been readily outclassed by a professional player, though even regular losses of large sums of money did not deter him from trying to do so. Haydn's pupil, Franz Seraph von Destouches (1772-1844), supplied the following information about Mozart for Sulpiz Boisserée's diary (Heidelberg, November 1815):

He was a passionate player of billiards, and played badly. Whenever a famous billiard player arrived in Vienna, it was of more interest to him than the arrival of a famous musician. The latter, he opined, would come to him all right, the former he looked up himself; he played for high stakes, whole nights long. He was very thoughtless, but his wife excused him.[32]

Now admittedly Sulpiz Boisserée's diary contains several errors of fact, and O. E. Deutsch considered the work unreliable. However, Destouches was Haydn's pupil in Vienna for a few years from 1787, and so would have been in touch with the local music scene during Mozart's latter years.

Karoline Pichler mentioned Mozart's "irresponsible way of life." The following notice appeared in the "Allgemeine Musikalische Zeitung" in 1825: "To Mozart's contemporaries it is unfortunately all too well known that only over-exertion at his work, and fast living in ill-chosen company, shortened his precious days!"[33]

If the gambling hypothesis is valid, then there must have been some mention of it in Mozart's correspondence with his family. Alas, all such evidence has been destroyed; all of Constanze's letters to her husband, all but one of Mozart's letters to his father after 12 June 1784, and all of Leopold's letters to his son after 22 January 1781. Nannerl told Nissen that her father destroyed the later letters from his son because of their allusions to Freemasonry.[34] Although this explanation is plausible, Constanze may also have been responsible, for we have seen that she chose to conceal Mozart's defects of character. Indeed, she attempted to buy out the entire 1794 Graz edition of Schlichtegroll's Necrolog. No doubt she took umbrage at the following passage:

Mozart's income was considerable; yet his unbridled passion for pleasure, together with the wild disorder that reigned in the housekeeping accounts, resulted in the fact that, at his death, he bequeathed nothing to his family save the glory of his name and the benevolent concern of the Viennese musical audiences.[35]

And there was more. Schlichtegroll followed with a short account of Mozart's failing health, melancholia, and bizarre state of mind toward the end. There was high praise for Constanze's devotion and care, and an interesting sketch of the human frailty of genius. The author then compared and contrasted Mozart's genius with Antoine Thomas, Raphael Mengs, Carlo Maratta, and Guido Reni. Schlichtegroll elaborated on Reni's passion for gambling:

Guido Reni, whose passion for gambling exceeded that of any normal person and who, towards the end of his life, would sometimes paint as many as three pictures in the course of the day in order to redeem those debts contracted during the course of the night.[36]

Before presenting evidence of Mozart's gambling proclivities with Schikaneder's Troupe during his last summer, let us first examine why Mozart was attracted to gambling.

Pathological gambling is considered to be a disorder of impulse control. The compulsive gambler is motivated largely by the indirect satisfaction of various unconscious forbidden libidinal and aggressive components.[37] Mozart fits very well into the following commonly observed prototype of the pathological gambler: an obsessionally neurotic male who is intelligent, industrious, proud, overconfident to the point of abrasiveness, athletically inclined, restless, impatient, impulsive, and an incurable optimist. Furthermore, the compulsive gambler often possesses an inherent volatility of mood, with a predisposition toward depression. Gambling serves as a defense against such depression.

Gambling bouts are sometimes attributed to such emotionally charged events as the death of a parent, the birth of a child, marital conflicts, and either business catastrophes or successes. The gambler is particularly vulnerable to a father's death, and we have seen that Leopold's demise had a profound influence on Mozart's psychic equilibrium and subsequent depressive trends. Each gambling bout is followed by intense guilt and renewed ardor to repent, but there persists an inability to resist the next gambling impulse. In the postscript of the letter to his father from Vienna, dated 4 April 1781, Mozart insisted that he had reformed: "Think no more of my follies, of which I have repented long ago from the bottom of my heart. Misfortune brings wisdom, and my thoughts now turn in a very different direction."[38]

Edmund Bergler's theory of psychic masochism offers a neat explanation of Mozart's attraction to the unique thrill of gambling. The compulsive gambler is driven by an overwhelming unconscious desire to lose.[39] Mozart unconsciously resented the loss of the megalomania of his childhood and bore a profound grudge against his parents and other authority figures, who sought to impose the reality principle on his infantile omnipotence. According to Bergler's theory, the aggression directed against these "deprivers" results in inordinate guilt and an intense need for punishment. Gambling recapitulates the cycle of rage, aggression, and remorse; its pleasures are found in the joy of grandiose rebellion. The anguish of the loss is eroticized and elaborated into a psychic masochism. The compulsive gambler savors his victimhood, relishes the collection of injustice, and revels in self-pity and spurious righteous indignation. It is to be emphasized that psychic masochism is quite distinct from perversion masochism, in which bodily pain is sought. The psychic masochist is quite unaware of his longing for defeat and consciously rejects it, as does a normal gambler. Unconsciously, however, the psychic masochist is a glutton for punishment, and so Mozart forever remained optimistic about his chances of defeating a professional billiard player or gambler.

The childhood of a compulsive gambler often contains a history of inconsistent or inappropriately harsh parental discipline. Such gamblers often believe that their parents had unreasonably high expectations of them, or denied them the approval and recognition readily granted to their siblings. Such a history fits well into Mozart's profile, and we have seen how Leopold favored Nannerl after his son's marriage.

The home of a pathological gambler is not a happy one, and we have gained the impression that Constanze was far from reticent to escape from her domestic chaos during her health cures at Baden. Had she not witnessed the gradual decline of Mozart's mental, physical, moral, and social well-being? It is not difficult to imagine how shocked and disillusioned she must have been to discover the serious nature of his pathological gambling. No doubt there were repeated tearful reconciliations after Mozart earnestly resolved again and again to abstain. However, the vicious cycle of gambling, bickering, guilt-ridden remorse, sincere endeavor to reform, depression, relapse, further quarrels, guilt and remorse, depression, and gambling so often leads to a crushing of mutual respect and a destructive pervasive mistrust in the marriage. Under such conditions what wife could avoid nagging and moaning? Naturally, Constanze would have become increasingly concerned about the precarious state of her future security. Under such conditions, it would have been difficult for her to maintain a warm love and affection for her husband, but she did continue to care for him and tried to restrain him from his folly. Constanze could not have known that Mozart's bipolar disorder made him prone to spectacular mood swings beyond his control.

It would appear that Mozart's gambling partners were his Masonic brothers. In this context, it is interesting to note that gamblers are often preoccupied with superstition and rituals. Although Wolfgang maintained a regular correspondence with his father after the latter's return to Salzburg, only one of these letters has been preserved. We have seen that Nannerl informed Nissen that Leopold had destroyed the others because of their allusions to Freemasonry. Could not Leopold have been soured by his son's gambling associations with the craft? Furthermore, Constanze is known to have destroyed incriminating documents during the persecution of the Freemasons after Mozart's death.[40]

During the spring of 1789, Mozart accompanied his Masonic pupil, Prince Karl Lichnowsky, on a journey to Germany. The two parted at Leipzig in mid-May, and according to Mozart, the Prince borrowed 100 gulden from him. Perhaps this loan was fabricated to conceal a gambling debt. On 16 October 1790, in Mainz, Mozart lodged opposite the casino.

Pathological gamblers are often, like Mozart, gregarious people who are easily led into shallow friendships, partnerships, or loose coalitions with other gamblers. No doubt, a satisfaction of their inner loneliness is partly responsible. Abstinence from gambling is accompanied by an intense boredom, and relapses are often precipitated by the prompting of a gambling associate. The career of the compulsive gambler is marked by repeated episodes of spiraling, closure, bail-out, and relapse.

Although his coalition with Emanuel Schikaneder resulted in his creation of *Die Zauberflöte*, we have seen how this dissolute fellow led the gregarious Wolfgang astray into a shameful pleasure-seeking life of dissipation during his last summer. Admittedly, Constanze's absence at Baden and uremic irritation of his brain were also contributing factors. However, in 1803 Schikaneder gave his libretto *Vestas Feuer* to Beethoven, who after having written some sketches for the first scene, rejected it and broke off relations because he would not alter it to the composer's satisfaction. Schikaneder's extravagant lifestyle resulted in frequent debts, and although he made a fortune out of *The Magic Flute*, he died bankrupt in Vienna in 1812. Such a history is characteristic of pathological gambling. We have yet more references to Mozart's unfortunate association with Schikaneder.

Benedikt Schack, who created Tamino, died at Munich on 11 December 1826. A posthumous anonymous tribute appeared in the AMZ, and the following quote from it refers to Mozart: "We learnt the right and also the wrong roads that even the greatest talent has to walk in the harsh reality of life."[41] Ignaz von Seyfried, a piano pupil of Mozart, made more specific mention of the composer's gambling:

In accordance with your wishes I permit myself the following observations, which I am prepared to attest on affidavit—Schikaneder's personal acquaintance with Mozart, and his later acquaintance with Zitterbarth, dates from a Masonic Lodge—to be sure, not the famous Lodge of Born's, which is said to have numbered Vienna's leading worthies & the élite of the literary caste of that period among its members—but merely a so-called peripheral or eating lodge, where the brethren busied themselves at the weekly evening meetings with games, music & the many pleasures of a well-covered table, as Gieseke often told me.[42]

We have already speculated that Michael Puchberg and Anton Stadler may have been gambling associates of Mozart. Perhaps Franz Anton Gilowsky, Franz Hofdemel, and Lorenzo Da Ponte also shared such a relationship.

Franz Hofdemel was a Chancery official at the Law Courts and the former private secretary of Count Seilern. He had loaned Mozart 100 gulden in April 1789, a debt that was repaid. Although Hofdemel's salary was only 400 gulden a year, he was a well-connected financier. In March 1791, for example, he requested repayment of 4,400 gulden from Count Gottfried von Walldorf of Brünn; the count repaid him 500 gulden in November of that year.[43] Is it not possible that Hofdemel's shock suicide was precipitated by catastrophic gambling losses?

Lorenzo Da Ponte was undoubtedly one of Mozart's most colorful friends, and their coalition is unsurpassed in operatic history. However, it would be surprising if Da Ponte was not a gambler, bearing in mind his propensity to splurge so large an income.[44] Joseph Wölfl, a pupil of Leopold Mozart and Michael Haydn, saw Mozart in Vienna in 1790. According to Wurzbach, a deep friendship developed, though this is not substantiated.[45] It is of interest that Wölfl was a passionate billiards player.[46]

Why was it intended to erase the name NN from Mozart's letters to his wife during 1789-90? Perhaps Joseph Goldhahn's involvement in Mozart's financial affairs was unsavory? Was Goldhahn a gambling associate of Mozart? We do not know, but the supposition is consistent with the thread of our hypothesis.

In conclusion, it is proposed that the gambling hypothesis fits reasonably well into Mozart's profile, despite the paucity of concrete evidence. There is no doubt that he lived extravagantly beyond his means, but the discrepancy in his ledger and the documented episodes of big splurge spending in 1781, 1787, and 1791 are most readily accounted for by gambling. His association with Casanova and Schikaneder provided tempting opportunities. The theory of psychic masochism blends comfortably into Mozart's personality. Admittedly, the case would be strengthened by one or two further eyewitness accounts from the contemporary literature, but we do have the testimony of Destouches and Seyfried. Gambling proclivities are understandably kept secret, and it is most unfortunate that so many of the letters of the Mozart family were destroyed. However, the strongest evidence of all is the knowledge that subjects with cyclothymic disorder are prone to wild, uncontrollable gambling sprees during their upward swings in mood, following a depressive episode.

Niemetschek explains why he erased some of Mozart's blemishes in his biography:

A desire to be fair to a man of such merit demands that we try to wipe out such blemishes from the portraits of the great. If the same fairness is shown to Mozart, as one would wish shown to oneself, even then he could not serve as a model of economy and thrift. It is true, he should have been more careful with his money; but is a genius not allowed any weaknesses or failings?[47]

PART III

Enigmatic Personality

14

MOZART'S PERSONALITY

No other composer presents such an intriguing enigma to posterity as does Mozart. His life, his personality, his character, and his music are full of the most fascinating contrasts and complexities. How does one reconcile his merriment and melancholy on the one hand, or the fervor of his sacred music and his bawdiness on the other? It would be impossible to clearly answer this question to our satisfaction, since our understanding of the complex interplay between the mind, body, soul, and emotions of a genius is appallingly inadequate. Let us, however, attempt to approach the mysterious interior world of Mozart's being. In doing so, let us also retain compassion for his sufferings, and especially let us remain eternally grateful for the treasury of his incomparable music.

The definition of a personality includes the comprehensive ensemble of an individual's projected tendencies to act or behave, and the arrangement of distinguishing character traits, attitudes, and habits. However, in exceptional or gifted children, an imbalance between intellectual development and emotional maturation tends to occur.[1] Mozart left us the legacy of his incomparable music; however, his genius led to a stunting of the development of his personality. During the process of his socialization and education, an imbalance arose between various facets of his development. The major outcome of this disparity was a retardation of his emotional maturation, which could not keep pace with his creativity. Evidence of this emotional insecurity is found in Leopold's letter to his wife and son (dated 16 February 1778):

As a child and a boy you were serious rather than childish and when you sat at the clavier or were otherwise intent on music, no one dared to have the slightest jest with you. Why, even your expression was so solemn that, observing the early efflorescence of your talent and your ever grave and thoughtful little face, many discerning people of different countries sadly doubted whether your life would be a long one.[2]

A further example, in the eight-year-old Mozart in London, is portrayed in Leopold's letter to Lorenz Hagenhauer (dated 27 November 1764):

Little Wolfgang wept when I read out this portion of your letter and, when he was asked why, he said that he was grieved, as he believed that he would never see him again. But we told him that it would not be so. He remembered that your son had often caught a fly for him and that he used to blow the organ and bring him his air-gun. As soon as he returns to Salzburg he is going to St. Peter's and Mr. Cajetan is. to catch a fly for him and shoot with him![3]

The most vital years in the development of personality are the first six years of life. Mozart was fortunate to have spent his first six years in a stable, happy home, and he was much loved by his parents and sister. However, he never attended school, and his upbringing was further insulated during those four tours of travel between 1762 and 1771, which occupied seven years of his life. Amidst the exciting exclusive fantasy world of the royal palaces and aristocratic mansions of the ancien régime, the prodigy was showered with every praise and flattery. Wolfgang hugged and kissed the empress of Austria and declared he would marry the Archduchess Marie Antoinette after she helped him to his feet after a fall. Mozart played the organ in the chapel of Versailles before the Bourbon Court, gazed on Madame Pompadour, and was hand-fed and kissed by the dauphine of France. In London the king and queen of England stopped their carriage to pay tribute to the prodigy, who later attended many glittering receptions throughout Europe. It is impossible for us fully to appreciate the influence of these remarkable experiences on Mozart's development, since we lack his astute perception, vivid imagination, and photographic memory.

The most famous example of Mozart's photographic memory is found in his fourteenth year. Mozart and his father arrived in Rome on the Wednesday of Holy Week, 11 April 1770. After lunch they explored St. Peter's Basilica. Of course, the pilgrims kissed the foot of the famous bronze statue of St. Peter, and they also attended Mass in the Sistine Chapel, where they heard the Miserere of Gregorio Allegri (1582-1652). By 14 April, Wolfgang had committed this nine-part choral work to paper from memory. A further example of his photographic memory is given in his letter from Milan nineteen months later: "There is a performance of Hasse's opera today, but as Papa is not going out, I cannot be there. Fortunately I know nearly all the arias by heart and so I can see and hear it at home in my head."[4] Two other illustrations will suffice. The Violin Sonata in B-flat (K.454) was entered in his catalogue on 21 April 1784, and eight days later he played the piano part from memory, before the emperor at the Kärntnertor Theater, with the famous Italian violinist Regina Strinasacchi. At Prague Mozart wrote the trumpet and drum parts of the second finale of *Don Giovanni* without a score, and during a rehearsal with the players, he was able from memory to alert them to a difficult passage, where an error was likely to occur.[5]

Both Nannerl and Wolfgang were child prodigies, and in addition their father was an extremely talented musician and composer. Although all three were highly intelligent, and probably shared the gift of absolute pitch, only Wolfgang was a genius. To be a genius a human being requires three extraordinary traits. First, he or she must possess an exceptionally high order of intelligence. It has been suggested, that a child with an IQ of 140 or higher is a potential genius; such a score is reached by about 1 in 250 of the general population. However, IQ tests are biased toward an identification of convergent thinking by a measurement of analytic reasoning, and such tests tend to favor the detection of mathematical skills over artistic ones. Attempts have also been made to assess divergent thinking through tests devised to measure richness of ideas and originality of thinking, but such a task is difficult, if not impossible, to achieve. Although a genius may have an exceptionally high general intelligence, as for example, in the case of Leonardo Da Vinci, it is not necessarily so. In Mozart's case, we have seen that outside of music he showed notable talent only in mathematics. Indeed, it would appear that Leopold possessed a higher level of general intelligence than his son. There is therefore some merit in subdividing intelligence, for the purpose of study or discussion, into different categories. For example, musical intelligence may be considered to be one of several fundamental types of intelligence which we all possess in varying degrees.[6] Tests have also been devised to assess musical talent by measuring the subject's aptitude and appreciation of pitch, time, intensity, consonance, timbre, and rhythm.[7]

The second prerequisite is the possession of an extraordinary capacity for imaginative creation, original thought, invention, or discovery. Third, a genius requires an overabundant zeal, exalted pertinacity, an astonishing power of working, so as to be able to achieve an original creation of unique and inestimable value for the betterment of humankind. It has been estimated that during his last decade, Mozart spent an average of eight hours a day writing down his music.[8]

Yet even a genius needs to undergo a period of education and learning in order to bring the inherent seeds of creativity to fruition. The development of musical competence is more receptive to an educational program that begins in childhood rather than the post pubertal years. Mozart's environment was unique and ideal in that his father was one of the most outstanding and best qualified music teachers of his time. Moreover, during the seven years of travel between 1762 and 1771, Wolfgang mingled with many of Europe's outstanding composers. It is little wonder that his musical genius matured at an early age.

As to the origin of his musical talents, if genes are linked with musical intelligence, then Wolfgang inherited his from both his father and mother, as did Nannerl. With regard to the origin of his genius, however, all members of the Mozart family believed it was a direct gift from God.

Mozart's mind was exceptionally well organized in composition, and he possessed an incredible ability to detach himself from the activities around him. When the composition was complete he could recall it, even in the minutest detail, with his photographic memory. Thus, he was able to write out a complete score even while engaging in casual conversation. Let us now discuss his obsessional traits, which were expressed from his early childhood, and which may have been inherited from his father.

Mozart continued the nightly ritual of singing "Oragna figata marina gamina fa" with his father until his tenth year. Indeed, he composed clavier variations on "Willem Van Nassau" (K. 25) in 1766. Other obsessional traits in his personality included his preoccupation with meticulous dress and hair grooming, as well as his fanaticism about accurate watches. Mozart kept a book of expenses between March 1784 and February 1785.[9] How fortunate for posterity that, albeit with minor omissions, the composer carefully maintained his "Verzeichnüs aller meiner Werke" from February 1784 until his death.[10]

Wolfgang's vivid imagination led him readily into profound reveries and fantasies in the world of make-believe. Not surprisingly, Mozart's favorite form was opera, a medium that offered him unique opportunities to indulge in fantasy. Such a tendency became manifest even in his eighth year, while living in London: "Not a day passes without Wolfgang's talking at least thirty times of Salzburg and of his and our friends and patrons. He has now continually in his head an opera which he wants to produce there with several young people."[11]

Let us now consider two of the psychodynamic sequelae of Mozart's sensational experiences as a prodigy, where the distortion of reality resulted in fantasied configurations of the narcissistic "subject" and "object." First, there developed in his psyche a powerful, inflated self-image; such megalomania is associated with excessive narcissism and omnipotence. When later Mozart felt threatened, the resurgence of his "grandiose self," the fantasied perception of his own importance and strength, would provide us with some insight into the composer's vanity, exhibitionism, and arrogance. Second, the prodigy's major enmeshment with his father resulted in an idealized parent imago, who was perceived as a source of unlimited power.[12] Mozart used to promise that when his father grew old he would place him in a glass case so as to protect him from all harm and so that he would never lose him but always pay him honor.[13] Leopold Mozart fostered Woferl's sense of infantile omnipotence, and there formed a vicarious, symbiotic relationship.[14] The stage was set for the development in Mozart of a peculiar narcissistic dependency.

Further consideration of Mozart's dependency trait helps us to understand better his ready compliance and submission to his father's will, as well as his vulnerability to parasitic exploitation by Cäcilia Weber, his mother-in-law. Such dependency also gives us further insight into Mozart's gullibility, his remarkable loyalty to Emperor Joseph II despite the machinations of the Italian court composers, and his vulnerability to exploitation by Franz Anton Gilowsky, Anton Stadler, and Emanuel Schikaneder. Sophie Haibl related how his gullibility made him an easy prey for hangers on.[15]

Friedrich Melchior Grimm, who had been such an enthusiastic admirer and champion of Mozart the prodigy, became very disenchanted on his reacquaintance with the twenty-two-year-old composer. The baron concluded that Mozart was unlikely to make a successful career in Paris. In a letter to Leopold on 27 July 1778, Grimm criticized Mozart's gullibility and his lack of enterprise, daring, and shrewdness. He also stated that Mozart's preoccupation with composing would prevent his becoming a successful clavier teacher. Leopold forwarded this letter to his son in Paris, and, of course, Wolfgang was deeply hurt by its contents and criticisms.[16]

During the spring of 1792, Nannerl wrote reminiscences for Schlichtegroll's Necrolog. In her final postscript, which she obviously wrote with some reluctance, she described her brother's immaturity and dependency:

Wolfgang was small, thin, pale in colour, and entirely lacking in any pretensions as to physiognomy and bodily appearance. Apart from his music he was almost always a child, and thus he remained: and this is a main feature of his character on the dark side; he always needed a father's, a mother's or some other guardian's care; he could not manage his financial affairs. He married a girl quite unsuited to him, and against the will of his father, and thus the great domestic chaos at and after his death.[17]

Sophie Haibel recalled that she had never seen Mozart in a temper. The composer would air his hostilities by the defensive adaptation of passive aggression.[18] This special combination of dependence and passive aggression is the basis of a self-destructive component in Mozart's personality. We have already seen how such psychic masochism may have influenced his gambling proclivities. Sophie Haibel recalled a remarkable incident that well illustrates Mozart's propensity to suffer in silence. It occurred during one of Constanze's prolonged illnesses, probably in 1789. Sophie nursed her sister for eight months; her mother was also close at hand in case of need. On one occasion when Constanze was asleep, an ill-mannered servant entered her room; Mozart, concerned that his wife not be awakened, beckoned to the servant to remain quiet. However, during this alarm, while pushing back a chair, Mozart's open pen-knife fell from his hand, and the blade lodged deeply in his thigh. The composer gritted his teeth and bore the pain in silence. He made his way into the next room where his mother-in-law bound up the wound with St. John's oil of Cubebs. Mozart concealed the injury from his wife, limping about in silence until the wound had healed.[19]

Although Leopold Mozart dearly loved his son and succeeded in the difficult and unenviable task of raising a genius, his strong obsessional personality soon began to dominate the boy, who submitted passively. Leopold endeavored to shield the boy from the mundane stresses of living, so that all the energy of his genius could be channeled into the composition of his music. An excellent example of Leopold's ambivalence of attitude is reflected in his letter of 26 February 1778:

My dear Wolfgang, you are young and you do not worry much, for so far you have never had to bother about anything; you banish all serious thought, you have long since forgotten the Salzburg cross, on which I am still hanging; you only listen to praises and flatteries and thus are becoming by degrees insensible and unable to realize our condition or to devise some means of relieving it. In short, you never think of the future. The present alone engulfs you completely, and sweeps you off your feet, although if you would only ponder the consequences of your actions and face them in good earnest, you would I know be horrified.[20]

Mozart was in debt at this time, and having fallen madly in love with Aloysia Weber, he was looking for excuses to defer his journey to Paris. He even entertained the idea of taking her to Italy. Leopold developed nervous palpitations, and he balked at his twenty-two-year-old son's efforts to break his chains of bondage. Jealousy and the generation gap contributed to Leopold's lack of empathy for his son's plight. When Leopold appealed for sympathy that he would have to make do with his tattered clothing and stockings, Mozart replied: "It is out of the question to be badly dressed for appearances must be kept up."[21]

The former harmonious rapport of their relationship was never restored. The rift widened further when Leopold held his son partly responsible for his mother's death in Paris. After Mozart resigned from the Salzburg Court and he married Constanze, Leopold gradually shifted his allegiance to Nannerl and her children. In doing so, he did not realize that he would threaten his son's narcissistic dependency. Leopold had built up too high an expectation of Mozart's material future, and he became disenchanted with his son's principal failings of pride, gullibility, uncritical acceptance of flattery, instability, and impulsiveness.[22] But then Leopold could not have known that Mozart was subject to pathological mood swings beyond his control.

And so the personal cost of Mozart's genius was very high indeed. In the exercise of his genius he left the wonderful legacy of his music, but in the process the growth of his personality was stunted. In particular, his emotional maturity lagged behind his intellectual growth. It is clear that Mozart remained a child in his emotional development. Nannerl's assessment of her brother's personality was most astute and accurate in this respect. We will return to the importance of stable object relations in the next chapter.

Mozart's anomy and love of practical jokes persisted throughout his life, and he was unable to resist making fun of his friends. Wolfgang would have enjoyed seeing the monster cask at Heidelberg Castle during his visit in July 1763. We have seen how he liked to frolic with Joseph Leitgeb. Mozart sometimes used a variety of colored inks when writing his autographs. He used green and red ink, for example, in the Horn Concerto in E-flat (K. 495), and Einstein concluded that he may have done so to confuse poor Joseph Leitgeb, when he first played it. Mozart's joker mentality even found its way into some of his compositions, as, for example, in his Echo pieces, K. 239, 286, the "Bandl-Terzett," K. 441, the Musical Joke, K. 522 (especially the Presto finale), and many of his canons.

A posthumous tribute to the composer appeared in a December 1791 issue of the Berlin *Musikalisches Wochenblatt*: "In his life he was constantly the object of cabals, which he at times may well have provoked by his sans souci manner."[23] *Sans Souci*, a term coined in 1718, offers an excellent description of Mozart's carefree manner and frivolity.[24] He was at times his own worst enemy with tactless, cutting outbursts from his careless tongue. Other unfortunate consequences of his sarcastic humor included his curt criticisms of the prevalent Italian opera style in Vienna, as well as his delight in satirical parodies at the keyboard and of grand operatic scenas in the style of well-known masters, with dramatic effect.[25] Mozart's humor will be discussed further within the context of his cyclothymic disorder.

The exceptional early maturation of the musical genius of both Mozart and Mendelssohn illustrates the importance of home environment and parental attitudes in such development.[26] Although the right (nondominant) cerebral hemisphere is vitally concerned with nonverbal expression and comprehension of emotions, it is at present not possible to localize creative activities such as composition or performance within the brain.[27] Yet split brain research theories postulate that creativity and

behavior are governed by fluidity and interchangeability of right versus
left hemispheric directional shifts.[28] Limitations of the scientific study of
certain of its aspects have engendered the fascinating perplexity of
musical experience.

15

PASTIMES AND STRESSES

Throughout his life Mozart was subject to periods of boredom, a tendency which he countered through his enthusiastic attachment to the pastime of the moment. He liked to day dream during times of sadness, and he was readily attracted to the excitement of travel.

In the Alpine countries during the eighteenth century, "Bölzischiessen," a form of crossbow shooting, was one of the most popular and enjoyable pastimes. Civic Riflemen's Societies were prevalent everywhere, and in Salzburg the Mozart family belonged to the Bolt-Marksmen's Company. Air-guns loaded with bolts were shot at targets with painted discs that measured up to a meter in diameter. Individual members were responsible for the ornamentation of the targets with amusing drawings, rhymes, and verses: scatological subjects were popular. The shooting competitions were conducted in the gardens or apartments of the members in rotation, and the winner was awarded a small prize from a special fund.

The letters of the Mozart family reveal that their home was a popular venue for the bolt-shooting competitions. Mozart was a member of the Bolt-marksmen's Company from the age of ten. In September 1780, Emanuel Schikaneder shot at targets with them while on tour with his theatrical company in Salzburg for the winter season. Other popular recreational pursuits in the garden included darts, ninepins, and fencing. Mozart and his father played a game of boccie after lunch in Rome in April 1770.[1]

Mozart became passionately fond of horse riding, and throughout his life he showed a fond attachment to pet animals and birds. He loved playing with a favorite cat in London. Much of the family correspondence mentions their pets in Salzburg—a canary, a robin, a tomtit, and the fox terrier bitch Bimperl. The dog was regularly taken on walks through the Mirabell Gardens. In Vienna Mozart owned a dog named Gauckerl to which he gave the pet name Schamanuzky. In May 1784 he purchased a starling for 34 kreuzers; this bird was able to whistle a near version of the finale theme of the Piano Concerto in G (K. 453).

While in Prague for the production of *Don Giovanni*, the Mozarts left their bitch Katherl in the care of the Jacquins. Gottfried's father took a liking to the dog, and Mozart was touched by his friend's description of her playful activities:

I am delighted to hear what you say about Katherl, that is, that she commands the respect of cats and knows how to retain the friendship of dogs. If your papa, to whom I send most cordial greetings, likes to keep her, well, let us pretend that she never belonged to me.[2]

Mozart was so fond of his last canary that he would become upset if he could not take the bird with him on outings.

During the Grand Tour of Europe, the prodigy attended many balls and receptions, and as an adult he was an accomplished dancer. He especially excelled in minuets and looked forward to attending the public ball.[3] In mid-January 1783, Mozart held a private ball at his lodgings for his friends; the festivities continued from 6:00 P.M. through 7:00 the next morning. During the Carnival in 1786, Mozart attended the masked ball dressed as an Indian philosopher. (We will return to his hypomanic activities at that time in the next chapter.) During the evening of his arrival in Prague on 11 January 1787, Mozart attended a ball at the Seminary Hall, where the greatest beauties of Prague were gathered. They danced to quadrilles and waltzes arranged from *Figaro*, but Wolfgang was too tired and bashful to join in![4]

Throughout his life Mozart would leave the confines of his apartment to take a favorite walk, either alone or in the company of his friends. He also enjoyed family outings to gardens such as the Prater. During one such outing in 1783 Constanze lost her ribbon; the tall Gottfried von Jacquin found it but refused to hand it over until she could catch it. This amusing incident inspired Mozart to compose a humorous three-part song for soprano, tenor, and bass, "The Bandl-Terzett" (K. 441).[5] In 1784, Mozart took a daily early morning walk through the Augarten; when composing *Die Zauberflöte*, he loved walking through the Glacis to the Freihaus Theater.

In 1829, Constanze Nissen told Vincent and Mary Novello that Mozart drew a little, manifested a fondness and talent for all the arts, and enjoyed reading. His comprehensive library contained books on philosophy, music, drama, poetry, geography, history, mathematics, travel, natural science, prose, religion, and fiction. Mozart's library included the works of Pietro Metastasio, awarded to him by Count Karl Firmian at Milan in 1770, and Molière's complete comedies, presented by Fridolin Weber as a farewell gift at Mannheim in 1778. Other books included the posthumous works of Frederick the Great, a biography of Emperor Joseph II, a dot-book, a 1679 (Cologne) edition of the Holy Bible, and a book on learning English.[6]

Mozart smoked a pipe. His favorite foods were roast capon, sauerkraut, trout, and liver dumplings; there is no mention of exotic extravagant tastes in food. He remained thin, so that it would appear that he was not prone to overindulge. In the letter to his wife from Frankfurt Am Main dated 28 September 1790, he wrote:

At Regensburg we lunched magnificently to the accompaniment of divine music, we had angelic cooking and some glorious Moselle wine . . . at Würzburg, a fine, magnificent town, we fortified our precious stomachs with coffee. The food was tolerable everywhere, but at Aschaffenburg, two and a half stages from here, mine host was kind enough to fleece us disgracefully.[7]

Mozart very much enjoyed fine black coffee and usually drank alcohol in moderation, so as to retain a clear mind for composing. Both Michael Kelly and Sophie Haibel reveal that he was remarkably fond of punch, though Haibel affirmed that she had never seen him inebriated. When writing the Overture to *Don Giovanni*, Mozart was up most of the night while Constanze kept him awake with frequent cups of coffee and story tales. After he finally fell asleep, she awakened him at five and supplied him with draughts of hot punch, so that the work could be completed in time for the dress rehearsal.

Mozart sometimes drank wine when composing. Jahn was informed that a neighbor named Loibl would respond to taps on the partitioning wall by sending wine from his cellar to the composer.[8] Mozart also made frequent visits to Deiner's no longer extant tavern in the Kärnthnerstrasse, where he relaxed over a stein of beer in the merry company of his friends.

Johann Friedrich Rochlitz suggested that Mozart drank wine to escape anxious thoughts. It would appear that he imbibed more often when depressed during his latter years. At any rate, according to Iqnaz E.F.K. Arnold he did so during his last summer, when in the rough company of Schikaneder's troupe[9] (see p. 151). Even so, Mozart was always preoccupied with his music: "You know that I am, so to speak, soaked in music, that I am immersed in it all day long and that I love to plan works, study and meditate."[10]

Mozart loved making music at home with friends and pupils, so that musical soirees were sometimes arranged on Sundays or special occasions. On 12 February 1784, Joseph Haydn and the Barons Anton and Bartholomäus Tinti were invited to Figaro House where they played three string quartets (K. 458, 464, 465). It was on this occasion that Haydn made his famous remark to Leopold Mozart: "Before God and as an honest man I tell you that your son is the greatest composer known to me either in person or by name. He has taste and, what is more, the most profound knowledge of composition."[11]

In his letter from Prague to Gottfried von Jacquin, dated 15 January 1787, Mozart wrote:

Immediately after our arrival at noon on Thursday, the 11th, we had a dreadful rush to get ready for lunch at one o'clock. After the meal old Count Thun entertained us with some music, performed by his own people, which lasted about an hour and a half. This kind of real entertainment I could enjoy every day.[12]

In private Mozart was reticent to play the piano unless his audience was appreciative and attentive. However, when he was in the mood, he would sometimes demonstrate his complete mastery of every aspect of the musician's art. His forte was free improvisation by means of variations and fugues.

The Mannheim orchestra, which was famous for its dynamic range, effectiveness of contrasts, and especially its finesse of the winds and strings, arranged a four-hour concert specially for the Mozart family at Schwetzingen on 18 July 1763. At that time Carl Stamitz, who was the second violinist with that orchestra, mastered a brilliant performing technique, and later achieved fame in playing the viola with extraordinary art and facility. After his return from Paris, Mozart was to instill a good deal of his creative energy into writing for the viola in his orchestral and chamber music. He was one of the first composers to fully exploit the darker, warmer, richer, less assertive, more mellow, and even subdued tone qualities of this instrument, and to more effectively contrast it with the brighter, more brilliant tones of the soprano violin. Mozart dedicated his longest chamber work, the Divertimento for String Trio (K. 563), to his friend Michael Puchberg, and he took the viola part in three performances of this trio. Mozart loved the viola, generally playing it in performances of chamber music. He also loved the clarinet, and he was overcome with the glorious effect of a symphony with flutes, oboes, and clarinets.

Constanze told the Novellos that Mozart's favorite instrument was the organ; indeed, he never wasted an opportunity to visit a church or cathedral to play it.[13] As noted earlier, Mozart's favorite form was opera, and above all else, he enjoyed composing choruses: "I am looking forward most particularly to the concert spirituel in Paris, for I shall probably be asked to compose something for it. The orchestra is said to be excellent and strong: and my favorite type of composition, the chorus, can be well performed there. I am indeed glad that the French value choruses highly."[14] He achieved the acme of perfection in the Act II finale of *Figaro*, where in unprecedented fashion every singer of the cast gathered on the stage to produce an unsurpassed grandeur of dramatic effect. It is little wonder that he composed six of the greatest operas in the repertoire.

Mozart's favorite aria was J. C. Bach's setting of "Non so d'onde viene" from Metastasio's *Olimpiade*. Mozart also set this text to music in his own beautiful aria (K. 294) dedicated to Aloysia Weber. In April 1784, he considered his quintet for oboe, clarinet, horn, bassoon, and pianoforte (K. 452) to be the best work he had ever composed.[15]

According to Constanze and Michael Kelly, Mozart's best loved work was the sextet in Act III of *Figaro*: "Riconosci in questo amplesso." There was even a rehearsal of it on his deathbed. One of his favorite piano pieces was the variations on Johann Christian Fischer's minuet, from the finale of his first oboe concerto, K. 179. Mozart often featured it as a virtuoso display piece. Constanze and Thomas Attwood informed the Novellos that his favorite symphonies were the last three, K. 543, 550, 551; his favorite piano concerto was the one in D Minor, K. 466 and another favorite was his Piano Quartet in G Minor, K. 478. Mozart's three favorite operas were *Don Giovanni*, *Figaro*, and *Idomeneo*.

Mozart's lack of handsome appearance was one of the constant stresses in his life. According to John Pettinger, who met the formally dressed composer on a hot day during the summer of 1785, Mozart was of very slight build and short stature with an estimated height of five feet four inches (163 cm). His hand was cold with a firm grip, in keeping with an anxiety state. On that occasion he was composing string quartets, even continuing to write occasional notes during the conversation.[16] Michael Kelly described Mozart as remarkably small, very thin, and pale. He referred to the composer's profusion of fine fair hair, of which he was rather vain. Kelly also said that it would be as difficult to describe the lighting up of Mozart's little animated countenance when conducting *Figaro*, with the glowing rays of genius, as it would be to paint sunbeams.[17] Mozart's head appeared to be too large, for his short, slim body, while his oversized nose was frequently caricatured. His prominent blue eyes were adorned with good lashes and bushy brows, while his left ear was deformed. We have already described his disfigured face after the smallpox. Little wonder that he was sensitive to comment about his personal appearance. For a time in Mannheim he grew a beard. In the letter to his father from Mannheim (dated 31 October 1777) he wrote:

I thought I should not be able to keep myself from laughing when I was introduced to the people there. Some who knew me by repute were very polite and fearfully respectful; others, however, who had never heard of me, stared at me wide-eyed, and certainly in a rather sneering manner. They probably think that because I am little and young, nothing great or mature can come out of me; but they will soon see.[18]

Nissen wrote that Mozart was very angry about the Prussian ambassador's letter of introduction in which he said that he hoped Mozart's insignificant personal appearance would cause no prejudice against him.[19]

We have already considered many of the stresses during Mozart's childhood, as well as the deprivations and frequent illnesses during the travel journeys. Yet it is worth recalling the profound psychic trauma he suffered following the abrupt amputation of his friendship with Thomas Linley, Jr., at Florence in April 1770. Their friendship was unique in that Linley was a genius and his same age. In his letter to Thomas from Bologna, Wolfgang concluded: "Keep me in your friendship and believe that my affection for you will endure for ever and that I am your most devoted servant and loving friend."[20]

How traumatic it must have been for Mozart when he realized that despite his unique genius he had been born a member of the socially disdained class of musicians. While away from home in his twenty-second year, he suffered the bereavement of his mother in Paris, and six months later he was rejected by Aloysia Weber. On 8 January 1779, Mozart presented his aria to Aloysia, "Popoli di Tessaglia" (K. 316), with words from Gluck's *Alceste,* and a magnificent obbligato accompaniment for oboe and bassoon. She accepted his aria but rejected his love; the only warmth he received from her was the two pairs of mittens she had knitted him in Mannheim. Edward Holmes, in his first English biography, colorfully added that the composer immediately sat down to the clavier and sang aloud: "Gladly I leave the girl who does not want me."[21]

Mozart's objections to living in Salzburg are clearly stated in his letters to his father and to Abbé Bullinger. His major reservations were the narrowmindedness and hostility of Archbishop Colloredo, and the lack of facilities for opera. The poor social standing of professional musicians placed severe restrictions on social intercourse, and the rudeness of the aristocracy was at times intolerable. Mozart detested the coarse language and rough manners of the natives of Salzburg. The lack of discipline and insobriety of the slovenly, dissolute court musicians filled him with disgust. In addition, he was frustrated by the court's lack of enthusiasm and appreciation of his compositions. To make matters worse, there was too much interference from the chief steward. He objected to being seated at the servants' table between the cooks and the valets. It would also appear that there was a personality clash between Mozart and Colloredo, and the prince disliked short people. As an enlightened absolutist, he was intent on making sweeping reforms, many of which were unpopular, such as shortening the Mass time and abolishing several holidays (i.e., the observance of holy feast days). As an autocrat, he had resented the frequent absences of the Mozarts "who were travelling around the world like beggars." Colloredo was an able violinist and sometimes performed in the court orchestra. Whether there was any jealousy of Mozart's superior musical talents remains a matter for conjecture. Mozart disobeyed his prince and postponed his departure from Vienna for eight days; the final break came on 9 May 1781 when he was summoned before his employer. Colloredo lost his feudal temper and dismissed his court organist. The next day Mozart handed in his resignation to Count Arco, who refused to accept it without his father's consent.

Leopold wrote to Arco and exhorted him to persuade his son to return to Salzburg. However, Mozart's wounded pride would not allow him to back down. Encouraged by his success with *Idomeneo* and the Annual Society of Musicians' benefit concert in April, he chose to ignore the count's prophetic advice during a second interview at the end of May:

Believe me, you allow yourself to be far too easily dazzled in Vienna. A man's reputation here lasts a very short time. At first, it is true, you are overwhelmed with praises and make a good deal of money into the bargain—but how long does that last? After a few months the Viennese want something new.

Mozart replied: "You are right Count, but do you suppose that I mean to settle in Vienna?"[22]

After a quarrel, Wolfgang was finally dismissed from service and was literally kicked out of the house of the Teutonic Order by Count Arco on 8 June 1781. However, two years later he still had not received his formal discharge.[23]

There is much to digest here. The possessive, jealous father failed in his desperate bid to keep his beloved son under his domination, and the rebellious Wolfgang fell victim to the parasitic exploitation of Cäcilia Weber. After his marriage, with the consequent further rupture of the binding chains to his father, Mozart gradually became estranged from his family in Salzburg. His personality was vulnerable to object loss, and after his sister's marriage in August 1784 and his father's death in May 1787, he felt rather alone during the last few years of his life.[24]

The psychic trauma of such inner loneliness was exacerbated by Constanze's frequent absences at Baden and the premature death of four of his six children in infancy. Another factor was the departure of his friends Thomas Attwood, the Storaces, and Michael Kelly in February 1787. Four months earlier, Mozart and his wife were planning to accompany their English friends to London, but such plans were frustrated by Mozart's father's reasonable refusal to care for the two children during his absence. Leopold Mozart justified his refusal with a triad of sound fatherly advice. First, in order to undertake such a journey, Leopold calculated that his son would need at least 2,000 gulden; second, there was nothing to be gained by arriving in England during the summer; and third, he should procure some definite engagement in London in advance.

Mozart loved and admired Joseph Haydn above all other composers; the productivity of their friendship was unsurpassed in the history of music. On 1 September 1785, Wolfgang had dedicated his six String Quartets (K. 387, 421, 458, 428, 464, and 465) to Haydn:

To my dear friend Haydn, a father who has resolved to send his children out into the great world took it to be his duty to confide them to the protection and guidance of a very celebrated man, especially when the latter by good fortune was at the same time his best friend. Here they are then, O great man and my dearest friend, these six children of mine. They are, it is true, the fruit of long and laborious endeavour, yet the hope inspired in me by several friends that it may be at least partly compensated encourages me, and I flatter myself that this offspring will serve to afford me some solace one day. You yourself, dearest friend, told me of your satisfaction with them during your last visit to this capital. It is this indulgence above all which urges me to commend them to you and encourages me to hope that they will not seem to you altogether unworthy of your favour. May it therefore please you to receive them kindly and to be their father, guide and friend! From this moment I resign to you all my rights in them, begging you however to look indulgently upon the defects which the partiality of a father's eye may have concealed from me, and in spite of them to continue in your generous friendship for him who so greatly values it, in expectation of which I am, with all my heart, my dearest friend, your most sincere friend.

W. A. Mozart.[25]

How laudable was that kind and generous nature of Joseph Haydn, who was not troubled with a trace of envy or jealousy toward Mozart. Franz Rott, the chief commissioner in Prague, had written to Haydn requesting him to write an opera. In December 1787 Haydn made the following reply:

You ask an opera buffa of me. With the greatest pleasure, if you have the desire to possess some vocal composition of mine all for yourself. But if it is to be performed on the stage in Prague I cannot oblige you in that case, since all my operas are too closely bound up with our personnel, and moreover would never produce the effect which I calculated according to local conditions. It would be quite another matter if I had the incalculable felicity of composing an entirely new libretto for the theatre there. But even in that event I should be taking a great risk, since the great Mozart can scarcely have his equal. For if I were able to impress the soul of every music-lover, and more especially the great ones, with my own understanding of and feeling for Mozart's incomparable works, so profound and so full of musical intelligence, as my own strong sentiment dictates, then the nations would vie with each other to possess such a jewel within their encircling walls. Let Prague hold fast to the precious man—but also reward him; for without that the story of great genius is a sad one and gives posterity little encouragement for further effort; for which reason, alas, so many hopeful spirits suffer defeat. It makes me angry to think that this unique Mozart has not yet found an appointment at some imperial or royal court! Forgive me if I stray from my path. I love the man too much.[26]

In 1790, Mozart invited Haydn and Michael Puchberg to his apartment for a mini-rehearsal of *Così Fan Tutte* (K. 588). These two friends also attended the first orchestral rehearsal of this opera in the Burgtheater. Later that year, on 14 December 1790, Mozart attended the farewell dinner in Vienna for Haydn. Wolfgang's loneliness was further magnified by the departure of his friend for London, and he was then vulnerable for his collusion with Schikaneder. Although this coalition resulted in the creation of *Die Zauberflöte,* on the negative side, Jahn claimed that under the bad influence of Schikaneder and his riotous companions, Mozart was drawn into the whirl of a pleasure-loving lifestyle. Such folly and dissipation soon reached the public ear, and before long there were added exaggerated accounts of orgies, riotous parties, loose-living and the like, so that Mozart's good name was smeared for some time.[27] But we will better understand Mozart's more provocative behavior after the discussion of his cyclothymic disorder in Chapter 16. While living in London in 1791, Joseph Haydn received the unexpected news from his wife, that Mozart was talking malevolently against him.[28] Such a paradoxical defamation of Haydn is in keeping with the disturbed paranoid trend in Mozart's personality at that time.

The success of *Così Fan Tutte* was interrupted by the death of Joseph II. Mozart's application for the post of second Kapellmeister to Salieri was not even acknowledged by the new emperor, Leopold II. In 1781, Mozart wrote of his ambition to succeed Bonno, Salieri, and Starzer as court Kapellmeister. His failure to secure such an appointment was one of the greatest frustrations in his life. Among the other stresses in Mozart's life were the lack of appreciation of his music by contemporaries and patrons, the many intrigues of other composers, and the latter years of economic chaos and frequent ill health. His depression is therefore readily understood.

16

MOZART'S CYCLOTHYMIC DISORDER

Every normal person is subject to cycloid mood swings of elation and sadness. Such changes of mood may be in reaction to environmental influences, but they often appear to emanate from within, without obvious cause. Bipolar affective disorder is marked by recurrence of pathological mood swings beyond the control of the subject. Jean Pierre Falret (1794-1870) first described manic-depressive disorder in 1854 under the title *Folie Circulaire*. The condition is now known to affect about 1 percent of the adult population. In manic-depressive psychosis depressive episodes are interspersed with one or more bouts of mania, and gross impairment in reality testing and frankly psychotic behavior develop. Mood disturbance persists for at least two years in cyclothymic disorder, though the affective symptoms are muted. Depression alternates with hypomania in the absence of psychotic features.[1]

There is convincing evidence for the insidious onset of cyclothymic disorder during Mozart's early adult life.[2] The composer's hypomanic swings were characterized by elevated or expansive mood, decreased need for sleep, excessive energy, inflated self-esteem, increased productivity, extreme gregariousness, physical hyperactivity, inappropriate joking and punning, and indulgence in frivolous behavior without appreciation of consequences.

In 1791, the historian and librarian Adolf Heinrich Friedrich von Schlichtegroll was appointed a professor, privy counselor, and member of the Academy of Sciences in Munich. Between 1791 and 1806, he published annual volumes of biographical sketches of remarkable persons in the relevant year of their death. Schlichtegroll's Necrolog of Mozart was first published in Gotha in 1793; Joseph Georg Hubeck had it reprinted in

Graz in 1794.³ The source material for it was gathered from Nannerl's memoirs, Schachtner's notes, and other contemporary sources. Stendhal (Henri Beyle) republished Schlichtegroll's article in 1814 in his *Lives of Haydn, Mozart and Metastasio*. It was written of Mozart:

> This same being who, considered as an artist, had reached the highest stage of development even from his very earliest years, remained to the end of his life completely childish in every other aspect of existence. Never, until he died, did he learn to exercise the most elementary forms of self-control. The ordering of his domestic affairs, the proper husbanding of money, temperance, or the rational choice of pleasures—these were never virtues with which he had the least acquaintance. Invariably it was the pleasure of the moment that swept away all other considerations.⁴

Constanze attempted to buy out the entire Graz edition of 1794. Many biographers have distrusted or rejected Schlichtegroll's remarks about the darker side of Mozart's personality, without just cause. Let us now discuss the hypomanic periods of Mozart's cyclothymic disorder. It is repeated that such pathological mood swings are beyond the control of the sufferer and are of variable severity.

Mozart was in high spirits at Hohen-Altheim after the success of his two concerts at Augsburg. On 27 October 1777, he played two of his piano sonatas (K. 281, 284) to his rival Ignaz von Beeke. Later that evening, he played his violin like a gypsy and behaved frivolously.⁵ Mozart was deeply hurt, when at the moment of his departure from Mannheim on 14 March 1778, neither Christian Cannabich nor his daughter Rosa offered him any parting gift or even any words of thanks or appreciation. The teenage Rosa Cannabich had acquired a fine taste in her playing, after Mozart had toiled with her over many hours, so as to improve her fingering and playing of trills. The andante of his Piano Sonata in C (K. 309) is unique in that it is a musical portrait of her. Perhaps Cannabich had been shocked and dismayed by Mozart's extraordinary outbursts of objectionable rhymes and verses during the vulgar evening diversions at his home. The details were supplied by Mozart in the letter to his father from Mannheim (dated 14 November 1777):

> I did frequently, without any difficulty, but quite easily, perpetrate—rhymes, the same being moreover, sheer garbage, that is, on such subjects as muck, shitting and arse-licking—and that too in thoughts, words—but not in deeds. I should not have behaved so godlessly, however, if our ringleader, known under the name of Lisel, had not egged me on and incited me; at the same time I must admit that I thoroughly enjoyed it.⁶

In a letter to his father twelve days later, Mozart freely admitted to being "quite off the rails":

If I could find some more room, I would send 100,000 compliments from us 2, I mean, from us two, to all our good friends: particularly to the A's:—the Adlgassers, Andretters and Arco (Count); B's:—Herren Bullinger, Barisani and Berantzky; C's:—Czernin (Count), Cusetti and the three organ blowers (Calcanten). . . . I can't write anything sensible today, as I am rails off the quite. Papa be annoyed not must. I that just like today feel. I help it cannot. Warefell. I gish you nood-wight. Sound sleeply. Next time I'll sensible more writely.[7]

Mozart at times felt compelled to write nonsense letters or quasi-nonsense passages in his correspondence. There are many examples of such nonsense doggerel in the letters to his family, especially in his Bäsle letters.[8] Mozart's tomfoolery with words and numbers utilizes a diverse range of examples and techniques of jargon paraphrasia, nonsense anagrams, cancrizans, polyglot sections, and all kinds of bizarre manipulations and variations of rhyme and verse. He sometimes created verbal echo effects or introduced surprise stories, and was fond of using repetitions of synonyms and phonetically similar words. These letters contain several passages that are scarcely susceptible to literal translation. However, such passages are a unique reflection of Mozart's hypomanic behavior, in his own words, by way of their tomfoolery, puns, plays on words, amusing irrelevancies, distractability, and clanging.

For example, Mozart's letter to his Bäsle from Mannheim, dated 28 February 1778, contains clang associations, which are characteristic of the manic syndrome:

So if you want to send a reply to me from that town of Augsburg yonder, you see, then write at once, the sooner the better, so that I may be sure to receive your letter, or else if I'm gone I'll have the bad luck, instead of a letter to get some muck. Muck! —Muck! —Ah, muck! Sweet word! Muck! Chuck! That too is fine. Muck, chuck! —muck! —suck—O charmante! muck, suck! that's what I like! Muck, chuck and suck! Chuck muck and suck muck![9]

Mozart's flirtations with his cousin, Maria Anna Thekla, achieved notoriety through the infamous Bäsle letters. Nine letters written by Mozart to his cousin between October 1777 and October 1781 are extant. Much of their content is nonsense doggerel, but there are some serious passages, especially in the latter ones. Two further extracts will suffice to illustrate Mozart's hypomanic tomfoolery with words and numbers. His letter of 28 February 1778 commences:

Perhaps you think or are even convinced that I am dead? That I have pegged out? Or hopped a twig? Not at all. Don't believe it, I implore you. For believing and shitting are two very different things! Now how could I be writing such a beautiful hand if I were dead? How could that be possible? I shan't apologize for my very long silence, for you would never believe me. Yet what is true is true. I have had so many things to do that I had time indeed to think of my little cousin, but not to write, you see. So I just had to let things be. But now I have the honour to enquire how you are and whether you perspire? Whether your stomach is still in good order? Whether indeed you have no disorder? Whether you still can like me at all? Whether with chalk you often scrawl? Whether now and then you have me in mind? Whether to hang yourself you sometimes feel inclined? Whether you have been wild? With this poor foolish child? I swear I'll let off one behind! Ah, you are laughing! Victoria! Our arses shall be the symbol of our peacemaking! I knew that you wouldn't be able to resist me much longer. Why, of course, I'm sure of success, even if today I should make a mess, though to Paris I go in a fortnight or less.[10]

Twenty-six months later, in the ending of his letter, dated 24 April 1780, Mozart treats even the number of greetings in cancrizans:

All sorts of messages from my papa and my sister Zizibe; and to your parents from us three, two boys and a girl, 1 2 3 4 5 6 7 8 9 8 7 6 5 4 3 2 1 greetings, and to all our good friends from myself 6 2 4, from my father 1 0 0, and from my sister 1 5 0, that is a total of 1 7 7 4, and summa summarum 1 2 3 4 5 6 7 8 9 8 7 6 5 6 0 9 5 compliments.[11]

Mozart's scatological language has been discussed at length in the literature, especially within the context of the Bäsle letters.[12] No doubt, the composer was influenced by his mother's "Salzburgisch" humor, which placed her at ease with such language. For example, she attempted to cheer up her husband, in her letter from Munich, dated 26 September 1777: "Keep well, my love. Into your mouth your arse you'll shove. I wish you good-night, my dear, but first shit in your bed and make it burst."[13]

Even the priggish Nannerl comments on the bodily functions of their pet fox-terrier bitch, Bimperl, in the letter to her mother and brother, dated 29 September 1777: "All the same she is quite well, eats, drinks, sleeps, shits and pisses."[14]

The diplomatic Leopold Mozart also occasionally used words that are no longer in polite usage. Indeed, both Mozart and his father made a point of criticizing the crude and slovenly manners of the Salzburg court musicians. However, there is an air of hypocrisy in this condemnation since they both encouraged the design of disgustingly uncouth targets for their bolt-shooting competitions.[15]

There is certainly no evidence of dementia or Gilles de la Tourette syndrome to account for Mozart's coprolalia.[16] These letters are not pornographic. Rather, Mozart's scatological language is yet another reflection of his satirical, hypomanic humor.

When Mozart replied to his father's concern about his relationship with Aloysia Weber, he alluded to the complexity of his personality and the excitement of his mood swings:

I am a Mozart, and a young and clean-minded Mozart. So you will forgive me, I hope, if in my eagerness I sometimes get excited,—if that is the expression I should use, though indeed I would much rather say, if I sometimes write naturally. I have much to say on this subject, but I cannot, for I find it impossible to do so. Among my many faults I have also this one, a persistent belief that my friends who know me, really do know me. Therefore many words are not necessary: for if they do not know me, Oh, then where could I ever find words enough? It is bad enough that one needs words at all—and letters into the bargain.[17]

Mozart composed the greater and most difficult part of *Idomeneo* during the last few days before the premiere. His father confused his son's flat periods of creativity with laziness; Mozart's reply provides a unique reflection of the effects of his moods on his productivity:

Believe me when I say that I do not like to be idle but to work. I confess that in Salzburg work was a burden to me and that I could hardly ever settle down to it. But why? Because I was never happy. You yourself must admit that in Salzburg—for me at least—there is not a farthing's worth of entertainment. . . . it is true that in Munich, without wishing to do so, I put myself in a false light as far as you were concerned, for I amused myself too much. But I swear to you on my honour that until the first performance of my opera I had never been to a theatre, or gone any where but to the Cannabich's. It is true that during the last few days I had to compose the greater and most difficult part of my opera; yet this was not from laziness or negligence—but because I had spent a fortnight without writing a note, simply because I found it impossible to do so. Of course I composed a lot, but wrote down nothing. I admit that I lost a great deal of time in this way, but I do not regret it.[18]

After the premiere during an upswing of mood, Mozart behaved frivolously. Indeed, his actions resulted in the accruement of a substantial debt, as we have seen. When the well-informed Leopold Mozart accused his son of revelling in pleasures and amusements at Munich, Mozart justified his folly as follows:

That I was afterwards too gay was only due to youthful folly. I thought to myself, where are you going to? To Salzburg! Well, you must have a good time. It is quite certain that when I am in Salzburg I long for a hundred amusements, but here not a single one. For just to be in Vienna is in itself entertainment enough. Do have confidence in me; I am no longer a fool, and still less can you believe that I am either Godless, or an ungrateful son![19]

Mozart's extraordinary flamboyant behavior, during the Carnival in February 1786 at the Hofburg Assembly Room is also in keeping with an upswing of hypomania. The printed solutions to his eight riddles were in anagram, while the composer had also recorded fourteen selections from "Zoroaster's Fragments" for the edification of the rout.[20]

During the anticipation of the premiere of *Don Giovanni,* at the Duscheks' villa in Prague in October 1787, Mozart again behaved frivolously and talked in rhymes.[21]

Joseph Lange also referred to Mozart's excited mood swings before an important work was to be presented. In his autobiography, published in 1808, Lange described his brother-in-law's self-demeaning clowning. He also referred to the composer's excited speech disturbance, which is in keeping with hypomanic flight of ideas and distractability:

Never was Mozart less recognizably a great man in his conversation and actions, than when he was busied with an important work. At such times he not only spoke confusedly and disconnectedly, but occasionally made jests of a nature which one did not expect of him, indeed he even deliberately forgot himself in his behaviour. But he did not appear to be brooding and thinking about anything. Either he intentionally concealed his inner tension behind superficial frivolity, for reasons which could not be fathomed, or he took delight in throwing into sharp contrast the divine ideas of his music and these sudden outbursts of vulgar platitudes, and in giving himself pleasure by seeming to make fun of himself. I can[not] understand that so exalted an artist can, out of a deep veneration for his art, belittle and as it were expose to ridicule his own personality.[22]

Sophie Haibel, writing for Nissen's biography in 1828, suggests Mozart's psychomotor agitation. This condition is a depressive reaction resulting from severe anxiety, arising from unresolved threatening factors deep in the mental life:

Even when he was washing his hands when he rose in the morning, he walked up and down in the room the while, never standing still, tapped one heel against the other the while and was always deep in thought. At table he often took the corner of a napkin, crumpled it up tightly, rubbed it round below his nose, and seemed in his reflections to know nothing of what he was doing, and often he would grimace with his mouth the while. In his pastimes he was always passionately attached to the latest of them, and so it was with riding, and also with billiards. To keep him from intercourse of an unworthy kind his wife patiently took part in everything with him. Also, his hands and feet were always in motion, he was always playing with something, e.g., his hat, pockets, watch-chain, tables, chairs, as if they were a clavier.[23]

Karoline Pichler took piano lessons from Mozart, and in her memoirs (1843-1844) she gave further testament of the composer's frequent episodes of scatty behavior. These episodes are characteristic of the hypomanic syndrome. She wrote:

One day when I was sitting at the pianoforte playing the "Non Più Andrai" from Figaro, Mozart, who was paying us a visit, came up behind me; I must have been playing to his satisfaction, for he hummed the melody as I played and beat the time on my shoulders; but then he suddenly moved a chair up, sat down, told me to carry on playing bass, and began to improvise such wonderfully beautiful variations that everyone listened to the tones of the German Orpheus with bated breath. But then he suddenly tired of it, jumped up, and, in the mad mood which so often came over him, he began to leap over tables and chairs, miaow like a cat, and turn somersaults like an unruly boy.

Later, she referred to the composer's "irresponsible way of life."[24]

Cyclothymic personalities are especially vulnerable to alcohol dependence for their consolation. Although Mozart usually drank alcohol in moderation when composing, it would appear that he imbibed more in his latter years. At any rate, there is evidence that he did so during his last summer. Arnold's description is also suggestive of hypomanic behavior: "The liberties he took with his health are well known; how he used to drink champagne with Schikaneder all morning, and punch all night, and go to work again after midnight, without any thought of his bodily health."[25]

Let us now return to the enigma of the eternal feminine. We have seen that Mozart's moral convictions and dread of venereal diseases encouraged him to suppress his sexual fancies. Even so, he was vulnerable to capricious infatuations with almost every woman he met: "If I had to marry all those with whom I have jested, I should have two hundred wives at least."[26] The reason is bound up with his special kind of infantile narcissistic dependency, which required a constant supply of love and moral support from valued love objects. Furthermore, his lively intrigues with Henriette Baranius, Barbara Gerl, and possibly other women are readily accounted for by the inappropriate increased sexual activity that accompanies the hypomanic swings of cyclothymic disorder. Further consideration of Mozart's narcissistic dependency and passive aggression also helps to account for the femininity, or lack of sexual provocativeness, in his music.[27]

The hypomanic episodes in cyclothymic disorder may last days to months, but in due course recurrent depressive spells of variable severity develop. Occasionally, there may be an intermingling of hypomanic and depressive symptoms, which either occur simultaneously or rapidly alternate within a few days. Mozart manifested such alternations of mood during the summer of 1788, as well as during his last year, in both Prague and Vienna.

Cyclothymic artists are capable of astonishing bursts of creative activity during their upswings in mood, and Mozart is the ultimate example. Let us briefly consider five of these extraordinary fertile periods in Mozart's life:

1. *Mannheim, 1777-78:* K. 285, 285a, 285b, 294-6, 301-3, 305, 307-9, 311, and 314 (Flute Concerto in D).
2. *Munich, 1780-81:* K. 341, 349, 351, 361, 366 *(Idomeneo)*, 368-70.
3. *Vienna—First half of 1786:* K. 485, 486, 488, 491, 492 *(Figaro)*, 493-5.
4. *Vienna—The Summer of 1788:* K. 542-551 (including the three last symphonies).
5. *Vienna—First Quarter of 1791:* K. 595-613.

Mozart's first well-documented episode of depression occurred in Paris in July 1778 during his bereavement:

As long as I live I shall never forget it. You know that I had never seen anyone die, although I had often wished to. How cruel that my first experience should be the death of my mother!. . . . Once during my dear departed mother's illness a dose (of powder) was almost necessary—but now, thank God, I am perfectly well and healthy. From time to time I have fits of melancholy—but I find that the best way to get rid of them is to write or receive letters, which invariably cheer me up again.[28]

During his latter years, Mozart attempted to escape from his melancholia by immersing himself in favorite compositions, especially opera, or by traveling, or by recreational pursuits and gambling. On the occasion of their meeting during the summer of 1785, John Pettinger described the composer's facial expression as rather melancholic until he spoke, when his eyes became animated and interested in the subject matter. Johann Nepomuk Hummel (1778-1837), who was Mozart's pupil during the years 1786-87, also described Mozart's expression.

His physiognomy had much that was pleasant and friendly, combined with a rather melancholy graveness; his large blue eyes shone brightly. In the circle of his good friends he could grow quite merry, lively, witty, even at times and on certain subjects satirical![29]

It is curious, that on direct questioning, Constanze denied her first husband's melancholia to the Novellos. She maintained, on the contrary, that he was always in good humor. Perhaps she was attempting to negate Jean-Baptiste-Antoine Suard's anecdote:

He was extremely irritable; his affections were lively, but superficial and of short duration. He was melancholic and dominated by an active and mercurial imagination, which he only feebly kept in check by his reason. . . . his wife encouraged him in his work and sustained him in his fits of melancholy.[30]

From the viewpoint of his mental health, 1787 was the most crucial year in Mozart's life. Admittedly, that year started off well with his hero's welcome in Prague, but even his triumphant success in that great city was marred by the death of his friend, Count August Hatzfeld (1754-87) on 30 January.[31] Then he had to contend with the departure of the Storaces and Michael Kelly in February. We should also recall that Mozart was himself seriously ill during the spring. He made the following entry in a friend's album: "Patience and tranquillity of mind contribute more to cure our distempers as the whole art of medicine."[32] Five days later, when Mozart heard of the serious nature of his father's illness, he wrote to him:

This very moment I have received a piece of news which greatly distresses me, the more so as I gathered from your last letter that, thank God, you were very well indeed. But now I hear that you are really ill. I need hardly tell you how greatly I am longing to receive some reassuring news from yourself. And I still expect it; although I have now made a habit of being prepared in all affairs of life for the worst. . . . I hope and trust that while I am writing this, you are feeling better. But if, contrary to all expectation, you are not recovering, I implore you by . . . not to hide it from me, but to tell me the whole truth or get someone to write it to me, so that as quickly as is humanly possible I may come to your arms. I entreat you by all that is sacred—to both of us.[33]

Mozart had expressed all that was sacred to both of them in his letter from Mannheim, dated 28 February 1778:

You yourself know even better than I do how often things go awry—but they will soon go straight—only do have patience! Let us place our trust in God, Who will never forsake us. . . . I have full confidence in three friends, all of them powerful and invincible, God, your head and mine. Our heads, I admit, are very different, but each in its own way is good, serviceable and useful, and I hope that in time mine will by degrees equal yours in those branches in which it is now inferior.[34]

Unfortunately, Mozart's last letter to his father, dated 10 May 1787, is not extant, and alas, such a reunion was not to be.

Leopold was already in his grave when Mozart received the sad news of his father's death.[35] There are just three brief references to the composer's grief at this time:

I inform you that on returning home today I received the sad news of my most beloved father's death. You can imagine the state that I am in.[36]

You can easily imagine, as our loss is equally great, how pained I was by the sad news of the sudden death of our dearest father.[37]

I was not at all surprised, as I could easily guess the reason, that you yourself did not inform me of the sad death of our most dear father, which to me was quite unexpected.[38]

A certain coolness had crept into the brother-sister relationship. Mozart had written to Nannerl six days before her marriage, offering his congratulations, along with a witty verse.[39] He apologized for not attending her wedding since Constanze was in a state of advanced pregnancy. Mozart's narcissistic dependency was threatened by Leopold's transferral of his allegiance to Nannerl, and it is ludicrous to suggest, as some do, that the composer was not troubled by his alienation from his father.[40] His true feelings were expressed when Wolfgang wrote to congratulate him on his name-day in 1781:[41]

Dearest, most beloved father! I wish you every imaginable good that one can possibly wish. Nay rather, I wish nothing for you, but everything for myself. So I wish for my own sake that you may continue to enjoy good health, and that you may live many, many years for my happiness and my infinite pleasure. I wish for my own sake that everything I do and undertake may be in accordance with your desire and pleasure, or rather that I may never do anything which may not cause you the very greatest joy.[42]

Leopold Mozart's death is of immense importance in any study of Mozart's personality. When his father died, a vital part of Wolfgang also died.[43] Mozart's narcissistic dependency, so vulnerable to object loss, was shattered by his father's death, resulting in loss of self-esteem. The result was depression and a gradual withdrawal from his life as a celebrity, which had been bolstered by his brilliant success as a virtuoso; periodic elevated mood swings; and a determination to fulfill his father's ambitions for his success. It is no coincidence that he began to decline.[44]

Nine days after his father's death, Mozart buried his pet starling in the garden of his apartment in the Landstrasse district. He composed a serio-comic verse as an epitaph and arranged a solemn chanting funeral procession in which all veiled mourners were obliged to participate.[45] Such behavior is consistent with cyclothymic depression during bereavement.

The first work entered in Mozart's thematic catalogue, following news of his father's death, was "Ein Musikalischer Spass" (K. 522), entered on 14 June. This divertimento has posed a riddle for musicologists. Alan Tyson believes that the whole of the first movement was written out in parts before the end of 1786. Daniel Heartz notes that a near version of the fugue in the last movement was entered by Thomas Attwood in his sketchbook on 13 August 1786. Yet it seems reasonable to conclude that the clumsy discordant error at the end of the work was the result of Mozart's bereavement.[46]

Mozart escaped his depression for a while by immersing himself in the composition of *Don Giovanni*. Perhaps reflections of his dominating father were transferred into the creation of that most extraordinary character, Il Commendatore.[47] His most popular work, "Eine Kleine Nachtmusik" (K. 525), was entered on 10 August 1787, while he was working on the second act of *Don Giovanni*. Then on 3 September Mozart was shattered by the sudden death of his protector and childhood friend, Dr. Sigmund Barisani. Nor did his sinecure appointment as Kammer-musicus on 7 December relieve his frustrations.

Mozart's depression recurred during the productive summer of 1788. He was in debt, and he had moved to an inexpensive apartment away from the inner city: "During the ten days since I came to live here I have done more work than in two months in my former quarters, and if such black thoughts did not come to me so often, thoughts which I banish by a tremendous effort, things would be even better."[48]

After his father's death, Mozart became even more dependent on Constanze's affection for his well-being: "Take care of your health, for as long as you are well and are kind to me, I don't care a fig if everything else goes wrong."[49] During the summer of 1789 Constanze, who was in her fifth pregnancy, became ill with a varicose ulcer in the region of her ankle. Dr. Thomas Franz Closset applied leeches on 17 July and advised a cure at the spa. Constanze was frequently ill from that time, and on four occasions she was sent to Baden to take the warm sulphur baths—August 1789, May 1790, June-July 1791, and October 1791.

Although Constanze's frequent ill health during her pregnancies would appear to have been related to complications of varicose veins, a deficiency of iron and folic acid may also have contributed. However, there was also a psychosomatic element, and Constanze was often depressed. It is to be emphasized that cyclothymics are very difficult people to live with. Their emotional lability often results in marital conflicts and domestic chaos, as a consequence of their impulsive frivolous behavior. Mozart's worry about his wife's health precipitated further bouts of depression:

I have been living in such misery, that for very grief not only have I not been able to go out, but I could not even write. At the moment she is easier, and if she had not contracted bed-sores, which make her condition most wretched, she would be able to sleep. The only fear is that the bone may be affected. She is extraordinarily resigned and awaits recovery or death with true philosophic calm. My tears flow as I write.[50]

During Constanze's absences at Baden, Mozart sought companionship to lighten his burden during his melancholic spells:

If only I had someone to console me a little. It is not at all good for me to be alone, when I have something on my mind. . . . in the evening I again took a meal at the "Krone" simply in order not to be alone, and there at least I found someone to talk to.[51]

During 1790 Mozart was frequently ill and consumed by worries and anxieties. During the middle of spring he wrote to his friend Michael Puchberg: "For some time now you must have noticed my constant sadness. . . . What a pleasant sensation it is to reach one's goal at last—and what a blessed feeling it is when one has helped another to do so! Tears prevent me from completing the picture!"[52]

Even the anticipated pleasure of traveling to Frankfurt for the coronation of Emperor Leopold II was short-lived. Mozart was troubled with feelings of apathy: "I am as excited as a child at the thought of seeing you again. If people could see into my heart, I should almost feel ashamed. To me everything is cold—cold as ice."[53]

Let us now consider other manifestations of Mozart's melancholy. Depressed people are often troubled by insomnia, and there is reference to Mozart's early rising between 4:30 and 5:45, in the later letters to his wife. These letters also suggest a depressive paranoid trend and jealousy: "Do not torment yourself and me with unnecessary jealousy."[54]

Never go out walking alone. The very thought of this terrifies me.[55]

I seem to notice that you doubt my punctuality or rather my eagerness to write to you, and this pains me bitterly. Surely you ought to know me better. Good God! Only love me half as much as I love you, and I shall be content.[56]

Please do not go to the casino today even if Mme Schwingenschuhs should go out to Baden.[57]

I entreat you to take the Baths only every other day, and only for an hour. But if you want me to feel quite easy in my mind, do not take them at all, until I am with you again.[58]

I rely on your following my advice. If you do, I can feel a little calmer! As for my health, I feel pretty well. I trust that my affairs will improve as rapidly as possible. Until they are settled I cannot be quite easy in my mind.[59]

Mozart was prone to spells of exhaustion and fatigue, as, for example, in the July of his last year:

As soon as my business here is over, I shall be with you, for I mean to take a long rest in your arms; and indeed I shall need it, for this mental worry and anxiety and all the running about connected with it is really exhausting me.[60]

Yet despite his many sufferings and frequent depressive episodes, Mozart maintained an optimism about the future. None of his extant letters contains any thoughts of suicide; he did not despair but maintained hope. Although he must often have been left sleepless by his sad plight, even in the dismal year of 1790 he was able to write to his wife from Frankfurt: "I am firmly resolved to make as much money as I can here and then return to you with great joy. What a glorious life we shall have then! I will work—work so hard—that no unforeseen accidents shall ever reduce us to such desperate straits again."[61]

The nucleus of despair is suffering without meaning.[62] Despite his suffering, Mozart retained his will to live. His narcissistic dependency required a regular supply of love from an esteemed love object, though not necessarily a person, even a powerful cause or organization was sufficient. In addition to his love and concern for his family and his desire to create music for posterity, we have seen that Mozart gained further strength from his faith and trust in God. In times of stress he received consolation from his religion and moral support from his friends and Masonic Brothers.

The more severe episodes of depression are associated with a loss of interest or pleasure in most of the subject's usual activities and pastimes. When in addition decreased energy, difficulty in concentration or thinking, tearfulness, brooding, loss of appetite, fear, and anxiety exist, a diminution of creative outflow is inevitable. No doubt during those many flat, boring periods in his life, Mozart's indecisiveness plagued his creativity. It is to be noted that Mozart left over 100 fragments of incompleted compositions.

During the summer of 1789, Mozart was in debt and in desperate need of further income. Despite his enviable position of having twelve works commissioned by the king of Prussia, he managed to complete only one sonata (K. 576) and three string quartets (K. 575, 589, 590). In his letter to Michael Puchberg dated 17 May 1790, he wrote: "If only you knew what grief and worry all this causes me. It has prevented me all this time from finishing my quartets."[63]

During his last eleven years, Mozart composed an average of twenty-seven works each year. During 1790 he completed only nine, though four were masterpieces. Mozart's depression may have contributed to the cuts and corrections in Così Fan Tutte.[64] Let us now consider the melancholy in his music.

Many are attracted to the unreasonable sweetness of Mozart's music, and yet many of his compositions contain a central core of sadness hidden under the transparent disguise of a cheerful exterior. The mood of his work often hovers between tears and smiles. Mozart had an exceptionally deep awareness of his creative genius, and since he had difficulty verbalizing his emotions, the most natural outlet for expressing his frustrations and loneliness was through his music. Especially in those works in the minor key did Mozart seize the opportunity to express his inner pathos and melancholia. His compositions in the minor key include thirty-two works, fifteen fragments, and the *Requiem*.

With regard to some of these troubled works, there is sometimes a suggestion of a temporal relationship with a stressful event in the composer's life. The Piano Concerto in D Minor (K. 466) was composed in the knowledge that his father would be present at its first performance in the Mehlgrube Casino, on 11 February 1785. Could not the intense pathos, violence, and frenzied agitation of the first movement Allegro, in conjunction with the unsurpassed beauty of the opening theme of the Romance, have been inspired by the composer's love of his father and by a forlorn expectant hope of a warm reconciliation? Mozart's six-month-old daughter Theresia died on 29 June 1788; the G Minor Symphony (K. 550) was completed twenty-six days later. Perhaps his bereavement for his daughter exacerbated his depression, so that the turbulence of his mind expressed the profoundly impassioned and troubled melancholy of this symphony. Of course that is not necessarily so since very often sadness of mood emanates from the unconscious mental life.

The Adagio in B Minor (K. 540), entered in Mozart's catalogue on 19 March 1788, is one of the most profoundly moving and despondent of all his works. He had neglected his correspondence with Nannerl, and he dispatched this Adagio with a letter to her:

Indeed you have every reason to be vexed with me! But will you really be so, when you receive by this mail coach my very latest composition for the Clavier? Surely not! This, I hope, will make everything all right again.[65]

Einstein suggested that the Maurerische Trauermusik (K. 477) formed a link between the C Minor Mass (K. 427) and the *Requiem* (K. 626). The peculiar color of Mozart's Masonic music was achieved by replacing the horns with corni di bassetto or alto clarinets. The somber effect of these instruments was fully exploited in the *Requiem,* where they were blended with the lower registers of the strings, bassoons, trumpets, trombones, and timpani.

Many authorities consider cyclothymic disorder to be a less severe form of bipolar affective disorder, with absence of psychotic features. While it is true that, during the last six months of his life, Mozart suffered with mental delusions that he had been poisoned and that he had been commissioned to write his own requiem, such delusions may be accounted for by his development of chronic renal failure and cerebral vascular disease.[66]

Evidence from family, twin, and adoption studies supports the role of genetic factors in influencing the susceptibility of a population to the development of the major affective disorders. But the precise nature of such genetic linkages remains unknown.[67] Patients with cyclothymic disorder often present a family history of depression or bipolar disorder. Mozart's mother suffered a severe depression following the premature death of her first three children in infancy, but she made a good recovery following the spa cure at Bad Gastein.

Nannerl's family history is of much interest in this regard. Her son, Leopold Alois Pantaleon (1785-1840) died at age fifty-five. The second child, Johanna Jeanette, died on 1 September 1805, at age sixteen, of "Nervenfieber." This condition may have been due to meningitis, encephalitis, or even typhus fever. Nannerl's third child, Maria Barbara, died on 26 April 1791, aged five months, of "in der Fraiss" or infantile convulsions.[68] Nannerl's great granddaughter, Bertha Forschter, died at the age of seventy-seven on 9 January 1919, in the County Insane Asylum at Feldhof, near Graz, after a chronic illness of thirty years' duration. She was the daughter of Nannerl's granddaughter, Henriette von Sonnenburg, who had died in the same institution in 1890. However, it has been concluded that this lineage of insanity can be traced to the Berchtold side of the family, which Nannerl had married into.[69]

Any attempt to assess the effects of a mood disorder on musical creativity, after a lapse of two centuries, is at best difficult.[70] There are grey transition areas between normality and the two opposite poles of affectivity. Even subjects with cyclothymic disorder exhibit frequent intervening periods of normal mood, and there is difficulty in distinguishing pathological mood swings from the normal ups and downs of everyday life. The tendency to oversimplification is ever present. It is again to be emphasized that cyclothymic depression is muted. Mozart sometimes used the term *boring* to describe his flat periods of affect. We all know how dreary weather can depress mood. Consider, for example, Maria Anna Mozart's letter to her husband from Paris, dated 24 March 1778: "Wolfgang is bored, as he hasn't got a clavier yet. The weather has been so bad that he hasn't been able to see about one."[71] Yet there is no doubt that Mozart's mood profoundly affected his creativity. Three further examples from his family correspondence illustrate this idea. In the letter to his father from Mannheim, dated 14 February 1778, Wolfgang attempted to justify his slow progress with the flute quartets for M. de Jean:

It is not surprising that I have not been able to finish them, for I never have a single quiet hour here. I can only compose at night, so that I can't get up early as well; besides, one is not always in the mood for working. I could, to be sure, scribble off things the whole day long, but a composition of this kind goes out into the world, and naturally I do not want to have cause to be ashamed of my name on the title-page. Moreover, you know that I become quite powerless whenéver I am obliged to write for an instrument which I cannot bear. Hence as a diversion I compose something else, such as duets for clavier and violin, or I work at my mass.[72]

Three months later, in Paris, Mozart described his flat mood to his father: "I am tolerably well, thank God, but I often wonder whether life is worth living—I am neither hot nor cold—and don't find much pleasure in anything."[73] On 9 June 1781, in Vienna, Mozart's spirit was again at low ebb. On the previous day Count Arco had dismissed him from service, and his father had added insult to injury by accusing him of deserting his family:

Must I repeat it a hundred times that I can be of more use to you here than in Salzburg? I implore you, dearest, most beloved father, for the future to spare me such letters. I entreat you to do so, for they only irritate my mind and disturb my heart and spirit; and I, who must now keep on composing, need a cheerful mind and a calm disposition.[74]

And so there it is. When we are exhilarated by the exquisite music of *Die Zauberflöte*, we must not forget the torment and anguish Mozart suffered while composing it:

My one wish now is that my affairs should be settled, so that I can be with you again. You cannot imagine how I have been aching for you all this long while. I can't describe what I have been feeling—a kind of emptiness, which hurts me dreadfully—a kind of longing, which is never satisfied, which never ceases, and which persists, nay rather increases daily. When I think how merry we were together at Baden—like children—and what sad, weary hours I am spending here! Even my work gives me no pleasure, because I am accustomed to stop working now and then and exchange a few words with you. Alas! This pleasure is no longer possible. If I go to the piano and sing something out of my opera, I have to stop at once, for this stirs my emotions too deeply.[75]

PART IV

Death and Aftermath

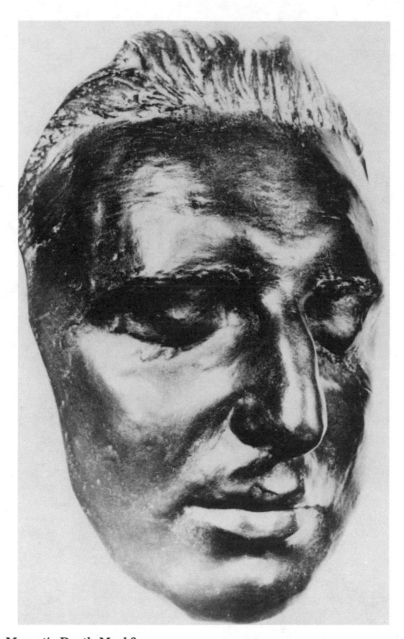

Mozart's Death Mask?
Cast in bronze by Thaddäus Ribola, Vienna. This mask was discovered in
Vienna in 1947 by the musician Jakob Jelinek. (Courtesy of the Inter-
national Foundation Mozarteum, Salzburg.)

17

TERMINAL ILLNESS AND BURIAL

On a cold November day in 1791, Mozart paid his last visit to a favorite tavern in the Kärnthnerstrasse. He flopped down wearily onto a chair and ordered a glass of wine. The waiter, Joseph Deiner, recalled that the composer looked wretched and unusually pale; his powdered wig was in disarray, and in his dejected mood he felt disinclined to drink his wine. Deiner's efforts to cheer up the composer were in vain, and he reported that Mozart said: "I feel that there won't be much more music-making. I've got a chill coming on that I can't account for." Prior to leaving, Mozart asked Deiner to call the next morning and assist Constanze in collecting some firewood. When Deiner visited the apartment in the Rauhensteingasse early next morning, the composer was on his death-bed, and he said: "Josef, there's nothing doing today; today we're going to be busy with doctors and apothecaries."[1]

Mozart took to his bed critically ill on 20 November 1791. His final illness had been contracted during an epidemic, probably at the lodge two days previously, and lasted only fifteen days.[2] During the night he had complained to Constanze of pain on moving in bed. She noted that his hands and feet were swollen and tender. Such symptoms suggest a polyarthritis. The swelling became more pronounced and widespread, suggesting the later development of edema. Mozart was febrile, and his fever was associated with drenching sweats. He suffered recurrent bouts of violent vomiting, especially at night, and also diarrhea.

In addition, a paralysis was present; Nissen mentions an almost total inability to move his limbs, while Holmes describes an almost total incapacity for motion; Jahn said that partial paralysis set in. Benedikt Schack, who was a frequent visitor, said that the composer was so weak that he had to be drawn forward whenever he required to sit up in bed. The combination of painful swellings and paralysis made it difficult for him either to move or to be moved. Sophie Weber and her mother therefore made him nightshirts, which could be put on him from the front, for he could not turn over in bed. Not appreciating the critical nature of his illness, they also made him a quilted dressing gown. It may be concluded that Mozart was afflicted with a hemiparesis and was paralyzed down one side of his body. He later became hypersensitive to the song of his beloved pet canary, which had to be removed from the adjacent room, because its song overtaxed his emotions. A skin rash was also present.

Mozart was being attended by Dr. Thomas Franz Closset, a physician at the General Hospital who had treated Constanze in July 1789.[3] Closset knew Mozart well, and he had seen the evolution of the composer's neuropsychiatric symptoms. Since in 1791 the syndrome of chronic renal failure was not recognized, Closset reasonably suspected that Mozart had developed a growth within his brain. He diagnosed "un deposito alla testa," which translates literally as a deposit in the head. Such a diagnosis would have accounted for the hemiparesis. However, Closset must have been puzzled by the composer's recent febrile illness associated with polyarthritis, edema, and skin rash, so that he called in the senior physician at the Vienna hospital, Dr. Mathias von Sallaba.[4] The consultation took place on 28 November. We know from Constanze that a venesection was performed, but no further details were given. Sallaba was also puzzled, for he diagnosed Hitziges Frieselfieber, which is the diagnosis in the Register of Deaths. It translates simply as a heated miliary fever, which is entirely nonspecific, and refers to an illness associated with fever and exanthem (skin rash).

Mozart's condition fluctuated a little from day to day. His attacks of vomiting were often worse during the night. During the evenings, in his imagination he would follow the events of *Die Zauberflöte* and even did a little more work on the *Requiem,* trying out parts of it with his wife, Süssmayr, and other friends. On Saturday, 3 December, there appeared to be a slight improvement in his condition, and he told Cäcilia Weber, his mother-in-law, that he would pay her a visit on the octave of her name-day, which, alas, was already past (29 November). On the Sunday afternoon at 2 o'clock, a kind of rehearsal of the *Requiem* was held at the composer's bedside; Mozart himself sang the alto part, Schack took the soprano, Franz Hofer the tenor, and Gerl the bass. They sang it through to the first bars of the "Lacrimosa," at which point Mozart broke down and wept. He later voiced his desire to hear *Die Zauberflöte* again, and when he began humming Papageno's bird-catcher song, Johann Roser sang it for him at his piano, much to his delight.

Later that Sunday, when Sophie Weber called, Constanze said: "Thank

God that you have come, dear Sophie. Last night he was so ill that I thought he would not be alive this morning. Do stay with me today, for if he has another bad turn, he will pass away tonight." When Sophie went in to see Mozart, he said: "Ah, dear Sophie, how glad I am that you have come. You must stay here tonight and see me die." Soon after, he added: "Why, I have already the taste of death on my tongue. If you do not stay, who will support my dearest Constanze when I am gone?"

Sophie hurried off to inform her mother of this grave situation, arranging for her to spend the night with her daughter Josefa Hofer. Then, as was Constanze's wish, Sophie hastened to St. Peter's Church and requested that a priest call on Mozart, as if by chance, so as not to alarm him. Initially, the clergy were reluctant to anoint Mozart, presumably because his apartment was situated within the parish of St. Stephen's, and more especially because the composer, who was still conscious, had not himself requested it. However, Sophie eventually succeeded in persuading a priest to call, and he administered the sacrament of Extreme Unction.[5] When Sophie returned to Mozart's apartment, she found Süssmayr at his bedside. The *Requiem* lay open on the quilt, and the composer was instructing his pupil as to how the work should be finished. "Did I not say that I was writing the Requiem for myself?"[6] he said, looking at it through his tears. Mozart also exhorted Constanze to keep his death a secret until his friend Johann Georg Albrechtsberger had been informed, so that he could secure the reversion to an appointment at St. Stephen's Cathedral which Mozart held.

Dr. Closset was eventually contacted at the theater. He came after the performance had ended, at about 11:00 P.M. Mozart had a high fever, and Closset told Süssmayr in confidence that there was no hope. He ordered Sophie to apply a towel, moistened with vinegar and cold water, to Mozart's burning forehead. There followed a convulsion (violent shuddering) followed by loss of consciousness. Constanze was hysterical, so that Closset administered a sedative to her. Towards midnight, Mozart attempted to raise himself up, opened his eyes wide, and then lay down with his face to the wall. Sophie Weber noted that he puffed out his cheeks, and she presumed that he was imitating the trumpets and drums in a passage from the *Requiem*. Mozart remained unconscious and expired at 12:55 A.M., on Monday, 5 December 1791, toward the end of his thirty-fifth year. He died in Sophie's arms. Constanze and Closset were also present.[7]

Constanze was extremely distraught following her husband's death; she threw herself onto her knees and implored God to have mercy on his soul. She then lay down next to his corpse in order to catch his disease and die with him. Baron van Swieten soon arrived and tried to console her. Constanze was taken to the house of Herr Bauernfeld, an associate of Schikaneder, and later she stayed with Herr Goldhahn.[8] And so it was that Mozart's widow did not attend his funeral. In view of these events, it is likely that her entry in his album, dated 5 December 1791, was made later: "Beloved husband Mozart, who cannot be forgotten by me and all of Europe."[9]

It is recorded in the Register of Deaths of St. Stephen's Parish, Vienna, on 6 December 1791, that W. A. Mozart, I & R Kapellmeister and Kammer Compositeur, had died of severe miliary fever, and having been examined, he was given a third-class burial in the cemetery outside St. Mark's. The cost was 4 florins, 36 kreuzers, in parish charges, 4 florins, 20 kreuzers in church expenses, and 3 florins for the hearse. This entry was examined by Jahn, Nohl, Wilder, Schurig, Paumgartner, Abert, Schenk, and Deutsch, all of whom accepted 6 December 1791 as the date of Mozart's funeral.[10] Yet, recent authors have supported Bär's hypothesis that the burial took place the following day.[11]

No details of Mozart's funeral were recorded in the earlier sources—Schlichtegroll, Niemetschek, Arnold, and Holmes. Nissen's main informer was Sophie Haibel, whose letter of 7 April 1825 gave the details of Mozart's last days. Sophie said that after his death, Count Josef Deym, alias Müller, came to take a cast of the death mask, and later that day crowds of people paid their respects.

It is stated in Nissen:

Baron van Swieten appeared immediately after his [Mozart's] death to mourn with the widow who had gone to rest on the bed of the deceased to take on his illness and die with him. In order not to be left alone in her despair, she was sent to Herrn Bauernfeind, an associate of Schikaneder, and then to Herrn Goldhahn. Mozart's death aroused the public's sympathy. On the day of his demise, many people gathered in front of his house, expressing their sympathy in various ways. Schikaneder went about crying: "His spirit pursues me all the time; he is constantly before me." . . . Mozart's remains were buried in the cemetery of St. Mark's near Vienna, where also his intimate friends Albrechtsberger and J. Haydn have rested since 1809. Mozart's widow became severely ill in view of Mozart's death. Therefore, Baron van Swieten took care of the funeral arrangements. Because he wanted to save the family's money, the coffin was buried in a common grave, and any luxury was avoided. According to the gravedigger, interments took place in the third and fourth row, beginning at the cross of the cemetery. The site of Mozart's remains could no longer be determined in 1808 on enquiry, because of the periodic shifts of the graves.[12]

Nissen mentions neither the date of Mozart's funeral nor the prevailing weather conditions. On 28 January 1856, the *Morgen-Post Vienna* gave an edited version of the recollections of an anonymous personal acquaintance of Mozart:

Süssmeyer remained at the side of the dying composer. At 12 o'clock in the night Mozart raised himself in his bed, his eyes staring, then he sank back with his head towards the wall, and seemed to fall asleep again. At 4 o'clock in the morning he was a corpse. At 5 o'clock in the morning the front door bell of the "Silver Snake" was violently rung. Deiner opened. Mozart's maid, Elise, stood before the door, sobbing. The landlord asked what she wanted.—"Herr Deiner," said the maid, "please come and dress our master!"—"To go for a walk?"—"No, he is dead; he died an hour ago; please hurry!"

Deiner found Mozart's widow dissolved in tears, and so weak that she could not stand upright. He performed for Mozart the services which it is usual to pay to the dead. In the morning Mozart was laid on the bier and covered with a black drapery from the burial society, as was then the custom, and which usage continued until the year 1818. The corpse was taken into the study and placed near his pianoforte.

Mozart's funeral took place at 3 o'clock in the afternoon of 7 December in St Stephen's Cathedral, not in the body of the church, but in the Crucifix Chapel on the north side, where the Capistrano pulpit stands. The committal was performed in the manner appropriate to a third-class funeral, at a cost of 8 fl., 36 kr. The hearse cost an extra 3 fl.

The night of Mozart's death was dark and stormy ; at the funeral too it began to rage and storm. Rain and snow fell at the same time, as if Nature wanted to shew her anger with the great composer's contemporaries, who had turned out extremely sparsely for his burial. Only a few friends and three women accompanied the corpse. Mozart's wife was not present. These few people with their umbrellas stood round the bier, which was then taken via the Grosse Schullerstrasse to the St Marx Cemetery. As the storm grew ever more violent, even these few friends determined to turn back at the Stuben Gate, and they betook themselves to the "Silver Snake." Deiner, the landlord, was also present for the funeral. He then went up to Mozart's wife and asked her if she did not want a cross erected for her dead husband. She answered, "They will give him one any way."—When in the year 1832 King Ludwig of Bavaria visited Mozart's widow in Salzburg (she drew a pension from him), he asked her how it had come about that she had had no memorial stone erected to her husband. She replied to the King, "I have often visited cemeteries both in the country and also in big towns, and everywhere, especially in Vienna, I have seen very many crosses in the cemeteries. I was accordingly of the opinion that the parish in which the funeral takes place is also responsible for the provision of a cross."

This error is the reason why we cannot today accurately determine the place where lie the remains of this great musician.[13]

The above account was reproduced in Jahn's classic biography, with, however, the date of Mozart's funeral corrected to 6 December 1791, and the funeral expenses to 8 florins 56 kreuzers, as stated in St. Stephen's Parish Register. Jahn believed that the probable author of these recollections was the late Joseph Deiner, but in that event, why was his name withheld? The many errors in this article, as highlighted by O. E. Deutsch, cast suspicion on the reliability of this document: Mozart died at 12:55 A.M. on 5 December 1791; the said tavern was the Golden, not the Silver Snake, and the proprietor in 1791 was Joseph Preisinger.

Erna Schwerin has pointed out that the word "landlord" is an erroneous translation of the German "hausmeister," which should read as janitor or caretaker.[14] Furthermore, the erection of a memorial cross over a common grave was forbidden at that time, and Constanze did not draw a pension from King Ludwig of Bavaria.

The alleged storm at Mozart's funeral was discredited by the brilliant detective studies of Nicolas Slonimsky and by O. E. Deutsch, who discovered independently that the records of Vienna's weather during the eighteenth century since 1750 are still extant. Three entries each day, at 8:00 A.M., 3:00 P.M., and 10:00 P.M., recorded barometric pressure, temperature, and wind conditions; from 1794 descriptions of the weather were also recorded. On 6 December 1791, the barometric pressure was steady, the temperature remained above zero (4° Celsius at 3:00 P.M.), and there was a light easterly breeze. Furthermore, the obsessional Count Karl Zinzendorf punctiliously recorded the weather in his diary each evening in French; the diary is kept in the Austrian State Archives. On 6 December 1791 (Vol. 36, p. 287), the entry was mild weather and frequent mist or drizzle.[15] Slonimsky also corrected the date of the funeral to 6 December, as recorded in the Parish Register, and discredited the alleged storm since two official sources precluded the possibility of violent rain and snow.[16] The *Morgen-Post* article also alleged that the weather was stormy on the night of Mozart's death. Yet in the official records mild weather conditions prevailed, with a light northerly wind on 4 December and a calm day on 5 December. On the latter date, Count Zinzendorf also recorded mild weather with mist three or four times a day.[17] However, Carl Bär checked the official weather records on 7 December 1791: a light southerly breeze at 3:00 P.M. that afternoon increased to strong south-westerly wind gusts of maximum velocity at 10:00 P.M. Bär concluded that such weather conditions were consistent with the alleged storm described in the *Morgen-Post* and that Mozart was buried on 7 December 1791.[18] Annette Kolb proposed that after the burial service at St. Stephen's on 6 December the coffin was deposited in the funeral chapel of St. Mark's overnight and interred the next day.[19] That would not have been so, however, since a graveside ceremony was forbidden. If Mozart was buried on 7 December, then the consecration of his corpse at St. Stephen's would also have taken place that same day. Let us now review recent research about eighteenth-century Viennese burial customs.

During Maria Theresa's era, ceremonial burials were popular and costly. Consider, for example, Joseph Lange's first wife, the singer Anna Maria Schindler, who died in 1779. Her funeral, including a Requiem Mass, candles, bell ringing, black drapery, and funeral oration, cost 341 gulden.[20]

Emperor Joseph II, among his many reforms, was particularly anxious to crack down on ceremonial burials and to crush the superstitious practices concerning tombs and graveyards. On 23 August 1784, burial in church crypts was outlawed. Some existing crypts were even dug up, and their contents were transported disrespectfully to cemeteries, much to the horror and disgust of the masses. Most funeral ceremonies were legally abolished, and a graveside ceremony by a priest was not permitted.[21] Although individual parishes might hire out a casket for the transportation of the corpse to the chapel and cemetery, such caskets were to be returned to the parish, and burial of a corpse in a casket was forbidden. Instead, the corpse was sewn into a sack at the cemetery and covered with quicklime before interment. The latter regulation was amended on 27 January 1785, following the righteous indignation and rioting of the common people: burial in a coffin was again reluctantly permitted if relatives of the deceased insisted on it.[22]

Only two choices of grave were available at that time. Individual family vaults with headstones were permitted only to the nobility or, by special dispensation, to wealthy members of special merit. All other corpses were interred in common graves ("Schachtgräber"). Such shaft graves were dug to a depth of about 7½ feet and could accommodate fifteen to twenty corpses, in three layers. These shaft graves were subsequently reused every seven to ten years, so that the setting of crosses on them was forbidden. However, the relatives were permitted to have memorial plaques attached to the walls of the cemetery.

In order to prevent premature interment, a waiting period of forty-eight hours after certification of death was usually stipulated. However, earlier burial was permitted in the interests of public health by special dispensation in cases of contagious diseases, and also for deceased members of the Orthodox Jewish faith. However, following a case of premature interment of a Jew, a new decree in 1787 forbade even the burial of Jews before a lapse of two days after death.[23]

Paupers were buried by the parish without charge. First-class funerals in individual vaults were restricted, as above, in Vienna until 1807. Second- and third-class funerals differed only in the church ceremony, the choice of bells and music, and the number of pall bearers. The site of interment in a shaft grave was common to both. In December 1791, 69 percent of all funerals in Vienna were of the third class.[24] The consecration of the corpse took place at the church, and no graveside ceremony was permitted. The transportation of the coffin to a cemetery outside the city walls was prohibited until 6:00 P.M. in the winter, or 9:00 P.M. in the summer. Little wonder then that it was not customary for the mourners to accompany the hearse to the cemetery, although it was not forbidden. If, on the other hand, the cemetery was situated within the church yard, the mourners did witness the interment.

It is to be noted that there is no record of rain or snow in Vienna during the afternoon and evening of 7 December 1791. Count Zinzendorf entered "beau temps, doux." Yet the late Carl Bär, who also overlooked the official record of mild weather on the night of Mozart's death, concluded that Mozart was buried on 7 December, as stated in the *Morgen-Post*. Bär proposed that the alleged snow was in fact a dust storm, in keeping with the official record of strong evening wind gusts, which would have disturbed the surface layer of limestone dust on the streets at that time.[25] Furthermore, Bär invoked the statutory forty-eight-hour waiting period after death. He argued that the official death register diagnosis of "an hizigem Frieselfieber" was unlikely to have been considered within the category of a contagious disease, which would have permitted an application for earlier burial. Such an argument supported Bär's diagnosis of death from rheumatic fever and heart failure, aggravated by venesections.

However, a fresh study of official burial regulations and imperial hygiene laws during this period sheds new light on this controversy. Let us consider two of the relevant decrees:

No corpse should be buried before the lapse of two days (twice 24 hours) unless death has been caused by black Petechiae ("schwarzen Petetschen") or plague.[26]

In those cases of death where a febrile illness has been preceded by a rash ("Ausschlage"), and it was certain that death had occurred because of the presence of the foul odour of putrefaction . . . and the physician had provided a written certification of death, and also accepted full responsibility, it was possible to obtain permission for burial a few hours earlier.[27]

Today we must interpret such regulations cautiously in view of the limitations of eighteenth-century medical knowledge. It is to be noted that Dr. Mathias Edler von Sallaba's entry of "hitziges Frieselfieber" is not a definitive diagnosis, but simply refers to a severe febrile illness associated with an exanthem (skin rash). However, such an illness would surely have qualified for the second escape clause above. Furthermore, Dr. Guldener von Lobes, who did attend the statutory examination of Mozart's corpse, stated that Mozart's terminal illness was also contracted by many others in Vienna during the late autumn of 1791 and that it proved fatal in several.[28] This suggests that an epidemic infection was responsible. Constanze also believed that Mozart's illness was contagious, for she confirmed to the Novellos that after his death she threw herself onto his bed and sought to catch his fever.[29]

The official Parish Register mentioned the examination of Mozart's corpse, so that there would not have been any difficulty in obtaining permission for burial a few hours earlier. If, as is proposed, Mozart was buried at 6:00 P.M. on Tuesday, 6 December 1791, the time lapse after his death would have been just forty-one hours. Braunbehrens has proposed that an error was made in the date of entry in the burial Register; but surely such a careless mistake involving so famous a person as Mozart would have been most unlikely. And so there is no valid reason to suppose that Mozart was not buried on 6 December 1791, as recorded in St. Stephen's Parish Register after all.[30]

The following reconstruction of Mozart's funeral is proposed. His corpse was consecrated in the Kreuzkapelle (Chapel of the Cross) of St. Stephen's Cathedral at 3:00 P.M. on 6 December 1791. (A memorial plaque was attached to the wall in 1931.) The priest entered this chapel via an internal entrance, adjacent to the stone pulpit, where St. John Capistran preached so eloquently in 1451, during the crusade against the Turks.

The identities of the mourners are not known with certainty, though it would appear that Constanze and Schikaneder were absent. There is agreement that van Swieten, Deiner, Süssmayr, Salieri, Roser, and Orssler were present, as were presumably also Hofer, Albrechtsberger, Lange, Schack, von Reiter, Freystädtler, Gerl, Scholl, Hatwig, and others.[31] The Austrian composer Anselm Hüttenbrenner (1794-1868) first claimed that Salieri attended Mozart's funeral. He wrote his obituary article in the *Allgemeine musikalische Zeitung* of November 1825 (see p. 184). Cäcilia Weber and three of her daughters (Sophie, Josefa, and Aloysia) may have been present, but Sophie Haibel volunteered no details when the Novellos questioned her about Mozart's funeral. The weather was mild. After the consecration of Mozart's corpse, the coffin was moved to the Kruzifixkapelle to await burial, and the mourners dispersed. At nightfall the coffin was transported 6 kilometers to the cemetery of St. Mark's by a hearse. None of Mozart's relatives or friends witnessed his interment in a common grave at 6:00 P.M. that evening on 6 December 1791.

The only person who knew the precise location of Mozart's grave was the sexton of St. Mark's, Joseph Rothmayer. He was a great admirer of the deceased composer, and it is alleged that he identified Mozart's corpse by encircling it with stout wire. Subsequently, during a moment of animated musical enthusiasm, Rothmayer raided the grave and he pilfered Mozart's skull. He kept it as a sacred, albeit ghoulish relic, until his death, when it came into the possession of his successor, Johann Joseph Radschopf (Ratshoff). The latter, in turn, presented the skull in 1842, to the copper engraver and musician, Jakob Hyrtl, who also then owned the now famous Boxwood medallion of Mozart, after Leonard Posch (May 1789). After his death in January 1868, the skull and the medallion were bequeathed to his brother, Professor Joseph Hyrtl, the eminent Viennese anatomist and anthropologist.[32]

Dr. Joseph Hyrtl verified the above history of the origin of the skull, though he was under the impression that Rothmayer had pilfered the cranium in 1801, when the ground was ploughed over in preparation for the new graves. Dr. Hyrtl noted that the upper four incisor teeth had been damaged prior to his acquisition of the cranium. During his examination of the skull, Dr. Hyrtl sawed it along a line parallel to the Frankfort horizontal plane, across the external auditory meatus: the upper four incisor teeth were further damaged. Dr. Hyrtl described the skull in 1875. He set it on a velvet cushion in a glass case, and inscribed a label, which was attached to the forehead:

> Wolfgang Amadeus Mozart,
> Gestorben 1791, geboren 1756,
> Musa vitat mori! Horaz![33]

After Joseph Hyrtl's death in 1894, the base of the skull, the lower jaw, and the four upper incisor teeth vanished. The Posch medallion was bequeathed to the Mozart museum in Salzburg. A judicial enquiry, after the death of Joseph Hyrtl's widow in 1899, verified Hyrtl's inscription and the likely authenticity of the skull. The relic remained in the Hyrtl orphanage at Mödling, until it was acquired by the Mozarteum on 6 October 1901. The skull was then exhibited for a time in the Mozart museum in Salzburg, until confusion and uncertainty about the missing upper incisor teeth, cast doubt upon its authenticity.[34] The skull was then transferred to the Mozarteum archives, where it is today. There is also damage to be noted to the orbits, the nasal bones, and the ethmoid.[35]

Such was the state of confusion about the authenticity of the skull until recently, when the Salzburg anthropologist, Dr. Gottfried Tichy, and his co-workers (Drs. B. Puech, P-F. Puech, P. Dhellemmes, P. Pellerin, and F. Lepoutre) undertook a fresh detailed examination of the cranium. During a two-year study, Dr. Tichy detected mineral and plant particles by microscopic analysis. He also discovered the presence of organic collagen and brain tissue remnants. From a comparison with other skulls from St. Mark's graveyard, he concluded that the cranium in the Mozarteum had not been buried in the earth for more than two years. A positive identification with Mozart was established by the techniques of portrait superimposition, facial indices, and specific features of the dentition.[36]

These recent studies by Dr. Tichy and his French medical colleagues have established that the cranium in the Mozarteum is that of a young man, an ultrabrachycephalic central European caucasian. The intracranial capacity has been estimated to be 1580 cc. The straight vertical forehead is flanked by widely separated frontal eminences. Both prominent eyebrow arches join and protrude above the root of the nose at the glabella to form a median superciliary protruberance. Both oval-shaped orbits are high, wide, and of diminished capacity: the one on the right is estimated to be 22.5 cc, while the capacity of the left orbit is also reduced to 21.5 cc.

The sockets of the upper front teeth protrude forward. The wide palate is of shallow depth. There is decay of one third of the coronal volume, and also the pulp of the first left upper molar. Less marked dental caries is evident in the second left molar. The third left molar had been dislodged after death. The closure of the apex of the roots of the wisdom teeth and the overall dental attrition indicate a dental age of between twenty-five and forty years.

When Dr. Tichy and his co-workers compared the unusual anatomical features of this skull to Mozart's image in the authentic portraits, there was fairly good correlation. Of course such comparisons must always take into account the varying degrees of artistic liberty which is inherent in such paintings. Consider, for example, the forehead, brows, eyes, nose, cheeks, and mouth in the portrait attributed to Pietro Antonio Lorenzoni in early 1763, the Watercolor by Louis Carrogis de Carmontelle in November 1763, the oil painting by Michel Barthélemy Ollivier in the summer of 1766, and the portrait by Saverio dalla Rosa in January 1770. The straight vertical forehead, prominent eyebrow arches, and naso-labial protrusion are depicted in the medallions by Leonard Posch from 1788-89, and the Silverpoint drawing by Doris Stock in April 1789. The prominent median glabellar protruberance, above the root of the nose, is visible in the posthumous oil painting by Barbara Krafft from 1819, but it is especially well marked in the unfinished oil painting by Joseph Lange in 1789. This latter portrait also displays a proptosis of Mozart's eyes, which is well accounted for by the documented diminished capacity of the orbits.

At this point, I would like to thank Dr. Tichy for his permission to discuss two exciting new discoveries, which at the time of writing in June 1988, were as yet unpublished. The unusual craniofacial anomalies in the skull owned by the Mozarteum are due to a premature synostosis of the metopic suture. This rare anomaly of the frontal bone is present in only 0.3 of every 1,000 newborn infants, and it was first described in 1862 by Dr. H. Welcker. This anomaly is responsible for the straight vertical forehead, the prominent brow arches, the glabellar protruberance, and the shallow orbits. Similarities are to be noted in the forehead of Mozart's mother.

The second discovery is of pathological significance. An oval, rosette-shaped imprint is present on the internal surface of the skull, in the left temporoparietal region. This imprint has three distinct concentric layers: the outer area is striated, the middle one is granular with scattered calcified bony deposits,while the central area is marked with vascular grooves. Standard X-ray pictures of the skull revealed a linear fracture in the left temporoparietal region. The undisplaced fracture is 10 cm long:

it radiates forward and downward from the left parietal eminence toward the temporal fossa. There is complete consolidation of the fracture along its entire length. The above described imprint is situated beneath the fracture, and it measures 8 × 6 cm. There is obliteration of the posterior branch of the middle meningeal vessels. The central area of the imprint measures 2.5 × 4 cm.

Dr. Tichy and his French medical colleagues have concluded that the imprint represents a calcified chronic extradural (epidural) hematoma. The initial lesion would have arisen from damaged blood vessels at the site of the fracture following a head injury: the volume of the hematoma has been estimated to be 45 to 65 cc. There followed a spontaneous partial resolution of the hematoma. Such an evolution of events would have taken place over a period of several months to over a year. The significance of this chronic extradural hematoma will be considered further in the discussion of the cause of Mozart's death.

Dr. Tichy's research is incomplete. He will attempt to identify Mozart's blood group from blood stains on the skull, and he plans to study strands of the composer's hair.

Let us now turn to the fascinating saga of Mozart's death mask. A young Austrian officer, Count Joseph Deym von Stritetz, fled the country to Holland after an unlawful duel. He changed his name to Müller and became a talented sculptor, working mainly in wax and plaster. Subsequently, he made a fortune in Naples by casting ancient statues. After returning to Vienna in 1780, the count opened Müller's Art Gallery on the Stock-im-Platz, near St. Stephen's Cathedral. It became a famous tourist attraction. The exhibits were later arranged as a panopticon and included ancient statues, wax figures of famous people, and a variety of mechanical toys. Leonard Posch worked there for a time.

Deym commissioned three works for mechanical organ from Mozart: K. 594, 608, and 616. In March 1791, Deym opened a mausoleum on the Himmelpfortgasse, in memory of the national hero, Field Marshal Baron von Loudon (1716-90). Mozart's adagio and allegro (K. 594) would chime out on the hour, between 8:00 A.M. and 10:00 P.M.[37] Loudon was subsequently displayed in Elysian colloquy with Joseph II; Loudon's mausoleum was removed to the main art gallery in August 1791.[38]

Sophie Haibel stated that soon after Mozart's death Deym came from the art gallery and took a plaster cast of the composer's face.[39] Constanze also confirmed this in her letter to Breitkopf & Härtel, dated 17 February 1802.[40] Mozart was subsequently exhibited as a wax figure dressed in his own clothing.[41] Deym also made a copy of the death mask for Constanze. That fragile gypsum mask was accidentally smashed in 1820, when she was dusting her apartment. It is alleged that she exclaimed that she was glad that the ugly old thing was broken.[42] It also seems probable that Deym would have had a bronze cast made for exhibition and safekeeping, but there is no record.

Müller's art gallery was moved to the Kohlmarkt in 1795. Finally, it was reconstructed as an eighty-room museum in 1798, near the Red Tower on the Danube Canal.[43] Deym married Beethoven's friend, Countess Josephine Brunsvik, in 1799; a year later, they were in serious financial straits. Joseph Deym, who also commissioned three works for mechanical instrument from Beethoven, died suddenly of galloping consumption in 1804. After his death, the art gallery remained in the possession of his widow until it was closed down in 1819. She died two years later, and the gallery was liquidated in 1825. Mozart's death mask and the other exhibits vanished without a trace. Ludwig Nohl prophesied that the mask might one day be rediscovered in Vienna.[44]

During the summer of 1947, the musician Jakob Jelinek purchased an old bronze mask from a second-hand antique shop in Vienna for 10 Austrian schillings.[45] Jelinek noted a similarity to Mozart's features in the portraits by Joseph Lange and Doris Stock, and he became excited that this might be the missing death mask. Upon inquiry, he was advised to consult a sculptor on the Schulerstrasse, Willy Kauer.[46] Jelinek left the mask with Kauer in August 1947, for a detailed examination. Kauer purchased the mask from Jelinek for 100 Austrian schillings on 31 March 1948.[47] Newspaper and magazine reports began to appear two months later. Willy Kauer approached the Austrian Ministry of Education to commission a scientific inquiry into the authenticity of the mask. A panel of experts had been appointed by December 1948.[48] Let us now review briefly the anatomical and pathological evidence.

There is no doubt that this is a death mask, as opposed to a life mask, by way of the following distinctive features. There is an absence of the characteristic wrinkles on the forehead, above the root of the nose. The other distinctive markings of a death mask present are the slightly rounded, depressed tip of the nose, the faintly blurred detail of the nostrils, and the well-structured head of hair.[49]

Could the features in the mask be those of Mozart? The high forehead, the large prominent nose, the fullness of the mouth, the slight pouting of the lower lip, the heart-shaped chin, and the line of the hair attachment are all compatible with Mozart's image in the authentic portraits. Not one of the appointed experts has argued that the features in the mask are not those of Mozart.

Pathological features are also to be noted in this mask. There is marked edematous swelling of the eyelids, forehead, and cheeks. Such swelling is consistent with nephritic edema. Furthermore, it is recorded that Mozart's body showed evidence of marked swelling at the time of his death.[50] Pockmarks are to be noted on the cheeks and forehead; we have seen that Mozart's face was disfigured by his attack of smallpox in 1767. There is also a suggestion of ulceration of the center of the upper lip: this may have been secondary to the edema or more likely an artifact. The case for the authenticity of the mask was looking strong, but obstacles arose from the conflicting conclusions derived from technical examinations. Finally, the process of scientific evaluation was upset by intrigue and prejudice.

Inscriptions were discovered on the interior surface of the mask. Orel, Schwarzacher (members of the expert panel of inquiry), and Kauer, through special photography, deciphered two letters, A and M. Both letters are, of course, in Mozart's name. Kauer was very confident the inquiry would conclude that the mask was authentic, but he drew hostile reaction from other members of the panel by his positive statements to the press, and his announcement of a lecture which he himself planned to give. At the first meeting of the panel, Erich Schenk advocated the technique of superimposing the mask onto the skull. This mask did not fit over the skull in the Mozarteum. It was concluded that the mask and the skull did not match the same person. Kauer correctly argued that since there was doubt about the authenticity of the skull in the Mozarteum, it was not possible to draw valid conclusions from such a comparison. At the second meeting of the panel, the personality clash between Schenk and Kauer reached its height. Schenk shouted out that as long as Kauer refused to disclose where he had obtained the mask, he would always declare the mask a forgery, from a musicological point of view. Kauer, insisting that the origin of the mask was irrelevant to the scientific findings, withdrew the mask and his consent from the examination procedure. Later that day, Schwarzacher and Chiari's report to the Ministry of Education, on 1 February 1949, was noncommittal but not negative. This sensational turn of events was transmitted to the nation in a radio broadcast on the following day.[51]

Meanwhile, Jakob Jelinek, convinced that Willy Kauer had withheld vital information, sued him for suspicion of fraud. During this hearing, both the bronze mask and a plaster copy were confiscated by the court.[52] However, the Ministry of Education ordered further expert reports on the mask—the Institute for Anorganic Technology on 9 March 1950, and the Anthropological Institute on 20 April 1950. Both issued a negative report: the bronze mask was unlikely to be Mozart's death mask. Kauer suspected foul play by the Freemasons. The court found no reason to pursue the matter further, and the mask was returned to Willy Kauer on 15 July 1950.[53]

Six years later during the bicentenary of Mozart's birth, the musicologist Dr. Alfred Orel (1883-1967) persuaded the Mozarteum to have the mask examined by the anthropologist Dr. Aemilian Kloiber. His report, dated 24 November 1956, was positive. Kloiber stated unequivocally that the bronze mask must be regarded as a casting of the death mask taken by Müller on 5 December 1791. He added that the inscriptions would require further expert evaluation.[54] Kauer offered the mask for sale to the Mozarteum for 250,000 schillings. The Mozarteum commissioned two chemical institutes to determine the date of casting of the bronze mask, using different methods. The report was rendered in collaboration on 15 July 1957: Professor K. Peters assumed circa 1869, and Professor Brukl stated after 1890. The Mozarteum wrote to Kauer on 28 September 1957: the mask was not authentic, and his offer of sale was rejected.[55]

Meanwhile, Kauer continued to examine the inscriptions. A single number and two marks were identified to be present on the inner aspect of the mask; they were partly destroyed by corrosion. On 3 October 1957, Kauer deciphered the letters "Th R." They were inverted and had originated in the sand form. Kauer concluded that "Th R' were the initial letters of the bronze caster and pewterer, Thaddäus Ribola, whose studio in the 1790s was situated near Müllers art gallery. The single number had been deciphered in the 1950s to be 1793.[56]

Following Willy Kauer's death in 1976, the mask was bequeathed to Dr. Gunther Duda of Dachau, who is the present owner. The mask has been further examined by A. Burmester of the Munich Doerner Institute. The reports, dated 21 July 1983 and 20 March 1984, stated that the single number was deciphered to be not 1793 but 1928. The inscription "Th R" was confirmed, but there was no trace of the letters A and M. It was concluded that in the 1940s they had likely been confused with "Th R." Burmester also discovered that, slanting above the "8" of "1928," there had been scratched in several times an oblique "8." The nature of these numbers has not yet been explained.[57]

Eva Badura-Skoda reviewed Dr. Duda's book in the 1986 Mozart-Jahrbuch. She concludes that the authenticity of the mask is highly likely and that the book is an important contribution to Mozartian iconography.[58] We are impressed with the compatibility of the mask with Mozart's image in the authentic portraits, as well as by the initials of the caster of the mask "Th R," as being likely to represent Thaddäus Ribola, whose studio in the 1790s was adjacent to Müllers art gallery. There are surely sufficient grounds for a further scientific inquiry, perhaps by an international panel of experts, utilizing all recent advances in allied technology. Only then could a definitive critical report about the authenticity of this bronze mask be written. The new light shed by Dr. Tichy's recent research on the skull in the Mozarteum provides yet another reason for a revaluation of the bronze mask. It should be noted that there is a prominent median glabellar protruberance evident in the mask. Furthermore, the facial edema, which was present at the time of Mozart's death, needs to be accounted for in any method of superimposition of the mask upon the skull.

St. Stephen's Cathedral, Vienna
Detail of the northern side with the Crucifix Chapel in the center. Engraving by
Karl Schütz, 1792. Mozart's corpse was blessed here at 3:00 P.M. on 6 December
1791. (Courtesy of the Historischen Museen der Stadt, Vienna.)

18

MOZART WAS NOT POISONED

Since Mozart's death, there have been repeated accusations and insinuations that the composer was poisoned.[1] As we will see, such theories originated in the mental delusions of Mozart and Salieri, and they were perpetuated by an extraordinary chain of events and circumstances. Not even Constanze has been spared of complicity in his death in this context. In this chapter we seek to decisively lay to rest the myths that Mozart was murdered by Salieri, or the Freemasons, or Süssmayr, or Hofdemel, or anyone else.

ANTONIO SALIERI

Salieri was born of wealthy parents at Legnano, near Verona. After being orphaned as a boy, he was sent to Venice to further his music studies. In 1766, he was taken under the wing of Florian Gassmann, who brought him to Vienna as a composition pupil and organized an excellent general education for Antonio. Gassmann also installed Salieri in the emperor's chamber music ensemble. Antonio was very taken with Metastasio and became a protege of Gluck. After Gassmann's death in 1774, Salieri, at the age of twenty-four, succeeded him as court composer and conductor of the Italian opera. The following year he married Theresia Helferstorfer (1755-1807) who bore him eight children. Despite their legendary rivalry, Salieri was too shrewd to openly criticize Mozart's music or his genius. Let us then trace the chronological sequence of events and circumstances that has sustained the myth to the present day.

In 1773, Mozart composed Clavier Variations on a Theme of Salieri (K.

180),[2] and during his composition of *Idomeneo* he asked his father to send him an aria with oboe solo by the Italian composer.[3] Seven years before the event, Mozart anticipated that Salieri would succeed Bonno. Following Bonno's death in 1788, Gluck's protege remained court Kappellmeister until 1 March 1824.[4]

Mozart's first recorded hostility against the Italian composer was expressed to his father, following Salieri's appointment as music teacher to the fourteen-year-old Princess Elisabeth, even though the Archduke Maximilian had recommended Wolfgang for the post.[5] Mozart was anxious to learn how his rival's opera *Semiramide* had been received during the Munich Carnival.[6] A year later he expressed concern that if Lorenzo Da Ponte was in league with Salieri, he would be unable to secure the poet as his librettist.[7] Finally, Mozart criticized *Der Rauchfangkehrer* (see p. 33) as a wretched work.[8]

Leopold Mozart informed Nannerl of the powerful cabals that Salieri and his supporters had conspired against the production of *Figaro*.[9] Michael Kelly confirmed these intrigues and described the court composer as a clever, shrewd man, possessed of crooked wisdom.[10] In his letter to Michael Puchberg dated 29 December 1789, Mozart wrote that, on their next meeting, he would provide details of Salieri's unsuccessful plots against the production of *Così Fan Tutte*. Five months later, although Mozart praised his rival as very gifted, Mozart supported his own application for the post of second Kapellmeister with mention of superior abilities as a composer of church music and his humble prowess at playing the pianoforte![11]

Only after the death of Joseph II did Salieri's influence at court begin to wane. At that time he relinquished his post as conductor of the Italian opera and was succeeded by Joseph Weigl. According to Da Ponte, the new Emperor Leopold II was critical of Salieri's insufferable egoistic intrigues and mischief-making.[12] Mozart was indignant that he had been passed over during the festivities to honor the visit of the king of Naples to the Viennese court in September 1790.[13] On the positive side, Salieri conducted a Grande Symphony of Mozart at the Society of Musicians Benefit Concert in the Burgtheater on 16 and 17 April 1791.[14] Nor is it to be forgotten that the two rivals appeared to be on friendly terms just seven and a half weeks before Mozart's death:

At six o'clock I called in the carriage for Salieri and Madame Cavalieri—and drove them to my box. Then I drove back quickly to fetch Mamma and Karl, whom I had left at Hofer's. You can hardly imagine how charming they were and how much they liked not only my music, but the libretto and everything. They both said that it was an operone, worthy to be performed for the grandest festival and before the greatest monarch, and that they would often go to see it, as they had never seen a more beautiful or delightful show. Salieri listened and watched most attentively and from the overture to the last chorus there was not a single number that did not call forth from him a Bravo! or Bello! It seemed as if they could not thank me enough for my kindness. They had intended in any case to go to the opera yesterday. But they would have had to be in their places by four o'clock. As it was, they saw and heard everything in comfort in my box. When it was over I drove them home and then had supper at Hofer's with Karl.[15]

The Dossier

It is to be remembered that during the eighteenth century poisoning was still a popular means of executing a "murder most foul." So it was that many of Mozart's contemporaries were inclined to take such allegations seriously. The first public notice to mention suspicion of poisoning appeared soon after his death:

Mozart is—dead. He returned home from Prague a sick man, and continued to get worse; he was said to be dropsical, and he died in Vienna at the end of last week. Because his body swelled up after death, some people believed that he was poisoned.[16]

Schlichtegroll's Necrolog of Mozart, which appeared in 1793, referred to the composers's bizarre, melancholic state of mind, and to his preoccupation with his fast-approaching end, but made no mention of poisoning. In 1799, two references to Mozart's alleged death by violence were tempered with doubt.[17] Four years later Arnold argued against poisoning, suggesting that Mozart's energies were worn out by overwork and loose living.[18]

Niemetschek's biography detailed Constanze's account that during a walk in the Prater Gardens her husband had confided his conviction that someone had poisoned him. Niemetschek stated that he attributed the composer's untimely death to lack of exercise and overwork, but he added that, in fact, it might have been hastened unnaturally.[19]

In April 1813, the rumor was prevalent in Vienna that Salieri had poisoned Mozart. As a result, Carl Maria von Weber (1786-1826), during his visit to the Austrian capital, refused to meet Salieri, despite the encouragement of his teacher Abbé Georg Vogler to do so.[20] Two years later, Haydn's pupil Franz Seraph von Destouches stated that Mozart was said to have been given aqua toffana. He also made reference to the deceased composer's intrigues against Salieri.[21]

Gioachino Rossini (1792-1868) was invited to Vienna during the spring of 1822, when six of his operas were performed with extraordinary success. The following unsubstantiated anecdote has been traced back to this visit. Rossini asked Salieri to introduce him to Beethoven. The court Kapellmeister obliged and took Rossini to the deaf composer's house. It was alleged that when Beethoven caught sight of Salieri, he turned to Rossini and cried out: "How dare you come to my house with Mozart's poisoner?"[22] On two subsequent occasions, however, Rossini stated that he had been introduced to Beethoven by Giuseppe Carpani (1752-1825), the Italian poet, librettist, translator, and critic, and, furthermore, that he had been politely received by him.[23] Ironically, the unexpected death of Rossini's friend Vincenzo Bellini (1801-35) in Paris was followed by rumors of poisoning.[24] However, Rossini insisted on an autopsy, which established that death was due to acute colitis and liver abscess.[25]

During the autumn of 1823 Salieri, in his seventy-third year, became senile and was admitted to the Vienna general hospital, where he remained until his death. He locked himself in his room, required constant supervision by his attendants, and was troubled by dark delusions. Salieri accused himself of terrible crimes, and he unsuccessfully attempted suicide by cutting his throat with a razor. Amidst his ramblings, he is said to have accused himself of having poisoned Mozart. Salieri's suicide attempt and his self-accusations soon found their way into most of the boulevard newspapers.

In October 1823, Ignaz Moscheles (1794-1870) visited his friend Salieri at the Vienna hospital, and he recorded the details in his diary. The reunion was a sad one. Salieri's gaze horrified him; he spoke in broken sentences of his imminent death, and he commented on the rumors:

Although this is my final illness, I can still assure you in good faith that there is no truth in the absurd rumours. You know of course—Mozart—I am supposed to have poisoned him. But no, spite, sheer spite. Tell the world, dear Moscheles; old Salieri who'll die soon, has told you this.[26]

Johann Schickh recorded in Beethoven's conversation books that the suicide attempt was unsuccessful and that the odds of Salieri having murdered Mozart were one hundred to one.[27] The Polish composer Karol Kazimierz Kurpinski who visited the Viennese music publisher Artaria at this time, noted in his travel journal on 27 November 1823 that he had wished to visit Salieri but was refused admission. It was said that Salieri had cut his throat.[28]

The rumors persisted. At the second performance of Beethoven's Ninth Symphony in Vienna on 23 May 1824, leaflets containing a poem by C. Bassi were distributed to the concert goers. The poem clearly portrayed Salieri as Mozart's rival, and a poison goblet stood by his hand.[29]

Karl Beethoven recorded in his uncle's conversation book in 1824: "Salieri maintains that he poisoned Mozart." Anton Schindler continued:

Salieri is very ill again. He is quite deranged. In his ravings he keeps claiming that he is guilty of Mozart's death and made away with him by poison.—This is the truth—for he wants to make confession of it—, so it is true once again that everything has its reward.[30]

Giuseppe Carpani, enraged over this scandal, set about collecting documents to defend his mentally deranged friend. These documents were published in the quarterly *Bibliotecca Italiana*.[31] Carpani's star witness was the senior physician, Dr. Guldener von Lobes (1763-1827), who was a friend of Constanze Nissen and who, during the summer of 1824, lived in the Vienna suburb of Döbling. Ten years previously, Guldener had been appointed medical superintendent for Lower Austria. Also included in Carpani's article in defensé of Salieri was the attestation of his two keepers who testified that neither had ever heard the alleged self-accusation.

The Testament of Dr. Guldener von Lobes

This document, written on 10 June 1824, is of great importance, for it is the only contemporary account by a medical authority on the subject of the cause of Mozart's death. Guldener did not personally attend Mozart, but he did discuss his case with Closset and Sallaba, with whom he was in touch almost daily:

[Mozart] fell sick in the late autumn of a rheumatic and inflammatory fever, which being fairly general among us at that time, attacked many people. [Dr. Closset] considered Mozart's illness to be dangerous, and from the very beginning feared a fatal conclusion, namely a deposit on the brain. One day he met Dr. Sallaba and he said positively, "Mozart is lost, it is no longer possible to restrain the deposit." Sallaba communicated this information to me at once, and in fact Mozart died a few days later with the usual symptoms of a deposit on the brain. His death aroused general interest, but the very slightest suspicion of his having been poisoned entered no one's mind. So many persons saw him during his illness, so many enquired after him, his family tended him with so much care, his doctor, highly regarded by all, the industrious and experienced Closset, treated him with all the attention of a scrupulous physician, and with the interest of a friend of many years' standing, in such a way that certainly it could not have escaped their notice then if even the slightest trace of poisoning had manifested itself. The illness took its accustomed course and had its usual duration; Closset had observed it and recognized it with such accuracy that he had forecast its outcome almost to the hour. This malady attacked at this time a great many of the inhabitants of Vienna, and for not a few of them it had the same fatal conclusion and the same symptoms as in the case of Mozart. The statutory examination of the corpse did not reveal anything at all unusual.[32]

Thus, although no autopsy was performed, Dr. Sallaba had a special interest in forensic medicine, and at no stage did Mozart's attending physicians have any suspicions that he had been poisoned.

Antonio Salieri died on 7 May 1825. His attending doctors diagnosed "am Brand des Alters," which suggests the presence of decubitus bed-sores and gangrene, arising from peripheral vascular disease and sepsis.[33] In death the rumors did not cease. Karl Beethoven recorded in his uncle's conversation book in May 1825: "Even now people still claim very forcefully that Salieri was Mozart's murderer."[34] In the AMZ, Leipzig, 25 May 1825, it was said: "In the frenzy of his imagination he is even said to accuse himself of complicity in Mozart's early death: a rambling of the mind believed in truth by no one other than the poor deluded old man himself."[35] In the AMZ of June 1825, Salieri's friend Rochlitz wrote: "Salieri lost himself in dark delusions. . . . He imagined that his reputation was ruined, and sometimes accused himself of dreadful crimes."[36]

In November 1825 Anselm Hüttenbrenner (1794-1868) wrote an obituary for his teacher in the AMZ. In it he countered the accusation as follows: "Salieri spoke of Mozart always with exceptional respect. . . . He visited Mozart two days before Mozart died, and was one of the few who accompanied the body."[37] Nonetheless, the calumny was spread in the public papers, so that in 1826 the Austrian composer Sigismund Neukomm (1778-1858) felt obliged to defend his friend. He acknowledged the lack of intimate friendship between Mozart and Salieri, but insisted on their mutual esteem, and he again emphasized the deranged state of Salieri's mind.[38]

The Nissen biography, published in 1828, referred to Salieri's rivalry, but rejected the poisoning theory. Nissen reported that Constanze attributed Mozart's suspicion of having been poisoned to illness and overwork. Dr. Guldener's testimony was incompletely and imperfectly translated into German. The biography also made reference to the first publication concerning Mozart's death by A. von Schaden in 1825, which dismissed the poisoning theory and attributed the composer's fears to his imagination.[39] Nissen also restated Constanze's account of the outing in the Prater, when Mozart voiced his suspicions about poisoning, as had been written by Niemetschek.[40]

On 15 July 1829, Vincent Novello noted in his travel diary that Mozart's son, Franz Xaver Wolfgang, denied that Salieri had poisoned his father, even though his father was given to that opinion. It was also stated that Salieri's enmity arose from Mozart's successful setting of Così

Fan Tutte, since he had previously given up his attempt to do so, having found the subject unworthy of musical invention.[41] Constanze also confirmed to the Novellos the specific mention of aqua toffana, as proposed by Destouches fourteen years previously.[42]

On 26 October 1830, the Russian poet Alexander Pushkin (1799-1837) completed his one-act drama *Mozart and Salieri.* Pushkin's theme was that Salieri's dismay over Mozart's superior talents gradually turned into all-consuming envy. Salieri justified his foul deed by concluding that Mozart was a divine being who was too good for this earthly world, and so had to die young because he was a god and did not know it.[43] Among Pushkin's papers was found the unsubstantiated anecdote that during the first performance of *Don Giovanni* Salieri, filled with envy, hissed and stormed out of the theater in a rage. The Russian poet was, of course, familiar with the reports in German periodicals that Salieri had allegedly confessed to Mozart's murder on his deathbed. His drama was conceived in 1826. Rimsky-Korsakov (1844-1908) set Pushkin's one-act drama to music. The fifty-minute performance premiered in Moscow in 1898.

It would appear that Constanze Nissen herself retained some suspicions. In her letter dated 25 August 1837 to the Munich official Herr Ziegler, she stated that since her son Karl showed no signs of his father's greatness, he would therefore have nothing to fear from envious attempts on his life.[44]

The first English biographer Edward Holmes expressly exonerated Salieri: "The tale of poisoning, however, having transpired, Salieri, the known inveterate foe of Mozart, was fixed upon as the imaginary criminal."[45]

After over twelve years of meticulous and laborious research, Otto Jahn's first German edition appeared in four volumes (Leipzig, 1856-1859). Jahn quoted a passage from Niemetschek's biography, which related a conversation, after Mozart's death, between a contemporary musician and his acquaintance. Jahn assumed that the contemporary musician was Salieri: "It is a pity to lose so great a genius, but a good thing for us that he is dead. For if he had lived much longer, we should not have earned a crust of bread by our compositions."[46]

It was later alleged that after Karl Mozart's death in 1858, among his papers was a handwritten document outlining an alternative theory that his father had been murdered with a vegetable poison.[47] M. Sessi remained convinced about the baneful legend.[48] Thirty-eight years later it was proposed that Salieri's alleged involvement in the crime was within the context of a sinister Masonic plot, as we will see.

The theme was taken up yet again by the Soviet musicologist Igor Boelza, who expanded on the poisoning theory in his book.[49] Boelza claimed that Guido Adler discovered in the Vienna archives a communication from Salieri's father confessor to the archbishop of Vienna, reporting that on his deathbed Salieri not only admitted poisoning Mozart, but also explained in detail how he administered the slow-working venom. According to Boelza, Adler had no time to publish the document but spoke about his findings to the Soviet music scholar Boris Asafiev. However, Asafiev never referred to such a story in his writings, and these alleged events are completely unsubstantiated. Furthermore, Boelza invoked the mysterious circumstances of Mozart's funeral as sinister. He proposed that Salieri confided in Baron van Swieten, who shared his fear of violent retribution from the working masses of imperialist Vienna, should they discover that Mozart had been poisoned by a foreign court musician. Constanze was innocent, and van Swieten saw to it that she did not attend the funeral. It was essential to suppress all traces of murder by ensuring that Mozart's site of interment remain unknown. And so it was, according to Boelza's theory, in a conspiracy of Mozart's friends and family, that none of the mourners accompanied the hearse to St. Mark's cemetery.[50]

The German physician Dr. Dieter Kerner, the most enthusiastic advocate of the poisoning theories, has written over thirty articles and several books that provide historical and medical arguments that Mozart was poisoned with mercury. However, he is much less dogmatic and intentionally vague in his exposure of the alleged murderer.[51] There is a wealth of material for fictional novels.[52]

Franz Xaver Wolfang Mozart told the Novellos that, in his view, Salieri's cabals and intrigues against his father had effectively poisoned his life and thought, and that toward the end of his life, the Italian maestro's mind was haunted and disturbed by the guilt of his actions.[53] In Peter Shaffer's *Amadeus* Salieri's perception of the disparate contrast between the divine music created by an uncouth mortal is highlighted and transformed into a brilliant play.[54]

ALLEGED POISONING BY THE FREEMASONS

A footnote in Otto Jahn's classic biography refers to a dreary novel alleging that Mozart had been poisoned by the Freemasons. Jahn also stated that Georg Friedrich Daumer had striven to support this untenable conjecture.[55] Herr Daumer was a researcher of antiquities and religious polemicist whose theory was published in 1861.[56] It was proposed that Mozart had incurred the wrath of the craft in *Die Zauberflöte* by his unflattering portrayal of the Queen of the Night, and his use of Christian religious music in the chorus of the Priests.[57] Furthermore, Daumer alleged that Mozart was thinking of establishing his own secret lodge, "The Grotto."[58]

The alleged craft conspiracy was further developed by Mathilde Ludendorff and her Nazi husband, General Erich Ludendorff, whose anti-Masonic and anti-Semitic books were published by the family printing press.[59] She theorized that Mozart betrayed lodge secrets in *Die Zauberflöte*, and she proposed that the opera contained a secret counterplot in which Mozart (Tamino) sought the release of Marie Antoinette (Pamina) from the bondage of her Masonic captors.[60] Nor was it a coincidence that the day of Jehovah was chosen for the ritual execution. Allegedly, the Freemasons responsible were Salieri, van Swieten, and the mysterious stranger who commissioned the *Requiem*. These three took advantage of the composer's friendship and slowly poisoned him. Nissen, also a Mason, covered up their crime in his biography of Mozart. Constanze was innocent and knew nothing about the plot. Ludendorff also offered a brilliant solution as to why the wealthy Baron van Swieten permitted Mozart to be buried in a pauper's grave. She suggested that, according to Masonic laws, the body of the transgressor must be cursed, that the skull should be removed so as to prevent decent burial, and that the grave should be unmarked. She suggested that Mozart's skull was removed for this purpose and that van Swieten kept Constanze away from the cemetery under the pretext of safeguarding her health. Such a theory is of course ludicrous: neither Salieri nor Baron Gottfried van Swieten were masons.

Dr. Gunther Duda also became a disciple of the Masonic murder theory. In his medical study of Mozart's illnesses and death, he was unconvinced of any evidence of chronic disease of the kidneys or heart, and favored the administration of poison during the summer of 1791, so as to account for the composer's illness in Prague and subsequent death. Duda proposed that the Masonic hierarchy exercised its right to execute disobedient members of the craft, and that this theory accounted for the manner of Mozart's death and the circumstances of his burial.[61] Duda also cast suspicion on the Masons for the deaths of the librettists of *Die Zauberflöte*, Emanuel Schikaneder in 1812 and Carl Ludwig Gieseke in 1833.

Dr. Johannes Dalchow collaborated with Duda and Kerner in the publication of two further books in support of the Masonic murder theory.[62] The second of these books proposes that the stranger who commissioned Mozart's *Requiem* (Anton Leitgeb) was sent by the Masonic court to announce his death sentence. Two different motives proposed were (1) a ritualistic sacrifice to Masonic deities and (2) punishment, with the participation of Salieri, for betrayal of lodge secrets in *Die Zauberflöte*. The recurrence of the number 18 in the music and libretto of the opera is given a sinister association with the Eighteenth Rosicrucian Degree of Freemasonry. As further evidence to support their theory, the authors point out that Mozart's Little Masonic Cantata (K. 623) was performed precisely eighteen days before his death on 18 November 1791.[63]

A detailed discussion of the literary sources of *Die Zauberflöte* is beyond the scope of this book; the reader is referred to the excellent works of Dent, Mann, Osborne, and Batley listed in the Bibliography. *The Magic Flute* was originally nothing more than a spectacular comedy with music, but under a veil of mystery, it was transformed into one of the world's greatest operatic masterpieces. The main literary source was a book of oriental fairy tales in three volumes collected by Christoph Martin Wieland, called *Dschinnistan*, published in 1785-89. Schikaneder took the foundation material and the title from one of the stories in this collection called "Lulu" by Liebeskind. There were also borrowings from Wieland's *Oberon*, a poem later recast for Weber's masterpiece. The characters of the Queen of the Night, her Ladies, and the Three Genii were also taken from other stories in the same collection. The Egyptian source of the work was based on the legend of Prince Sethos, written by the Abbé Jean Terrason in 1731. Mozart had already written incidental music for Gebler's adaptation of the Sethos Legend: *Thamos, König in Aegypten* (K. 345) in 1779. Furthermore, Mozart had used the opening three groups of three chords in the overture of *The Magic Flute* to introduce the first entre acte of *Thamos*. The reader's attention is also drawn to the fascinating article by Alec Hyatt King on the melodic sources and affinities of *Die Zauberflöte*.[64]

FRANZ XAVER SÜSSMAYR

This Austrian composer settled in Vienna as a private music teacher in July 1788. Later, he became a composition pupil of Mozart, who first made reference to him in his letter to Constanze dated 7 June 1791. Mozart also employed Süssmayr as a composer, and they collaborated in *Die Zauberflöte* and *La Clemenza di Tito*. Following Mozart's death, Süssmayr took instruction from Salieri in vocal composition, and from 1794 until his death he was Kapellmeister of the German opera at the National Theater in Vienna.

After Mozart's death, Constanze, who was in desperate financial straits, was anxious not to lose the commission of the *Requiem*. First, she handed over the score to Joseph Eybler, who completed the orchestration of the "Dies Irae" only as far as the "Confutatis" and then gave it up. After Nissen's death, Constanze admitted that she had first chosen Eybler to complete it because she was angry with Süssmayr, but she refused to disclose the reason. When Eybler refused to press on with it, the work was entrusted to Süssmayr, who completed it. Constanze maintained that Mozart left additional sketches of his *Requiem*, which she handed over to Süssmayr; these have vanished. Because Eybler and Süssmayr's handwriting was similar to Mozart's, controversy persists as to who wrote what.[65] When the anonymous patron, Count Franz Walsegg-

Stuppach, who was Michael Puchberg's landlord, later heard about Constanze's deceit, he brought an action against her. He was finally satisfied with copies of some unpublished works of Mozart.

Eric Blom, while rejecting the proposal that Mozart was murdered by Salieri, was attracted to Dr. Dieter Kerner's theory that Mozart died of quicksilver poisoning. It was suggested that Mozart's doctors, unable to deal with his complaint, may have given him a trial of treatment with mercury in desperation and that the composer died of accidental mercury poisoning.[66] Hildesheimer raised the possibility that Mozart was a syphilitic genius who was treated with mercury and who died from iatrogenic poisoning.[67] However, a careful medical study by an English venereologist concluded that Mozart bore no evidence of syphilis, and we support Fluker's view.[68] Nevertheless, the question of syphilis needs to be discussed again in relation to the terminal illness (see p. 198).

Blom also jestingly proposed, at the extremes of ridiculous conjecture, that Süssmayr and Constanze may have had a love affair and then poisoned Mozart in collusion.[69] Dieter Schickling took up this theme and even argued that Süssmayr was the father of Franz Xaver Wolfgang Mozart, a view that was restated by Hildesheimer and Francis Carr.[70] It was argued that Constanze's frequent absences at Baden offered tempting opportunities for love affairs with Süssmayr and/or others. Mozart's admonitions in his letters to Constanze and her hostility toward Süssmayr after his death were put forward as evidence.[71] The rendering illegible by a later hand (Constanze? Nissen?) of references to Süssmayr and other Nomen Nescio's was also submitted. One fantastic proposal was that Mozart was on tour in Frankfurt when Franz Xaver Wolfgang was conceived.

Schickling's hypothesis was decisively squashed by Joseph Heinz Eibl.[72] There is no substantiated evidence that Süssmayr and Constanze were together at Baden in 1790 or the previous year. Mozart's younger surviving son was born on 26 July 1791. It is erroneous to assume that he was conceived nine months previously on 26 October 1790. While it is true that the expected date of confinement, as calculated by the obstetrician from the date of the last menstrual period, anticipates a pregnancy of forty weeks duration, a span of thirty-eight to forty-two weeks is normal. There is then no objection to the likelihood that the child was conceived on or soon after Mozart's return to Vienna on 10 November 1790. Furthermore, Mozart's ear is a trump card for the defense. Franz Xaver Wolfgang's birth with the same rare congenital malformation of his left external ear provides the strongest possible proof of Mozart's paternity. It should also be emphasized that, in view of the composer's depressive paranoid trends, his admonitions to Constanze need to be interpreted with caution. We have seen that a

Nomen Nescio was first entered in Mozart's letter to his wife at Baden in mid-August 1789 and that subsequently, in the autumn of 1790, he asked her to negotiate a loan through the intermediary of this person, whom Constanze later distrusted (see p. 108). The exorbitant interest rate is in keeping with a desperate "black market" negotiation. The subsequent rendering illegible of such a shady dealer's identity is understandable enough.

THE HOFDEMEL AFFAIR

Yet another theory has been advanced with regard to Mozart's possible murder. Franz Hofdemel was a chancery clerk, and his wife, Maria Magdalena, was a pianoforte pupil of Mozart. We have seen that Franz Hofdemel had loaned the composer 100 gulden for three months in April 1789. The Bill of Exchange was signed just prior to Franz's entry into Mozart's lodge and this debt was repaid prior to the composer's death. On the day of Mozart's funeral, 6 December 1791, Franz Hofdemel viciously attacked and wounded his pregnant wife, inflicting lacerations to her face and throat with a razor, and he then committed suicide. The poor woman and her child survived. Such a terrible crime of passion may indeed have been perpetrated by the disturbed mind of an insanely jealous husband, but no lover was mentioned. Furthermore, the following notice appeared in December 1791:

Wien, 18 December. The widow of the suicide who, as is now known, took his life from faint-heartedness rather than jealousy, is still alive, and not only several ladies, but also her majesty the Empress herself, have promised assistance to this woman, whose conduct is known to be unexceptionable.[73]

Maria Magdalena Hofdemel was granted an annual pension of 560 gulden by Emperor Leopold II. Nevertheless, the momentum of the public scandal impelled her to leave Vienna and return to her father's home in Brünn, where on 10 May 1792, she gave birth to a son named Johann Alexander Franz. True, Johann was the first name entered at Mozart's christening, but Magdalena's son was christened Johann von Nepomuk Alexander Franz, after his godfather (Fidel Holderer) and her husband. Although Francis Carr has provided circumstantial evidence of Mozart's involvement with Magdalena, Franz Hofdemel cannot as a result be indicted as Mozart's murderer.[74] Nor is there any convincing evidence that this was so.

The *Pressburger Zeitung* notice made reference to Hofdemel's "faint-heartedness." What does this imply? Clearly, we need to know more about his personality. Was he subject to depression? How much had he been drinking prior to the tragic deed? In the absence of such vital information, our proposal that catastrophic gambling losses may have contributed to his shock suicide is submitted as a reasonable alternative (see p. 122). We cannot be sure, and further evidence is plainly needed. However, the poisoning theory can be dismissed on medical grounds.

AQUA TOFFANA

Aqua Toffana was a familiar slow poison in the eighteenth century. When administered in repeated small doses, it was difficult to detect. It was named after its inventor Signora Teofania de Adamo, and its major toxic ingredients were the oxides of arsenic, lead, and antimony.

The symptoms of acute arsenic poisoning include severe burning pain in the mouth and throat, scalding tears, abdominal pain, vomiting, diarrhea, and muscle spasms. Later, jaundice, heart failure, kidney failure, a blistery skin rash, or gastrointestinal hemorrhage may develop. Chronic arsenic ingestion leads to anemia, a characteristic irregular yellowish-brown pigmentation, thickening of the skin and nails, and a peripheral neuropathy. Although chronic ingestion of lead may result in anemia, mental changes, vomiting, headache, abdominal pain, and a nephrotic syndrome, a blue line on the gum, develops, as does a neuropathy causing foot-drop or wrist-drop. Acute antimony poisoning causes vomiting and bloody diarrhea. Chronic exposure to antimony gives rise to dermatitis, conjunctivitis, weight loss, and anemia.[75]

The vomiting and dropsy of Mozart's fatal illness were linked with poisoning by aqua toffana. However, there is lack of more specific manifestations of toxicity from arsenic, lead, or antimony, such as the blue gum line, peripheral neuropathy, and characteristic dermatitis. It is clear that Mozart was not poisoned with aqua toffana.[76]

CORROSIVE SUBLIMATE

Acute mercury poisoning results in nasty corrosive injury to the entire gastrointestinal tract and serious kidney damage. The symptoms are severe abdominal pain, vomiting, bloody diarrhea, metallic taste, thirst, salivation, and foul ulceration of the mouth and throat. Death may occur within a few hours from shock but more often results from acute renal failure within one to fourteen days.

Chronic mercury poisoning is associated with toxicity and brain damage. There is usually present a characteristic psychic disturbance referred to as erythism, which is often more pronounced during the morning. There is an embarrassing nervous excitability, irritability, shyness, insomnia, phobic anxiety, and deterioration of social intercourse. Mercury poisoning used to be common in the felt hat industry, when the acid nitrate of mercury was used in treating the felt.

Such is the origin of the term "mad as a hatter." Headaches are common, and the erythism is usually associated with a disabling tremor of the eyelids, lips, tongue, fingers, and extremities. Speech disturbance and cold shivers are common, while other manifestations include violent painful convulsive attacks without loss of consciousness, neuritic pains, loss of sensation, impotence, exaggeration of the special senses, loss of balance, dementia, oscillations of the head, muscular weakness, vertigo, choreiform movements, and paralysis. A chronic gingivitis of the gums is usually present, sometimes with a blue line, while gastrointestinal symptoms, weight loss, anemia, salivation, urticaria, metallic taste, and various skin rashes are not uncommon.[77]

Dieter Kerner and Gunther Duda undermined the testament of Dr. Guldener and took advantage of the controversy over the uremic and rheumatic fever hypotheses. Even so, the majority of medical writers have argued strongly against poisoning on medical grounds.[78] Kerner and Duda appreciated that Mozart suffered chronic ill health during the last six months of his life. They argued that Mozart's symptoms presented a classic picture of mercury intoxication. It was proposed that repeated sublethal doses of corrosive sublimate (mercuric bichloride), administered during the summer of 1791, caused the composer's symptoms of fainting fits, tiredness, anxiety, loin pains, along with his mental changes of persecution complex and paranoid behavior. The final lethal dose, they proposed, was administered toward the end of November, and this caused generalized edema due to a nephrotic syndrome about eighteen days before the end, and finally death from uremic coma. Mercury poisoning would also account for Mozart's headaches, vomiting, paralysis, metallic taste, and his hypersensitivity to the song of his canary. They proposed that Salieri or some other anonymous Freemason would have had ample opportunities to administer the poison. Kerner discovered that Dr. Gerhard van Swieten was one of the pioneers in treating syphilis with a mercury compound diluted in alcohol. In 1756, van Swieten demonstrated that, in the treatment of syphilis, repeated small doses of mercury over a period of several weeks were more efficacious than a short course of high-dose therapy.[79] Kerner also explored the possibility that Mozart contracted syphilis from a woman in Schikaneder's troupe and was treated by Dr. van Swieten with small doses of mercury. That would have been impossible since the founder of the old Vienna School of Medicine died in 1772.[80]

While these arguments have some merit, there are several major objections to this hypothesis which render it untenable on medical grounds. Dr. Guldener stated that Mozart's rheumatic inflammatory fever was contracted by many others in Vienna at that time and that there were also several deaths from it. This strongly suggests that Mozart's final illness was precipitated by an infection, contracted during an epidemic. The febrile onset and sweating are also in keeping with an infection. Although mercury poisoning may cause joint pain, it does not give rise to a polyarthritis. Furthermore, *the absence in Mozart* of the following characteristic symptoms of quicksilver poisoning is further argument against it: gingivitis, stomatitis, salivation, bloody diarrhea, and painful muscular spasms. Mozart's symptoms were worse during the night, but the disabilities of chronic mercury poisoning are worse during the morning.

The main objection to the mercury poisoning hypothesis is the absence of tremor. Both Dr. Kerner and Dr. Duda have proposed that Mozart's neuropsychiatric symptoms during the latter months of his life were the consequence of chronic mercury poisoning. If this be true, it is inconceivable that there would be no tremor. The characteristic tremor is the cardinal feature of mercury poisoning and is usually associated with erythism, in greater or lesser degree from the onset. In the early stages the tremor is absent at rest, but it appears upon voluntary effort, and especially upon finely coordinated movements such as writing. The tremor may be slight and of small amplitude, but it is usually rapid and gross. Frequently, it is so severe that it is impossible for the subject to write legibly. The hands and lips chiefly are affected by the tremor in the early stages, but later it may spread to involve most of the facial muscles and all of the extremities. In severe cases, it is impossible for the subject to speak coherently or feed or stand or walk. It is to be noted that Mozart showed no evidence of impairment of his speech.

Dr. Kerner, aware of the importance of tremor in cases of mercury poisoning, busied himself with study of the autograph of Mozart's *Requiem*. In 1960, he even proposed that Süssmayr claimed for himself the Domine and Hostias sections of the Offertory, but Friedrich Blume rejected such a proposition.[81] However, there is no evidence of tremor in the autograph of Mozart's *Requiem*, particularly the first eight bars of the Lacrimosa which are written with a steady hand.[82] Nor is there the slightest suggestion of tremor in Mozart's last entries in his personal thematic catalogue. Mozart's "Verzeichnüss aller meiner Werke" is the crown of Stefan Zweig's collection in the British Library. Between July and 15 November 1791, Mozart entered the Cantata (K. 619), *Die Zauberflöte* (K. 620), *La Clemenza di Tito* (K. 621), the Clarinet Concerto (K. 622), and the Little Masonic Cantata (K. 623) in his catalogue.[83] The absence of tremor in Mozart's hand, during the period of alleged poisoning with mercury, seals the lid on the coffin to this hypothesis.[84]

Today a coroner would not accept a verdict of death by poisoning unless the following evidence was presented: (1) Autopsy confirmation of compatibility with poisoning; (2) absence of evidence of death from natural causes; and (3) a pharmacological demonstration of the poison in tissue samples from the corpse. An autopsy was not performed on

Mozart, so that we can never be certain of the cause of his death. Clearly, however, the proposed poisoning hypotheses can be dismissed on medical grounds. Having taken all the evidence into account, we are now able to render a medically acceptable account of Mozart's death from natural causes.[85] Let the fantastic myths that Mozart was poisoned be laid to rest forever.

19

THE CAUSE OF MOZART'S DEATH

Controversy about the cause of Mozart's death has persisted for several reasons: none of his medical records survives; no autopsy was performed; and laymen recounted his symptoms. The clinical features of his terminal illness have been detailed in Chapter 17, and they are both unusual and perplexing. The entry in the Register of Deaths and the testament of Dr. Guldener von Lobes need to be cautiously interpreted in view of the limitations of medical knowledge in the eighteenth century. The complexities have posed an enigma to all authors on the subject. The major controversies have centered around the interpretation of the swelling of Mozart's body, the reality of pre-existing illness, and the alleged poisoning. Having refuted the poisoning theory in Chapter 18, let us now attempt to identify the natural cause of his death.

"HITZIGES FRIESELFIEBER"

Nissen stated that Mozart's last illness lasted fifteen days, and he called it "hitziges Frieselfieber."[1] This diagnosis was made by Dr. Sallaba and is entered in the Register of Deaths. No death certificate signed by Mozart's attending doctors is extant. The entry from the Register of Deaths of St. Stephen's Cathedral on 5 December 1791 is reproduced in Deutsch.[2] Jahn copied an extract of entry from the year 1847. The diagnosis recorded in the Register is "an hizigem Frieselfieber," which translates as a severe or heated miliary fever.[3] The entry from the Register of Deaths of St. Stephen's Parish on 6 December 1791 is "an hitzigem Frieselfieber."[4] Bär concluded that this term was the German equivalent of the Latin "febris miliaris."[5] It is not a definitive diagnosis but simply describes a severe febrile illness

Mozart
Oil painting by Ellen Douglas, Melbourne, 1979; after Joseph Lange, 1789. Photograph by Mario Cotela. The artist has completed the unfinished portrait by Mozart's brother-in-law. (Courtesy Mario Cotela.)

associated with an exanthem. This is of importance since the two key witnesses, Constanze and Sophie Haibl, made no mention of a rash. However, their accounts were penned thirty-seven years after the event for Nissen's biography. Even so, it may imply that the rash caused him no great discomfort in the way of itch or sting. Jahn's extract of entry was translated in *The Musical Times* as "brain fever."[6]

"UN DEPOSITO ALLA TESTA"

Guldener's testament was written in Italian, and an incomplete version was reproduced in Nissen.[7] The full text in English was published in the centenary issue of *The Musical Times*.[8] Dr. Closset diagnosed "un deposito alla testa" which translates as "a deposit in the head." Dr. Guldener clearly implies that it referred to a serious life-threatening disorder of the brain, a diagnosis that would account for the paralysis Closset had observed. It is unlikely to have been a quadriplegia which results from a cervical cord lesion, and fortunately it is rare.[9] Mozart's partial paralysis was almost certainly a hemiplegia, which is most commonly due to cerebral ischaemia, but it may also arise from serious infection or a brain tumor. It is recorded that Mozart's attacks of violent vomiting were worse during the night, a feature that is typical of raised intracranial pressure.[10] Bär argued that the deposit may have been a rheumatic nodule in Mozart's scalp, but in that event Guldener would have written "un deposito su la testa." Some of the earlier medical writers concluded that the diagnosis of a serious intracranial infection such as meningitis or encephalitis or brain fever would account for the diagnosis. However, such diagnoses would not account for the gross swelling of Mozart's body, nor do they take into account the composer's retention of consciousness until near the end.

RHEUMATIC INFLAMMATORY FEVER

Dr. Guldener's testament not only refutes the poisoning theory, but also provides the important clue that Mozart was one of many victims in Vienna who died as a result of an illness contracted during an epidemic. Guldener was present at the statutory examination of Mozart's corpse, and he described the composer's illness as a rheumatic inflammatory fever. As observed earlier, this is not a specific diagnosis; it simply refers to a serious febrile illness in which there is evidence of inflammation of the joints.

SUMMARY OF EVIDENCE FROM THE ORIGINAL SOURCES

It may be concluded that Mozart's fatal illness was ushered in by an acute infection, which was contracted during an epidemic and which was associated with an exanthem, inflammation of the joints, gross swelling of the body, and serious intracranial pathology. Let us now consider the two diagnoses that were suggested in Nissen's biography: tabes dorsalis and phthisis nervosa.[11] Georg Nikolaus von Nissen died before completing his biography, and Constanze sought the assistance of the physician and Mozart admirer, Dr. Johann Feuerstein, who wrote the Preface at Pirna in July 1828.

TABES DORSALIS (NEUROSYPHILIS)

In 1791, tabes dorsalis was a term used without specific connotation to describe unusual cases of paralysis. The first adequate description of tabes dorsalis (locomotor ataxia) was written in 1846 by Moritz Heinrich Romberg. The neurosyphilitic pathogenesis was not substantiated until the earlier part of the twentieth century.[12] It may be argued that Mozart's neuropsychiatric symptoms during the last six months of his life might conceivably have been due to tabes, contracted a few years previously, albeit most unlikely in the absence of ataxia. However, since syphilis was prevalent in Vienna in the eighteenth century and is known to be a notorious mimic of most other disorders, let us consider the possibility further. Mozart suffered with paralysis during his final illness, and tabes is a known cause of hemiplegia. The case is looking stronger.

Let us now, for a moment, ignore what has just been said and focus on Mozart's fatal disorder. A febrile illness with exanthem, vomiting, diarrhea, and nephrotic syndrome is quite compatible with secondary syphilis, contracted during the previous six months. Furthermore, it is apparent from Suard's anecdotes (1804, Paris) that it was rumored that Mozart had contracted venereal disease from Barbara Gerl, so that secondary syphilis is indeed a possibility.

When the information in the last two paragraphs is laid side by side, we see that a diagnosis of syphilis is impossible. Patients suffering from tertiary syphilis are immune from the secondary manifestations of the disease. Although the evidence is against Mozart having syphilis, the exercise does give us insight into the reasons why his symptoms raise such a possibility.

PHTHISIS NERVOSA (PULMONARY TUBERCULOSIS)

During Mozart's lifetime, it was still widely believed that consumption was related to overwork and irregular living. We have seen that this diagnosis was considered at the time of Leopold Mozart's illness in London in July 1764 and that it may have caused his death. There is no record of symptoms of cough or hemoptysis during Mozart's last illness, but a remote case can be made for a diagnosis of tuberculosis, according to the following sequence. Mozart may have contracted cervical tuberculosis in October 1762, and this was responsible for his erythema nodosum. Then in August 1784 he developed renal tuberculosis, which presented with renal colic, and recurred in 1787. Mozart's chronic ill health during the last six months of his life may have been due to a cerebral tuberculoma, which disseminated at the time of his last illness to cause death from miliary tuberculosis or tuberculous meningitis. However, although several years may elapse between the onset of renal colic and the subsequent diagnosis of advanced renal tuberculosis, the above sequence of events seems far too remote for further consideration. Nor does it take into account the epidemic nature of the illness of 1784 and the fatal illness.[13]

WHICH EPIDEMIC INFECTION WAS IT?

Other diagnoses favored by early authors include typhus and grippe, while more recently streptococcal infection has been proposed.[14]

TYPHUS FEVER

In 1883, Dr. F. Gehring argued that Mozart had died with malignant typhus fever, a disease from which he had previously suffered.[15] We have seen that typhus was the likely cause of his mother's death in Paris. Although typhus fever may cause a febrile illness with exanthem, dropsy, and death from heart failure or kidney failure, the absence of cough and deafness in Mozart render it unlikely. Furthermore, the absence of stupor or delirium tends to exclude it from further consideration. Clouding of consciousness is the cardinal feature of typhus, from which the term was derived. It is to be remembered that Mozart retained consciousness until two hours before his death.

TYPHOID FEVER

There is good evidence that Mozart and his sister suffered with typhoid fever at the Hague in 1765. There is confusion in terminology with typhus. Typhoid fever in German is sometimes referred to as typhus biliosus, or typhus abdominalis; louse-borne typhus is referred to as Fleckfieber. However, Mozart's retention of alertness argues strongly against a diagnosis of enteric fever.

GRIPPE

Schurig favored a diagnosis of a severe grippe, which is an alternative term for influenza.[16] A fatal termination is usually related to bronchopneumonia. This is uncommon except during pandemics and in subjects with chronic lung disease or immune-deficiency states. There were twenty million deaths during the Great Pandemic of 1918-19. Grippe would not account for the swelling or paralysis.

INFECTIOUS POLYARTHRITIS

The epidemic nature of Mozart's fatal illness excludes from further consideration several disorders which might have otherwise been considered because of their association with polyarthritis, such as acute rheumatoid arthritis, Reiter's disease, other connective tissue disorders such as systemic lupus erythematosis, drug hypersensitivity, Behcet's disease, sarcoidosis, and Whipple's disease.

A wide variety of bacteria, viruses, rickettsia, mycoplasma, fungi, and parasites need to be considered in relation not only to polyarthritis, but also to the pathogenesis of nephritis. We will return to the latter in our discussion of immune-complex disease. Within the context of the clinical setting of Mozart's fatal illness, however, the long list of potential microorganisms is reduced to a consideration of streptococci, rubella, yersinia, and some of the viruses. Mozart bore no evidence of a septic arthritis or hepatitis B infection. The tick-transmitted Lyme arthritis is worthy of mention because it may be associated with a skin rash, neurological syndromes, and myocardial abnormalities. However a fatal outcome is unusual.[17]

STREPTOCOCCAL INFECTION

That sounds more like it. We have seen that throughout his life Mozart was prone to recurrent streptococcal infections, which were then prevalent. Shapiro proposed that Mozart's fatal illness was due to streptococcal septicemia complicated by acute renal failure.[18] Bär argued in favor of rheumatic fever.[19] Franken diagnosed a toxic carditis and heart failure following staphylococcal, streptococcal, or meningococcal sepsis, or toxic scarlet fever.[20] We have argued in favor of Schönlein-Henoch Syndrome.[21]

DROPSY

The biblical term *dropsy* refers to the abnormal accumulation of serous fluid in a body cavity or in cellular tissues, when it is called edema. The medical term for generalized massive edema is anasarca. Generalized edema is related to the body's retention of water and salt; the causes include heart failure, renal failure, nephrotic syndrome, liver failure, and hypoproteinemic states. Massive edema also occurs in certain allergic types of urticaria and angioedema, including the Schönlein-Henoch Syndrome. In the acute nephritic syndrome, the edema initially tends to occur in the face, hands, and feet. When Sophie Haibl described Mozart's fatal illness to the Novellos in 1829, she said that on that last evening: "(his) arms and limbs were much inflamed and swollen."[22] It may be concluded that there was an inflammatory component to his edema.

BACTERIAL ENDOCARDITIS

There is much merit in a diagnosis of bacterial endocarditis, which was included in Clein's differential diagnosis and proposed by Sakula.[23] One could argue that Mozart's serious illness in August 1784 was rheumatic fever and that subsequently he developed chronic rheumatic carditis. In May 1790, Mozart complained of a toothache, and it is possible, though not recorded, that he underwent a tooth extraction and then contracted bacterial endocarditis. As a consequence of septic emboli, he then developed glomerular nephritis and a brain abscess, with eventual death from septicemia and renal failure. However, the course seems too prolonged, and such a diagnosis does not account for the epidemic nature of Mozart's fatal illness.[24]

TOXIC GOITER (HYPERTHYROIDISM, THYROTOXICOSIS, GRAVES' DISEASE)

The latter argument also dismisses a diagnosis of Graves' disease, which was proposed by Sederholm.[25] It was argued that Mozart's prominent protruding eyes in the unfinished portrait by Joseph Lange, as well as in the engraving by Sasso (after G. B. Bosia, 1785), suggested a diagnosis of exophthalmos, and furthermore that there was a hint of goiter in the latter engraving.[26] It was proposed that Mozart's nervousness, weakness, weight loss, and vomiting were compatible with Graves' disease. The composer's paralysis was dismissed, and his edema was attributed to heart failure, which is known to occur in hyperthyroidism.

Even when we leave aside the authenticity of Bosio's portrait, we see that Nannerl was known to have suffered with goiter. Since the condition may be familial, Mozart's thyroid gland may have been slightly enlarged, even though there is no mention of it in the literature. However, it is difficult to diagnose exophthalmos from a painting, and in borderline cases a special measuring device is required.[27] Robert James Graves (1796-1853) described primary thyrotoxicosis in 1835. There is no evidence of even fine tremor in Mozart's handwriting, and Graves' disease does not fit well into the clinical spectrum of Mozart's fatal illness which was contracted in an epidemic. Furthermore, the recent research on Mozart's skull has provided a satisfactory explanation for Mozart's prominent eyes: we have seen that the capacity of his orbits was reduced by a rare anomaly of the frontal bone.

UREMIC COMA

In Chapter 8 we documented the substantial medical view that Mozart's chronic ill health during the last six months of his life was related to chronic renal failure and that there was lack of agreement as to the nature of the kidney disorder. The majority of medical writers, including the poisoning advocates, have also concluded that a uremic coma was responsible for Mozart's death. This view was also shared by Erich Schenk and O. E. Deutsch.[28] The pioneer of the uremic theory was Barraud, and it was also proposed by Casseroller, Holtz, Marx, and Willms.[29] The theory was further developed by Greither, Clein, Scarlett, Carp, Roe, Fluker, Böhme, and Rappoport.[30] These uremic advocates, headed by Greither, attributed the swelling of Mozart's body to edema, due to fluid and salt retention, related to nephrotic syndrome or renal failure. The taste of death on Mozart's tongue was also attributed to uremia. A foul taste in the mouth is a frequent complaint in chronic renal failure, and the taste of ammonia, especially on awakening, is related to a decomposition of urea by anerobic bacteria in the mouth.[31] The exanthem could be accounted for by purpura, which may form part of the uremic syndrome. However, Mozart's joint symptoms and the epidemic nature of his fatal illness are not readily accounted for.

ACUTE RHEUMATIC FEVER

In 1906, Dr. J. Bókay diagnosed rheumatic heart disease.[32] Carl Bär argued against uremic coma as the cause of Mozart's death. He undermined the symptoms of chronic ill health as depressive in origin, and he diagnosed acute rheumatic fever as the cause of the fatal illness. This diagnosis accounts for the epidemic nature of this illness, as well as the polyarthritis. Bär argued that Sophie Haibl's description of the swellings pointed toward an inflammatory component, and he also invoked the venesections as contributing to Mozart's death. Wilhelm Katner, William Stein, and Erna Schwerin, and more recently Anton Neumayr, have supported Bär's theory.[33]

Although Franken also argued against Mozart's chronic ill health during the last months of his life, we share the view of the majority of authors, who favor chronic renal failure as the cause of his symptoms at that time. Nor does Carl Bär's hypothesis account for the neurological symptoms of the final illness.[34] An exanthem is uncommon in rheumatic fever. Although we support Bär's view on the probable inflammatory component of the swellings, their distribution also favors a nephritic origin. Furthermore, we have seen that the bronze cast of Mozart's death mask also shows evidence of edema of the face and eyelids.

THE VENESECTIONS

We know from Sophie Haibl that venesections were performed, but no details were given.[35] Bär studied the practice of blood-letting in Vienna at that time, and on the basis of his calculations with regard to Sallaba's patients, he concluded that the small-built Mozart could have been drained of four or more pints of blood and that this would have given rise to hemorrhagic shock.[36] We would agree that the venesections would have contributed to Mozart's death since they are contraindicated in patients with chronic renal failure and anemia.[37]

SCHÖNLEIN-HENOCH SYNDROME (SHS)

This diagnosis ties up the loose ends and accounts for the febrile terminal illness of fifteen days' duration, precipitated by an acute infection contracted in an epidemic, with manifest symptoms of exanthem, strange swellings, vomiting, diarrhea, paralysis, and retention of consciousness until near the end.[38]

The probable streptococcal infection may have been contracted during his last public attendance at the lodge on 18 November 1791. The latent period of two or three days is in keeping with the medical literature: that the latent interval in recurrent attacks of SHS, between upper respiratory tract infection and onset of symptoms, is shortened to between one and seven days.[39] On the other hand, the latent interval in recurrences of rheumatic fever is not shortened.[40]

The SHS began on 20 November with fever and polyarthritis. The asymptomatic exanthem may have been purpuric and was not recalled by the key witnesses thirty-seven years after the event. SHS also accounts for Mozart's peculiar swellings through the development of an acute nephritic syndrome and localized edema. Edema is common in SHS and may even occur in the absence of arthritis or renal involvement. The most common sites of such edema are around the eyes and the dorsum of the hands and feet; such edema may also be unilateral and recurrent.[41] The case for the exacerbation of nephritis would be strengthened by some mention of blood in Mozart's urine, but there is no record.[42] His renal failure would have been aggravated by the vomiting, diarrhea, and venesections. It is to be remembered that laxatives were commonly administered in cases of inflammatory fever. Moreover, Mozart's tendency to dose himself with analgesics and proprietary powders may have further damaged his kidneys. Nor is there any record of alimentary bleeding, but such a manifestation is recorded in only 19 percent of adult cases.[43]

CEREBRAL HEMORRHAGE

Mozart's paralysis is readily accounted for by cerebral hemorrhage. Even in childhood cases of SHS, there are recorded instances of multiple small brain hemorrhages, which are related to the necrotizing arteritis of this condition.[44] Such tiny hemorrhages could account for a hemiplegia without marked impairment of consciousness.

About two hours before his death, Mozart convulsed and became comatose. Then an hour later, he attempted to sit up, opened his eyes wide, and fell back with his head turned to the wall; his cheeks were puffed out. These symptoms suggest paralysis of conjugate gaze and facial nerve palsy. They are consistent with a massive hemorrhage in either one of the frontal lobes or brain stem. Such a stroke could also be accounted for by uremic malignant hypertension. On the evening before his death, Mozart was suffering with high fever and drenching sweats. Bronchopneumonia is frequently the immediate cause of death in uremic patients, and it often develops when the patient is already moribund.[45] It has also been proposed that Mozart died of a subarachnoid hemorrhage from a ruptured Berry aneurysm, in association with polycystic kidneys and uremia.[46] However, Mozart's retention of consciousness and the epidemic nature of his fatal illness argue heavily against this theory.

IMMUNE-COMPLEX DISEASE

It is of interest to comment further on the pathogenesis of Mozart's illnesses and death. Throughout his life, the composer's immune system was bombarded by frequent and serious infections. Such a chain of events is likely to have profoundly affected his immune tolerance. Mozart manifested a tendency to develop immune-complex diseases. The clinical spectrum of these disorders is broad and protean. The resulting clinical syndrome is named according to the predominant organ involvement. In erythema nodosum it is the skin and joints. The heart and joints are afflicted in rheumatic fever, chorea occurs in some 19 percent of cases, while abdominal pain is an occasional manifestation. Mozart showed no evidence of chorea. In Schönlein-Henoch Syndrome, the organs involved are the skin, joints, gastrointestinal tract, kidneys, and, less commonly, other internal organs such as the brain and lungs.

The kidney is commonly involved in the systemic diseases. In a susceptible individual, a wide range of antigens may contribute to the development of glomerularnephritis. The list includes drugs, tumors, chemicals, and a varied assortment of infectious microorganisms such as bacteria, viruses, rickettsia, mycoplasma, fungi, and parasites.[47]

There are documented accounts in the literature of patients who have suffered consecutive attacks of rheumatic fever and Schönlein-Henoch

Syndrome.[48] Our hypothesis is that following recurrent streptococcal infections, Mozart developed in turn erythema nodosum, rheumatic fever, and Schönlein-Henoch Syndrome.[49] It is also possible that Mozart suffered with Berger's IgA nephropathy.[50]

A review of the literature readily accounts for the heated controversies about the cause of Mozart's death. In an undated note, discovered among the personal effects of Karl Thomas Mozart, the elder son, it was stated that an exacerbation of the gross swelling of Mozart's corpse after his death, rendered an autopsy impossible.[51] This is nonsense: an autopsy would have been performed if there was suspicion of homicide. We know from Dr. Guldener that this was not so. Yet even if an autopsy had have been performed, it may not have completely resolved the enigma, because of the limitations of medical knowledge in the eighteenth century. In most major controversies, there is often some merit in many of the proposed arguments. We submit that the Schönlein-Henoch diagnosis accounts very well for the known facts.

The significance of the recent discovery, of a calcified chronic extradural hematoma in the skull in the Mozarteum, needs now to be considered. Dr. Tichy and his French medical colleagues have concluded that this skull is probably genuine, though they admit that this is not absolutely certain. Let us assume, during this discussion, that the relic is in fact Mozart's skull. Serial computerized tomographic skull scans, performed on head injury patients, have established that the initial headaches in cases of extradural hematoma, may subside after a week or two. When spontaneous resolution of the hematoma proceeds, there may be no further symptoms.[52] We have seen that, although there is no documented history that Mozart suffered a head injury, such a possibility is not excluded, since there is no medical record. The onset of chronic renal failure and hypertension during the latter half of 1791, however, is likely to have aggravated the chronic extradural hematoma and contributed to his symptoms of recurrent headaches and blackouts.

Furthermore, we have seen that, in some cases of Schönlein-Henoch Syndrome, there is affliction of the cerebral vessels, which causes hemorrhages within the brain. It seems reasonable to conclude that a patient with a chronic extradural hematoma would be even more susceptible to aggravation of the hematoma during an attack of Schönlein-Henoch Syndrome. During his final illness, Mozart's symptoms of recurrent violent headaches, vomiting, and hemiplegia led Dr. Closset to diagnose "a deposit in the head." An aggravation of the extradural hematoma by the Schönlein-Henoch Syndrome accounts well for these symptoms. Then finally, a massive cerebral hemorrhage occurred two hours before death and caused coma with paralysis of conjugate gaze and facial nerve palsy.

EPILOGUE

If Mozart had lived, he would have become wealthy through benefits from *Die Zauberflöte*, which had an unprecedented run of success. Shortly before his death, he was assured of an annual subscription of 1,000 gulden from devoted members of the Hungarian nobility, and even more from Dutch admirers in Amsterdam. The mind boggles at what new masterpieces would have been forthcoming, but that was not to be. At the time of his death, Mozart had made entries on only twenty-nine of the forty-three pages of his "Verzeichnüss aller meiner Werke."

The Czechs in Prague remained loyal to Mozart, whose *Figaro* and *Don Giovanni* had triumphed in that great city. On 14 December 1791, over 4,000 people attended a Requiem Mass for the composer in the small side parish church of St. Niklas in Prague. For that occasion Franz Anton Rosetti was commissioned to compose the Requiem, and Josepha Duschek was one of the 120 musicians to take part.

Baron Gottfried van Swieten arranged a benefit concert for Constanze at the Burgtheater on 23 December 1791. The emperor kindly donated 150 ducats, and the receipts of 1,500 gulden enabled the widow to pay off her debts. Constanze was awarded an annual pension of 266 florins, 40 kreuzers, by Leopold II. She offered the score of *Tito* and *Zauberflöte* to the leading tenor of the elector's court in Cologne, while in February 1792 she was paid 800 ducats by King Frederick William II of Prussia for the manuscripts of eight of Mozart's compositions, including *La Betulia Liberata* (K. 118) and two litanies (K. 125, 243).

A Masonic tribute was read by the playwright Karl Friedrich Hensler at New-crowned Hope Lodge during April 1792. After a reference to the decay of the body, it concluded:

The ability courageously to conquer such repugnant thoughts and to take the great and important step into the unknown fields of eternity with a calm smile, can only be attained by him who has learned in this very place the great art of living in virtue that he may die as a mason, as a christian.[1]

Two months later this lodge took up a collection for the widow and children.

Josepha Duschek took part in a benefit concert for Constanze on 13 June 1792 at the Prague National Theater. Mozart's dying wish was fulfilled, when following the death of Leopold Hofmann on 17 March 1793 Johann Georg Albrechtsberger was appointed organist to St. Stephen's. Two special benefit concert performances of *La Clemenza di Tito* were held for Constanze in Vienna in December 1794 and March 1795 before the new Emperor Francis II.

In the absence of further pregnancies, Constanze maintained excellent health and proved herself a capable businesswoman. During 1795-96, she undertook a concert tour of North Germany, accompanied by her sister Aloysia Lange and the Viennese pianist and composer Anton Eberl. Constanze later established a boarding house in Vienna, and in 1797, the Danish diplomat Georg Nikolaus Nissen took lodgings with her. In August 1808, Nissen and Constanze made a futile search for Mozart's grave in the cemetery of St. Mark's.

After Abbé Maximilian Stadler and Nissen set Mozart's remaining manuscripts into order, Constanze sold fifteen packets of autographs and engraved copies to Johann André of Offenbach during 1799-1800, for 3,150 florins. André subsequently published about 55 of Mozart's works between 1800 and 1830.

Constanze married Nissen on 26 June 1809. For a time they lived in Copenhagen, returning to Salzburg in 1821. There Nissen took the baths at Gastein and wrote his biography. Nissen and Constanze enjoyed a happy marriage and were very devoted to each other. In her affluence Constanze assisted her two sons and was able to lend the Duscheks 3,500 gulden at 6 percent on the mortgage of their Villa Bertramka. Despite every effort to promote Nissen's biography, it was not a success. The text was poorly written, it lacked objectivity, and, despite its wealth of original source material, it did not prove popular. After Nissen's death, Constanze lived with her sisters Aloysia Lange and Sophie Haibel. She handed over the book to Dr. Feuerstein, who edited it, wrote the Preface, and also possibly the final chapter on "Mozart as an Artistic Personality." Feuerstein later lost interest in his Mozart research and cheated Constanze, who unsuccessfully sued him for 1,500 thaler. He died in poverty, neglected and mentally ill, in a poorhouse in Dresden on 2 January 1850.[2] Constanze last resided in an apartment at Mozart Platz 8, and she died on 6 March 1842, at age eighty. Nissen and Constanze were buried in Leopold Mozart's grave in St. Sebastian's Cemetery.

After his father's death, the elder son, Karl Thomas (1784-1858), was boarded with Franz Xaver Niemetschek in Prague. Karl attended the Kleinseitner Gymnasium from 1792 until 1797 and was instructed in the piano by Franz Duschek. Although quite a gifted pianist, he later abandoned a musical career and entered the civil service in Milan. A copyright law yielded him royalties on three Paris performances of *Figaro* to the tune of 10,000 francs, and he purchased a country estate at Caversaccio in Como province. His musical soirees were well known, and he became a friend of Felix Mendelssohn. Karl may have sired a daughter named Constanze, who died in 1833.[3] He had a warm relationship with his mother and stepfather. Karl bequeathed valuable relics and autographs to the Mozart museum at Salzburg, and the Zavertal collection at Glascow. He died in Milan on 2 November 1858, at seventy-four years of age.

Neither of Mozart's two sons ever married. Both attended the unveiling of the bronze Mozart monument at Salzburg on 4 September 1842, for which Wolfgang, Jr., composed and conducted a festival Cantata. He also played his father's D Minor Piano Concerto (K. 466) at the festival concert. For the Cantata he set themes from his father's *Tito*, and the Adagio in B minor (K. 540) to a text by Franz Grillparzer, who also wrote Beethoven's funeral oration.

Franz Xaver Wolfgang Mozart also received his early education in the households of the Niemetscheks and the Duscheks at Prague. He returned to Vienna in 1798. Among his teachers were Neukomm, Streicher, Hummel, Salieri, Vogler, and Albrechtsberger. He was very fond of his aunt Nannerl, and he became a respected composer, teacher, and pianist. Between 1807 and 1838, he lived in Lemberg (now L'vov), Podkamien, and Sarki as a music teacher and freelance musician, having undertaken an extensive concert tour of Europe (1819-21). Franz Xaver fell in love with and remained devoted to Josephine von Baroni-Cavalcabó. He bequeathed his father's portrait and piano to the Mozarteum in Salzburg. He was buried at Carlsbad, where he died at age fifty-three on 29 July 1844, while taking a cure there for a gastric ailment.

Mozart's sister Nannerl, after her husband's death in 1801, returned with her children to Salzburg where she lived almost opposite the home of her birth, at Sigmund Haffner Gasse 12. She was a popular piano teacher. Her relationship with Constanze remained one of mere civility; Nannerl had never liked Constanze. She heard of Constanze's remarriage only through strangers. The relationship was further strained when Constanze buried Nissen in the Mozart family grave in St. Sebastian's Cemetery. Constanze had an elaborate monument erected, which made no mention of the grave's earlier occupants—Eva Rosina Pertl (1755), Leopold Mozart (1787), and Nannerl's eldest daughter, Jeanette von Berchtold zu Sonnenburg (1805).[4] Nannerl became blind in 1825 and later was partially paralyzed after a stroke. She was lovingly cared for by a fellow-lodger, Joseph Metzger, but spent her last years in loneliness and simplicity. When Beethoven's friend, the harpmaker J. A. Stumpff, heard of Nannerl's sad plight, he and Vincent Novello collected a subscription of 60 guineas from seventeen London musicians, who included Thomas Attwood (the organist at St. Paul's Cathedral), J. B. Cramer, and Ignaz Moscheles. The subscription was personally delivered to Nannerl by Vincent Novello in 1829, and Mozart's blind sister was deeply moved. Nannerl died soon after on 29 October 1829 at seventy-eight. In accordance with her will she was buried in the churchyard of St. Peter's Abbey in Salzburg.

When the victorious French troops invaded the Archbishopric of Salzburg, Count Hieronymus Colloredo fled that city on 10 December 1800, just four days before Salzburg was taken. After his retirement, Haydn was succeeded at Esterhazy by Johann Nepomuk Hummel. The post had been offered to Michael Haydn, who instead chose to remain in Salzburg, where he died just one month short of his sixty-ninth birthday, in 1806. Joseph Haydn died at age seventy-seven at his home in Gumpendorf on 31 May 1809, just three weeks after the French army had taken command of the outer walls of the city of Vienna. His brother's requiem was performed at his funeral, and on 15 June 1809 Joseph Eybler conducted Mozart's *Requiem* for Haydn at the Schotten church in Vienna.

Ludwig Alois Ferdinand Ritter von Köchel was born at Stein, on the Danube in Austria, and he became a noted botanist, minerologist, and music bibliographer. He graduated in law at Vienna University and was appointed tutor to the four sons of the Archduke Carl. Köchel, an ardent devotee of Mozart, was alerted by his friend Franz Lorenz to the appallingly inadequate state of knowledge about Mozart's music and its sources. With admirable pertinacity, Köchel based himself at Salzburg from 1850 to 1863; he traveled all over Europe to collect autographs and manuscript copies. Köchel's labors were rewarded with Breitkopf and Härtel's publication of the *Chronologisch-Thematischen Verzeichnisses sämtlicher Tonwerke Wolfgang Amade Mozarts* in 1862. Each of Mozart's works was given a K number (K.1-626) and listed in order of their composition. The Catalogue was appropriately dedicated to Jahn. Köchel generously contributed 15,000 gulden to the first complete Mozart edition by Breitkopf and Härtel, which was completed in 1905. Köchel died on 3 June 1877, and Mozart's *Requiem*, recently edited by Brahms, was performed at his funeral. After more than seven years of meticulous research, Alfred Einstein produced a considerably revised and expanded third edition of Köchel's Catalogue in 1937 and added an Appendix in 1947. The sixth edition (1964) was used for this book. Although Köchel did not intend it, it is possible to calculate Mozart's age at the time of composition of a work by dividing the K number by 25 and adding 10. There are a few exceptions. (This method works only for K numbers over 100.)

Over the past five decades, more and more music lovers have learned to appreciate and love Mozart's music, with its subtle and paradoxical blending of passion with purity, and yet absence of false or exaggerated earthly sentiment. How satisfying are the profound serenity, grace, and dignity which are molded into a perfection of balance and proportion. Yet another highlight are those spontaneous passages of indescribable ethereal beauty.

It is true that had Mozart lived today his life could have been prolonged with artificial kidneys and renal transplants. However, the world has improved little since the composer's death. The hardness of men's hearts has resulted in two terrible world wars, and today East and West are poised on the verge of nuclear warfare and catastrophe. Too many people are obsessed with the pursuit of pleasure, money, and power. Despite the extraordinary advances in medicine, science, and technology, there are millions who are suffering with stress, anxiety, and depression. There is no easy solution to these problems, but listening to music can provide a healthy relaxation. After a serious illness and breakdown of his health, Otto Jahn found tremendous consolation in Mozart's music and after his recovery, his love of and dedication to Mozart provided the astonishing strength, courage, and pertinacity, to undertake and complete his monumental biography. There are few composers to rival the classical elegance and peaceful fulfillment of Wolfgang Amadeus Mozart, in such impeccable symmetry of melodic refinement and tonal drama.

Let us conclude with this charming, inspired reflection from the pen of Mozart's friend, Franz Xaver Niemetschek:

In his mind the work was already complete before he sat down at his desk. When he received the libretto for a vocal composition, he went about for some time, concentrating on it until his imagination was fired. Then he proceeded to work out his ideas at the piano; and only then did he sit down and write. That is why he found the writing itself so easy. While at work on it he would often joke and chatter . . . he spent half the night at the piano. It was then that he created his loveliest songs. In the peaceful hours of the night, when there was nothing to distract his thoughts, his imagination came alive and unfolded a whole wealth of sound, which nature had implanted in his mind. Then Mozart was filled with sentiment and well-being—most beautiful harmonies seemed to flow from his very fingers. Only those who have heard him at such moments can really appreciate the depth and, in fact, the full extent of his genius: free and indifferent to anything else, his spirit soared aloft to the very highest regions of his art. In such moments of poetic mood, Mozart laid up inexhaustible stores. On these stores he was able subsequently to draw for use in his immortal works.[5]

APPENDIX: DEATH CERTIFICATE

ČESKOSLOVENSKÁ SOCIALISTICKÁ REPUBLIKA
MINISTERSTVO VNITRA ČESKÉ SOCIALISTICKÉ REPUBLIKY

č. j. VS/3-61/9973/87

ÚMRTNÍ LIST

(úmrtní matrice)
Karlovy Vary

svazek 27, ročník 1844, strana 97, poř. č. 1 jest zapsáno

Den, měsíc, rok a místo úmrtí	29.7.1844 - dvacátý devátý červenec jeden tisíc osm set čtyřicet čtyři Karlovy Vary
Jméno a příjmení	Wolfgang Amadeus M o z a r t
Pohlaví	mužské
Stav	svobodný
Povolání	kapelník
Bydliště	Karlovy Vary č. 448
Den, měsíc, rok a místo narození	neuvedeno - 53 let
Jméno a příjmení rodičů zemřelého	neuvedeno
Příčina smrti	Ztvrdnutí žaludku
Místo a datum pohřbu (kremace)	neuvedeno - 1.8.1844 - neuvedeno
Poznámky	---

V Praze dne 10. 11. 19 87

vedoucí oddělení

SEVT - 03 006 0 - Úmrtní list pro cizinu   11/86   TZ 43-5676-86-G

The following entry appears in the Register of Deaths of the Registry District of Karlovy Vary, Volume 27, for the year 1844, page 97, reference number 1.

On 7-29-1844—the twenty-ninth of July one thousand eight hundred and forty four, at Karlovy Vary, died Wolfgang Amadeus Mozart, male, single, conductor, of Karlovy Vary No. 448, aged 53 years, of stomach hardness. The Date of Burial was 1-8-1844 (the first of August 1844). The Date and Place of Birth, the Full Names of the Parents of the Deceased, and the Place of Burial or Cremation were not indicated.

Extracted at Prague on 10-11-1987: Number VS/ 3-61/ 9973/ 87, and translated by the Ministry of Interior of the Czechoslovak Socialist Republic. (Courtesy of Dr. Gabriel Brenka, Czechoslovak Consul, Washington, D.C.)

NOTES

CHAPTER 1

1. King, 1974, 11-13.
2. Layer, 62-77.
3. Leopold Mozart, Preface by Alfred Einstein, xi. His employer was Count Thurn-Valsassina und Taxis; see Schwerin, 1987, 10.
4. Deutsch, 1966, 9.
5. Wilder, II, 224, fn.
6. H. J. Herbort, "Hatte Mozart einen silberblick?" *Die zeit,* 20 February 1981; T. Engström "Zu dem angeblichen Mozart-porträt (*Acta Mozartiana,* 1981—III), in *Acta Mozartiana* 29 (February 1982), Heft 1, 29-30.
7. F. C. Blodi, "Was Mozart Cross-Eyed?," *Arch Ophthalmol* 99 (1981), 823.
8. Bory, 1-225; Valentin, 1970, 1-144; Zenger and Deutsch, 1-404.
9. Landon and Mitchell, 1-9; Zenger and Deutsch, 1-23.
10. Bauer and Deutsch, No. 1233, IV, 224.
11. Nissen, 586.
12. In the museum catalogue of 1882, it was listed as Exhibit No. 38, donated by Arthur Gaye.
13. See Wolfgang Rehm, "Mozartiana in der sammlung varnhagen," in E. Herttrich and H. Schneider, eds., *Festschrift Rudolf Elvers zum 60. Geburtstag,* trans. Erna Schwerin, verlegt bei Hans Schneider, Tutzing, 1985, 407-23, 410-12. On 19 September 1879, the archivist of the Mozarteum, Franz Jellinek, stated that the watercolor had been purchased from the heirs of Mrs. Josephine von Baroni-Cavalcabo, with whom Mozart's son resided in Vienna. The original was sold to Mrs. Cora Kennedy Aitken of Boston and is now in the Houghton Library at Harvard University. A copy of the watercolor is retained in the Mozarteum Archives at Getreidegasse 14 in Salzburg. It was believed that G. N. Nissen had corrected the inscription in good faith.
14. Anonymous, "L'oreille de Mozart," *La Chronique Médicale* 5 (1898), 576; P.

H. Gerber, Mozart's Ohr," *Dtsch Med Wochenschr* 24 (1898), 351-52; M. Holl, "Mozart's Ohr," *Mitt Anthropol Gesellsch* (Wien), 21 (1901), 1-12.

15. A. Paton, A. L. Pahor, and G. R. Graham, "Looking for Mozart ears," *Brit Med J* 293, (1986), 1622-24.

16. D. Kerner, "Mozart's Äusseres Ohr." *Zeitschr für laryngol rhinol otol, und ihre grenzgebiete* 40 (1961), 475-78.

17. La V. Bergstrom, "Mozart Ear," in: D. Bergsma, ed., *Birth Defects Compendium*, London: Macmillan, 1979, 376.

18. Nissen, opposite, 586.

19. Zenger and Deutsch, xviii.

20. Davies, 1987d, 581.

21. L. Bernadi, "Mozart duro d'orecchio," trans. Lidia Rebeschini, in *Oggi*, Roma, Vol. 40, No. 38, 19 September 1984, 84-86. Professor G. Cavicchioli of Rome owns an anonymous oil portrait of a child, possibly by Johann Zoffany (properly Zauffely). The subject resembles the child in the unauthenticated portrait, London 1764-65, of "Mozart with the Bird's Nest," now in the Mozarteum, Salzburg. The portrait in Rome was subjected to detailed chemical analysis, radiographic, and X-ray examinations by the Scientific Bureau of Restoration in the Vatican. It was discovered that the left ear lacked a lobe and had been painted over so as to mask the malformation. A myopia was also present.

22. See Andreas Schachtner's letter to Nannerl, dated 24 April 1792, in Jahn, 1, 21-4, 23.

23. Hanson, 5.

24. Niemetschek, 1966, 20.

25. Deutsch, 1966, 453. See also Schlichtegroll, 83-84, and Niemetschek, 1966, 17-18.

CHAPTER 2

1. See Anderson, No. 7, 12.

2. See Anderson, No. 4, 9.

3. Hanson, 12.

4. Barraud, 740; Turner, 429-30.

5. H. Holz, "Mozarts Krankheiten und sein Tod," Dissertation, Jena, 1939. Quoted by Deutsch, 1966, 17.

6. Rothman, 33; Bett, 90; Davies, 1983, 777.

7. R. Willan, *On Cutaneous Diseases*, London, 1808, 483.

8. Desmond O'Shaughnessy, *Music and Medicine*, Privately printed, Melbourne, 1984, p. 11.

9. Bär, 1972, 94; Davies, 1983, 777.

10. Medical Research Council, Special Report Series, 1927, No. 114.

11. Hanson, 12.

12. Wood, 594.

13. F. W. Denny, "The Mystery of Acute Rheumatic Fever and Post-streptococcal Glomerulonephritis," *J Laboratory & Clinical Med* 108 (1986), 523-24.

14. Engel, Vol. 2, 104.

15. T. Faulkner, *A Description of Patagonia and the Adjoining Parts of South America*, Hereford, 1774, 115.

CHAPTER 3

1. Now 68 Rue François-Miron.
2. Davies, 1983, 777.
3. F. D. Sylvius, *Opera Medica,* de Tournes, Geneva, 1680, 526.
4. Deutsch, 1966, 494.
5. Daines Barrington, "Account of a Very Remarkable Young Musician," Royal Society of London, *Philosophical Transactions,* 40 (1770), 54-64. See also discussion by Donald Scott and Adrienne Moffett, in Critchley and Henson, 175-77.
6. King, 1984a, 157-79.
7. Davies, 1984a, 438.
8. Anderson, No. 427, 772.
9. Clein, 41; Shapiro, 18; Davies, 1983, 778.
10. Katner, 4-6; Fluker, 841.
11. Scarlett, 314.
12. Singer and Underwood, 453.
13. Bär, 1972, 94; Davies, 1983, 778.

CHAPTER 4

1. K. Dewhurst, "Sydenham's Original Treatise on Smallpox with a Preface, and dedication to the Earl of Shaftesbury, by John Locke," *Medical History* 3 (1959), 278-302.
2. Frank Fenner, "Smallpox, 'The Most Dreadful Scourge of the Human Species,'" *Medical Journal of Australia* 141 (1984), 728-35.
3. Engel, II, 94.
4. Anderson, No. 23, 40.
5. Singer and Underwood, 507-10.
6. World Health Organization, *The Global Eradication of Smallpox,* Final report of the Global Commission for the Certification of Smallpox Eradication, *History of International Public Health,* No. 4, Geneva, WHO, 1980.

CHAPTER 5

1. See P. J. Bishop, "A List of Papers, etc., on Leopold Auenbrugger (1722-1809) and the History of Percussion." *Medical History,* 5 (1961), 192-95; P. J. Bishop, "A Bibliography of Auenbrugger's 'Inventum Novum' " (1761), *Tubercle,* London, 42 (1961), 78-90.
2. Mozart criticized it as "a wretched work" in the letter to his father dated 10 December 1783. See Anderson, No. 501, 863.
3. Landon, 1978, 792.
4. A. R. G. Owen, *Hysteria, Hypnosis and Healing: The Work of J-M Charcot,* London: Dennis Dobson, 1971, 171-72.
5. Anonymous, "Modern Faith Healing: Anton Mesmer," *Brit Med J,* 9 December 1911, 1556-57.
6. H. Ullrich, "Maria Theresia Paradies and Mozart," *Music & Letters* 27 (1946), 224-33.

7. F. A. Mesmer, "Mémoire sur la découverte du magnétisme animal," Geneva and Paris, 1779.

8. Anonymous, "Modern Faith Healing: Anton Mesmer," *Brit Med J,* 20 January 1912, 133-37.

9. A. R. G. Owen (see note 4), 85-123.

10. Lorenzo Da Ponte, 197.

11. Peter Murray Jones, *Medieval Medical Miniatures,* B.L., London, 1984, 60-62.

12. Douglas Guthrie, *A History of Medicine,* 2nd ed., London: Thomas Nelson & Sons Ltd., London, 1960, 277.

13. Hemochromatosis is a metabolic disorder resulting from an excessive absorption of metallic iron from the small intestine. Polycythemia is a blood disorder associated with an excessive production of red blood corpuscles.

14. T. G. H. Drake, "Infant Feeding in England and France from 1750 to 1800," *Amer J Dis Children* 39 (1930), 1049-61.

15. Anderson, No. 22, 36-37.

16. T. G. H. Drake (see note 14), 1049.

17. A. E. Imhof, "From the Old Mortality Pattern to the New: Implications of a Radical Change from the Sixteenth to the Twentieth Century," *Bull Hist of Med* 59 (1985), 1-29.

18. J. J. Walsh, *Medieval Medicine,* London: A & C Black, 1920, 136-46.

CHAPTER 6

1. Davies, 1984a, 439.

2. Anderson, No. 144, 199.

3. Jones F. Avery, J. W. P. Gummer, and J. E. Lennard-Jones, *Clinical Gastroenterology,* 2nd ed., Oxford: Blackwell Scientific Pub., 1968, p. 57.

4. Deutsch, 1966, 134.

5. Anderson, No. 143a, 197.

6. Deutsch, 1966, 520.

7. Davies, 1983, 778.

8. Davies, 1984a, 439.

9. Anderson, No. 289, 487.

10. Davies, 1984a, 440.

11. G. B. Risse, "'Typhus' Fever in Eighteenth-Century Hospitals: New Approaches to Medical Treatment," *Bull Hist Med* 59 (1985), 176-95.

12. Anderson, No. 381, 698.

13. Anderson, No. 491, 850.

14. Jahn, II, 305.

15. Jahn, II, 315.

CHAPTER 7

1. Anderson, No. 518, 883.

2. Now Graben 29.

3. Now Domgasse 5, Schulerstrasse 8, First Floor.

4. Greither, 1956b, 165; 1967, 725; Clein, 42; Schenk, 350; Scarlett, 314; Deutsch, 1966, 227; Fluker, 841.

5. Bär, 1972, 121; Shapiro, 19.

6. Bauer and Deutsch, III, No. 808, 331.

7. Davies, 1983, 778-9; 1984a, 441.

8. E. Henoch, *Vorlesungen über Kinderkrankheiten,* X, Berlin, 1899, 839.

9. E.G.L. Bywaters, I. Isdale, and J. J. Kempton, "Schönlein-Henoch Purpura," *Quarterly Journal of Medicine* 26 (1957), 161-75.

10. J. J. Cream, J. M. Gumpel, and R. D. G. Peachey, "Schönlein-Henoch Purpura in the Adult," *Quarterly Journal of Medicine* 39 (1970), 461-84; H. S. Ballard, R. P. Eisinger, and G. Gallo, "Renal Manifestations of the Henoch-Schoenlein Syndrome in Adults," *American Journal of Medicine* 49 (1970), 328-35.

11. S. R. Meadow, E. F. Glascow, R. H. R. White, M. W. Moncrieff, J. S. Cameron, and C. S. Ogg, "Schönlein-Henoch Nephritis," *Quarterly Journal of Medicine* 41 (1972), 241-58.

12. Jean Berger, "IgA Glomerular Deposits in Renal Disease," *Transplantation Proceedings* 1 (1969), 939-44.

13. Anderson, No. 536, 896.

14. Deutsch, 1966, 289.

15. Engel, II, 109-10. It was believed that prolonged piano playing resulted in an unnatural overloading of the circulation of blood through the chest.

16. Jahn, II, 306.

17. Stendhal, 193.

18. William Osler, "The Visceral Lesions of Purpura and Allied Conditions," *British Medical Journal,* 7 March 1914, 517-25; Cream et al., op. cit., 466 n.10.

19. N. E. Gary, J. T. Mazzara, and L. Holfelder, "The Schönlein-Henoch Syndrome," *Annals of Internal Medicine* 72 (1970), 229-34.

20. Jahn, II, 322; Bauer and Deutsch, IV, No. 1034, 26.

21. Bauer and Deutsch, IV, No. 1048, 43, trans. Erna Schwerin.

22. Bauer and Deutsch, IV, No. 1052, 47-48, trans. Erna Schwerin. This remedy was the so-called Spiritus Salis dulcificatus Brecheri. The active ingredient may have been salep-root, obtained from the round or pear-shaped tubers of various orchids growing in Germany and the East. The chief constituent was a mucilage named Bassorin, and it was a popular remedy for intestinal catarrh. Pliny had extolled the virtues of orchis bulbs as an aphrodisiac as well as a cure for ulceration of the mouth, respiratory catarrh, and, if taken in wine, diarrhea. See C. Binz, *Lectures on Pharmacology,* trans. from the second German ed., by Peter W. Latham, 2 vols., London: New Sydenham Society 1897, II, 384.

23. Deutsch, 1966, 293.

24. Juhn, 192.

25. Anderson, No. 576, 937.

26. Anderson, No. 578, 938.

27. Anderson, No. 583, 941.

28. Bywaters et al., op. cit., 161 n.9.

CHAPTER 8

1. The count subsequently wrote out the *Requiem* in his own hand and conducted it in the church of the Cistercian Monastery of Neukloster at Wiener-

Neustadt on 14 December 1793. The copy used by the count carried the title "Requiem Composto del Conte Walsegg."

2. Medici and Hughes, 125. According to Niemetschek, this incident took place shortly after Mozart's return from Prague in September 1791.

3. Holmes, 337.

4. Jahn, III, 353.

5. Deutsch, 1966, 405.

6. Deutsch, 1966, 510. See also Niemetschek, 1966, 43.

7. Davies, 1983, 780-81; 1984b, 554-55.

8. R. Bright, "Cases and Observations, Illustrative of Renal Disease Accompanied with the Secretion of Albuminous Urine," *Guy's Hospital Reports* 1 (1836), 338.

9. A. S. Lyons, and R. J. Petrucelli, II, *Medicine, an Illustrated History,* Macmillan Co. of Australia, South Melbourne, 1979, 593.

10. De Wardener, 181-239.

11. W. Hughes, M. C. H. Dodgson, and D. C. Mac Lennan, "Chronic Cerebral Hypertensive Disease," *The Lancet* II (1954), 770-74.

12. Barraud, 744; Greither, 1956b, 167; 1967, 725; Clein, 43; Scarlett, 316; Carp, 279; Fluker, 843; Reinhard, 321.

13. Medici and Hughes, 128.

14. A. E. Rappoport, "A Unique and Hitherto Unreported Theory Concerning a Genetic pathologic Anatomic Basis for Mozart's Death," Dissertation IV, European Congress of Clinical Chemistry, Vienna, 3 September 1981; L. Karhausen, "Mozart Ear and Mozart's Death: letter to the Editor," *Brit Med J* 294 (1987), 511-12.

15. Davies, 1987 d, 583.

16. E. Wasserman, I. Sagel and N. Bingol, "Renal Disease: Polycystic Adult Type," in D. Bergsma, ed., *Birth Defects Compendium,* London: Macmillan, 1979, 925-26.

17. La V. Bergstrom, op. cit. (see Chapter 1, note 17). "Mozart Ear," by current definition, excludes microtia, atresia, ear pits, Darwin tubercle, earlobe pit, and ear flare.

18. W. Hummel, "W. A. Mozart's Söhne," *Bärenreiter Verlag,* Kassel & Basel, 1956, 207.

19. Bett, 90.

20. D. M. Bear, "Behavioural Symptoms in Temporal Lobe Epilepsy." *Arch Gen Psych* 40 (1983), 467-68.

CHAPTER 9

1. Jahn, I, 19 n. 26.

2. Anderson, No. 13, 26.

3. Anderson, No. 18, 31.

4. Betty Matthews, "Frau Mozart as Godmother," *The Musical Times* 123 (1982), 612.

5. Joan C. Cruz, *The Incorruptibles,* Rockford, Ill.: Tan Publishers, 1977, 142-45.

6. Cruz, op. cit. 85 n.5.

7. Kerst, 137.

8. Anderson, No. 115a, 163.

9. Anderson, No. 229, 341.

10. Anderson, No. 283a, 468.

11. Anderson, No. 311, 558.

12. Anderson, No. 313, 561.

13. Anderson, No. 313, 561-62.

14. Anderson, No. 311, 558.

15. Anderson, No. 459, 814.

16. Deutsch, 1966, 605.

17. The Salzburg Loretto-Kindl measures 10 cm in height. The Kindl's blessing is still administered today by one of the nuns through the convent grill to the kneeling subject. A prayer is recited as the Kindl touches the head. I am most grateful for personal communications from Dr. Rudolph Angermüller, Padre Rettore of Salzburg, and Padre Joseph Santarelli of Loreto in Italy, for the information about this Loretto-Jesulein, which has been a popular figure of devotion in the Capuchin order at Salzburg since the middle of the seventeenth century.

18. Anderson, No. 103 and 103a, 149.

19. Bauer and Deutsch, IV, No. 1212, 195.

20. Anderson, No. 95, 140.

21. Anderson, No. 89, 131.

22. Anderson, No. 39, 62.

23. Anderson, No. 546, 907.

24. Jahn, II, 306.

25. Anderson, No. 616, 970-71.

26. Deutsch, 1966, 304-5.

27. Anderson, No. 322, 593.

28. Kerst, 142-43.

29. Anderson, No. 410, 743.

30. Ghéon, 50-66; Kolb, 355-61; Einstein, 77-86; Hutchings, 1976, 112 and 117; Hildesheimer, 361-65; Kupferberg, 156-63; Barth, 25-41.

31. There is no surviving record of when Mozart was raised to the third degree, that of master Mason. See Landon, 1982, 10.

32. Listed in O. E. Deutsch's documentary biography of Mozart are at least forty-two names of Masons whom the composer knew personally.

33. Landon, 1982, 8.

34. Katherine Thomson, "Mozart and Freemasonry," *Music and Letters* 57 (1976), 25-46, 27.

35. Braunbehrens, 258.

36. Bauer and Deutsch, III, No. 885, para. 20, 425, trans. Erna Schwerin.

37. Landon, 1981, 86.

38. Edgar Istel, "Mozart's Magic Flute and Freemasonry," *The Musical Quarterly* 13 (1927), 510-27.

CHAPTER 10

1. Deutsch, 1966, 462.

2. Anderson, No. 436, 783.

3. Anderson, No. 551, 913.

4. Anderson, No. 285, 476.

5. Anderson, No. 288, 485.

6. Hildesheimer, 106; Valentin, 1985a, 140; Kupferberg, 66.

7. Anderson, No. 436, 784.

8. Anderson, No. 436, 784.

9. Anderson, No. 404, 733.

10. Einstein, 74.

11. See Betty Matthews, "Nancy Storace and the Royal Society of Musicians," *The Musical Times,* 128 (1987), 325-27. See also Jane Girdham, "The Last of the Storaces," *The Musical Times* 129 (1988), 17-18.

12. Anderson, No. 292, 497.

13. Schenk, 415.

14. Jahn, III, 234.

15. Anderson, No. 426, 769.

16. Anderson, No. 528, 890. Mozart also included Aloysia Lange, Frau Adamberger, and Therese Teyber.

17. Anderson, No. 571, 933-34. The date of this letter is ?19 August.

18. Jahn, III, 282.

19. Jahn, II, 271; Breakspeare, 238.

20. Deutsch, 1966, 498.

21. Anderson, No. 283a, 468.

22. Anderson, No. 544, 904.

23. Anderson, No. 547, 908. This letter was written toward the end of May.

24. Medici and Hughes, 144.

25. Medici and Hughes, 159.

26. Jahn, II, 302, F.N., No. 91.

27. Anderson, No. 616, 971.

CHAPTER 11

1. Anderson, li.

2. Kraemer, 1976; Bär, 1978; Angermüller, 1983; Steptoe, 1984; Braunbehrens, 146-56.

3. Anderson, No. 406, 737.

4. See letters to his father, dated 8 and 11 April 1781; Anderson, No. 397, 722; No. 398, 723-24.

5. See Anderson, No. 418, 754.

6. Josepha Auernhammer's concert at the Kärntnertor Theater on 3 November 1782.

7. K. 387, 421, 458, 428, 464, and 465.

8. K. 479, 480.

9. Mozart adapted his Munich opera of 1781 and added two new numbers, K. 489, 490.

10. Deutsch, 1966, 269.

11. See Leopold Mozart's letter to Nannerl, dated 1 March 1787; Anderson, No. 545, 906.

12. Hildesheimer, 211.

13. Mozart received 450 gulden for the commission of *Don Giovanni,* which was

given its premiere on 29 October 1787. The performance for his benefit was given on 3 November. *Figaro* was revived on 14 October.

14. See letter to Michael Puchberg, early in June 1788: Anderson, No. 553, 915.

15. Mary Sue Morrow, "Mozart and Viennese Concert Life," *The Musical Times* 126 (1985), 453-54.

16. Medici and Hughes, 82. However a recent estimate suggests that Mozart was paid 306 gulden for the manuscript and publication rights of his Redoutensaal Dances in 1791. See Landon, 1988, 46.

17. The Elector Frederick Augustus III of Saxony.

18. Jahn, III, 227.

19. Deutsch, 1966, 347.

20. Anderson, No. 563, 925.

21. Holmes, 321-22; Jahn, III, 230-31. Schlichtegroll quoted a figure of 3,000 crowns, equivalent to 11,000 francs; Stendhal, 189.

22. Medici and Hughes, 81-82.

23. Schenk, 416.

24. Steptoe, 1982.

25. Deutsch, 1966, 310.

26. K. 577, 579.

27. K. 578, 582, 583.

28. This loan was taken for a two-year term and was repaid before his death.

29. Jahn, II, 309.

30. K. 594, 608, 616.

31. Anderson, No. 586, 943-44.

32. O'Reilly offered Mozart 300 pounds to compose two operas between December 1790 and June 1791, with the additional right to give private concerts.

33. See letter to Baron Raimund Wetzlar, Anderson, 2nd ed., 1966, No. 609, 962; Bauer and Deutsch, IV, No. 1168, 140-41.

34. Deutsch, 1966, 402-3.

35. Bär, 1978, 51.

36. Nissen, 549.

37. King, 1970, 8-9.

38. Hans Lenneberg, "The Myth of Unappreciated Genius," *The Musical Quarterly* 66 (1980), 219-31, 227.

39. Deutsch, 1966, 212.

40. See Leopold Mozart's letter to Breitkopf & Son, dated 10 August 1781: Anderson, No. 420, 759. Mozart was also given thirty copies and a free hand in regard to their dedication.

41. See Anderson, No. 541, 901 fn 1.

42. K. 179, 180, 264, 265, 352, 353, 354, 398, 455, 500, 613; Sadie, 1982, 213-14; Landon and Mitchell, 50-51.

43. Deutsch, 1966, 516. Artaria may have paid Mozart 108 gulden for the Piano Concerto B Flat, K. 595. See Landon, 1988, 46.

44. Bär, 1978, 52.

45. Kraemer, 203; Angermüller, 1983, 8.

46. Steptoe, 1984, 198; Braunbehrens, 154. H. C. Robbins Landon has estimated that Mozart's income during 1791 was precisely 5763 Fl. 10 Kr. See Landon, 1988, 61.

47. See Anderson, No. 12, 23.

48. See Anderson, No. 524, 888.

49. Crankshaw, 134.

50. Crankshaw, 152.

51. W. H. Bruford, *Germany in the Eighteenth Century*, London, 1959; Eda Sagarra, *A Social History of Germany*, London, 1977.

52. Pezzl's Guidebook in 1786; see Hansen, 18. J. Gerold's Guidebook in 1792; see Bär, 1978, 38.

53. Deutsch, 1966, 585.

54. Bär, 1978, 42; Schwerin, 1978c, 1-11.

55. Now Wipplingerstrasse 14.

56. Now Kohlmarkt 7.

57. Now Judenplatz 3.

58. The landlord was the printer, Johann Thomas von Trattner, whose wife Therese was already a piano pupil of Mozart.

59. Now Domgasse 5. Mozart's apartment here at Figaro-haus was restored during the winter of 1964-65 and now houses the Mozart Museum.

60. The official was Otto Heinrich Freiherr von Gemmingen-Homberg (1753-1836); see Anderson, No. 299, 516.

61. Deutsch, 1966, 314.

62. Bär, 1978, 37. This estimate may be inflated, since Beethoven was offered a new six-octave piano by Johann Schanz in Vienna in March 1815 for 400 gulden.

63. This building is no longer extant. The site is now occupied by Steffel's Department Store. For a detailed description of Mozart's last apartment, see Landon, 1988, 201-8.

64. Bär, 1978, 47.

65. Nissen, 693.

66. Tyson, 1975.

67. Braunbehrens, 391.

68. Landon, 1982, 23. The fragment is from the year 1785 (Köchel-Einstein 467a).

69. Landon, 1988, 60.

CHAPTER 12

1. Angermüller, 1983, 8.

2. Dr. Rudolph Angermüller, personal communication on 25 August 1986.

3. Kelly, 126.

4. Nissen, 692.

5. Anderson, No. 345, 642-43.

6. Deutsch, 1966, 516.

7. Bauer and Deutsch, III, No. 861, 387-88.

8. Einstein, 69-70.

9. Angermüller, 1983, 5-6.

10. Schenk, 367.

11. Anderson, No. 466, 823.

12. Angermüller, 1983, 14.

13. Jahn, II, 309.

14. Jahn, II, 308-9.

15. Jahn, II, 340-41.

16. Jahn, II, 309.

17. The witness at Mozart's wedding was Dr. Franz Wenzel Gilowsky.

18. Deutsch, 1966, 585.

19. Jahn, II, 309.

20. Deutsch, 1966, 600.

21. Bauer and Deutsch, IV, 156.

22. See Anderson, No. 282, 464.

23. See Anderson, No. 340, 634.

24. Holmes, 230.

25. See Anderson, No. 533, 894.

26. See Anderson, No. 408, 739; No. 411, 745; No. 417, 753.

27. Anderson, No. 411, 745.

28. Anderson, No. 500, 861.

29. Letters to Puchberg, early June, 17 June, 27 June, and beginning of July 1788.

30. Letters to Puchberg, 12 July, 17 July, second half of July and 29 December 1789.

31. Letters to Puchberg, 20 January, 20 February, March-April, 8 April, 23 April, beginning of May, 17 May, 12 June, and 14 August 1790.

32. The name NN, first mentioned in Mozart's letter to his wife at Baden in mid-August 1789, was crossed out of several of the autographs by a later hand. Mozart's letters to Constanze from Frankfurt were dated 28 September, 30 September, and 3 October 1790. The mysterious NN may have been Joseph Odilio Goldhahn, with whom Constanze stayed after Mozart's death. See Landon, 1988, 50.

33. Anderson, No. 603, 957.

34. Anderson, No. 583, 941.

35. Nissen, 686.

36. Deutsch, 1966, 583-604.

37. See Deutsch, 1966, 236.

38. Niemetschek, 1966, 39 and 49.

39. Deutsch, 1966, 564.

CHAPTER 13

1. Leopold Mozart's court salary was about 600 gulden.

2. Astragali are the knucklebones of cloven-footed animals.

3. Deutsch, 1977, 380.

4. Kraemer, 203-11.

5. Angermüller, 1983, 12.

6. Anderson, 908, fn. 5; Bauer and Deutsch, IV, No. 1048, 44.

7. See Da Ponte, 115, and Schenk, 104-5.

8. See Schenk, 384.

9. Casanova wrote a letter in Prague, dated 25 October 1787, to Count Max Lamberg; see Deutsch, 1966, 301.

10. Hodges, 88-91. Professor Meissner recounted this anecdote to his grandson, Alfred Meissner, who included it in his book *Rococo-Bilder* (Gumbinnen, 1871).

11. Paul Nettl, *Mozart in Böhmen,* Prague, 1938, 146-48; P. Nettl, *Don Giovanni und Casanova, Mozart Jahrbuch,* 1957, 108. Paul Nettl discovered this fragmentary textual alteration in the Bohemian Casanova archives.

12. Angermüller, 1983, 12.

13. Jahn, 1, 64.

14. King, 1974, 13 and 16.

15. Anderson, No. 149a, 203-4.

16. Anderson, No. 13, 25.

17. See Anderson, No. 313, 562.

18. See Anderson, No. 267, 435.

19. Kelly, 135-36.

20. Crankshaw, 4 and 111.

21. Deutsch, 1977, xxvii, 305, 569-70, 703-4, 743.

22. Today's Ambassador Hotel in Vienna was built on the site of the old Mehlgrube.

23. *Antony and Cleopatra,* Act 2, Scene 5. This play was first published in 1623.

24. Jahn, II, 280.

25. Niemetschek, 1808, 100; Jahn, II, 305.

26. Medici and Hughes, 95.

27. Nissen, 559.

28. Holmes, 259.

29. Nissen, 627; Deutsch, 1966, 537.

30. Anderson, No. 614, 967.

31. Kelly, 113.

32. Deutsch, 1966, 515-16.

33. Deutsch, 1966, 527; AMZ, Vol. 27, No. 27, Col. 349. Leipzig, 25 May 1825.

34. Nissen, Vorrede des Verfassers, XVi.

35. Stendhal, 193.

36. Stendhal, 195.

37. American Psychiatric Association, *Diagnostic and Statistical Manual of Mental Disorders,* 3rd ed., Revised, Washington, D.C.: American Psychiatric Association, 1987, 324-25. Recent estimates indicate that 2 to 3 percent of the adult population are pathological gamblers.

38. Anderson, No. 396, 721.

39. E. Bergler, "The Psychology of the Gambler," *Imago* 22 (1936), 409; E. Bergler, *The Psychology of Gambling* New York, 1957; rep. 1970.

40. Katherine Thomson, "Mozart and Freemasonry," *Music and Letters* 57 (1976), 25-46, 28.

41. Deutsch, 1966, 536.

42. Deutsch, 1966, 555, Letter to Georg Friedrich Treitschke, Vienna, 1840? H. C. Robbins Landon, 1982, 52; in his translation, he uses the term gambling in lieu of games.

43. Carr, 95.

44. In his memoirs (p. 95) Da Ponte refers to his own excessive liberality.

45. Heinz Wolfgang Hamann, Joseph Wölfl, in the New Grove; see Sadie, 1980, 20, 508-10.

46. See Paul Nettl, *Beethoven Encyclopedia*. Peter Owen Ltd; London, 1957, 308.

47. Niemetschek, 1966, 49-50.

CHAPTER 14

1. Myre Sim, *Guide to Psychiatry*, 3rd ed., London: Churchill-Livingstone, 1974, 768.

2. Anderson, No. 287, 483.

3. Anderson, No. 32, 52-53. Dominicus (Cajetan) Hagenauer entered St. Peter's Monastery at Salzburg in 1764, and he became abbot in 1786. His calendar for 1769 is preserved in the Monastery Archives. Mozart's "Pater Dominicus" Mass in C (K. 66) was first performed at Father Dominic's first Mass at 9:00 A.M. in St. Peter's Church on 15 October 1769.

4. Anderson, No. 150a, 205.

5. Jahn, II, 422; Nissen, 560.

6. Howard Gardner, *Frames of Mind: The Theory of Multiple Intelligences*, London: William Heinemann, 1984, 99-127.

7. Sadie, 1980, Vol. 15, 421-23.

8. Franken, 302.

9. Robert Waissenberger, "Mozart's Apartment (Figaro House), Domgasse 5, Vienna 1," *Museums of the City of Vienna*, 1981, 4-5.

10. Mueller von Asow, 39-97; King, 1984b, 53-56.

11. Anderson, No. 27, 47.

12. Heinz Kohut, *The Analysis of the Self*, New York: International University Press, 1971, 31 and 177; Davies, 1987a, 125.

13. Anderson, No. 285, 475.

14. Jan Ehrenwald, *Neurosis in the Family and Patterns of Psychosocial Defense: A Study of Psychiatric Epidemiology*, New York: Hoeber Medical Division, Harper & Row, 1963, 94-108; Schwerin, 1978a and 1978b.

15. Jahn, II, 309.

16. Anderson, No. 323, 597-600.

17. Deutsch, 1966, 462.

18. Deutsch, 1966, 526; Davies, 1987a, 125.

19. Deutsch, 1966, 526.

20. Anderson, No. 291, 495-96.

21. Anderson, No. 296, 506.

22. See Anderson, No. 287, 483; No. 290, 492-93; No. 460, 816.

23. Deutsch, 1966, 432.

24. P. Robert, *Petit Robert Dictionnaire*, 12th ed., Paris, 1973, 1604.

25. Jahn, II, 341.

26. See R. T. C. Pratt, "The Inheritance of Musicality," in Critchley and Henson, 22-31.

27. See R. A. Henson, "Neurological Aspects of Musical Experience," in Critchley and Henson, 3-21, 17.

28. See Jan Ehrenwald, "Mozart, Father and Son: Talent Versus Genius," in *Anatomy of Genius*, New York: Human Sciences Press, 1986, 102-16.

CHAPTER 15

1. Boccie is an old Italian bowling game.
2. Anderson, No. 550, 912.
3. Nissen, 692.
4. See Anderson, No. 544, 903.
5. Jahn, II, 362.
6. The details of the forty-one titles in Mozart's library are given in Deutsch, 1966, 601-2.
7. Anderson, No. 584, 942.
8. Jahn, II, 307.
9. See Jahn, II, 302.
10. Anderson, No. 319, 587.
11. Anderson, No. 523, 886.
12. Anderson, No. 544, 903.
13. For a discussion of Mozart and the organ, see King, 1970, 228-41.
14. Anderson, No. 292, 498.
15. See Anderson, No. 508, 873.
16. P. Gammond, *One Man's Music*, London, 1971, 110-11.
17. Kelly, 131.
18. Anderson, No. 232a, 350.
19. Nissen, 692.
20. Anderson, No. 112, 161.
21. Holmes, 163.
22. Anderson, No. 408, 739.
23. See Anderson, No. 490, 849.
24. Franz Reichsman, "Life Experiences and Creativity of Great Composers: A Psychosomaticist's View," *Psychosomatic Medicine* 43 (1981), 291-300, 292-93.
25. Deutsch, 1966, 250.
26. Deutsch, 1966, 308. See also Niemetschek, 1966, 60-61.
27. Jahn, III, 285.
28. Landon, 1988, 61-62.

CHAPTER 16

1. American Psychiatric Association, *Diagnostic and Statistical Manual of Mental Disorders*, 3rd ed., revised, Washington, D.C., American Psychiatric Association, 1987, 226-28.
2. Davies, 1987a, 126; 1987b, 191-96.
3. Valentin, 1985, 173.
4. Stendhal, 182.
5. Anderson, No. 285, 476; Schenk, 190-91.
6. Anderson, No. 243a, 373.
7. Anderson, No. 249a, 391-92.

8. For a brilliant discussion of Mozart's nonsense letters, see E. Winternitz, "Gnagflow trazom: An Essay on Mozart's Script, Pastimes, and Nonsense Letters," *Journal of the American Musicological Society* 11 (1958), 200-16.

9. Anderson, No. 293, 500.

10. Anderson, No. 293, 499-500.

11. Anderson, No. 355, 655.

12. H. Eibl and W. Senn, eds., "Mozarts Bäsle-Briefe," *Bärenreiter Verlag,* December 1978; Hildesheimer, 105-23; Kupferberg, 64-68.

13. Anderson, No. 209a, 278.

14. Anderson, No. 211a, 283.

15. See Mozart's postscript on the cover of the letter to his father dated 4 November 1777; Anderson, No. 235b, 357-58.

16. At an international Congress of Psychiatry in Vienna in 1985, R. Fog and L. Regeur presented a paper: "Did W. A. Mozart suffer from Tourette's Syndrome?" Coprolalia, present in about two-thirds of cases, is associated with recurrent involuntary muscular and vocal tics. This rare disorder usually has an age of onset between two and fifteen years, and clearly, this diagnosis is untenable in Mozart. See A. K. Shapiro, E. S. Shapiro, R. D. Bruun, and R. D. Sweet, *Gilles de la Tourette Syndrome,* New York: Raven Press, 1978, 146-48; M. Lawden, "Gilles de la Tourette Syndrome: A Review," *Journal of the Royal Society of Medicine* 79 (1986), 282-87.

17. Anderson, No. 289, 487-88.

18. Anderson, No. 406, 736-37.

19. Anderson, No. 406, 737.

20. Deutsch, 1966, 265 and 268. For a discussion, see Maynard Solomon, "Mozart's Zoroastran Riddles," *American Imago* 42 (1985), 345-69.

21. Hodges, 88-91.

22. Deutsch, 1966, 503.

23. Deutsch, 1966, 537.

24. Deutsch, 1966, 556-57.

25. Jahn, II, 302.

26. Anderson, No. 417, 753.

27. Turner, 379.

28. Anderson, No. 319, 583-84.

29. Deutsch, 1966, 527.

30. Deutsch, 1966, 498.

31. Valentin, 1985, 84.

32. Deutsch, 1966, 287. The friend was Johann Georg Kronauer.

33. Anderson, No. 546, 907.

34. Anderson, No. 292, 498.

35. Franz D'Yppold's letter to Mozart from Salzburg, dated 28 May 1787, is not extant.

36. Anderson, No. 547, 908.

37. Anderson, No. 547, 909.

38. Anderson, No. 548, 909.

39. Anderson, No. 517, 881-82.

40. Hildesheimer, 130-32. See Sadie, 1983, and Solomon, 1983, for astute reviews of Hildesheimer's "Mozart."

41. The feast day of St. Leopold was on 15 November.

42. Anderson, No. 432, 777.

43. Schwerin, 1979.

44. Davies, 1987b, 194.

45. Deutsch, 1966, 225.

46. Einstein, 207; Hildesheimer, 207-9; Sadie, 1982, 118; Tyson, 1987b, 234-45. See also Daniel Heartz, "Thomas Attwood's Lessons in Composition with Mozart," *Proceedings of the Royal Musical Association* 100 (1973-74), 181.

47. For a discussion of the Commendatore, see Kaiser, 49-51.

48. Anderson, No. 555, 917.

49. Anderson, No. 605, 959.

50. Anderson, No. 569, 932.

51. Anderson, No. 600, 954.

52. Anderson, No. 575, 936.

53. Anderson, No. 585, 943.

54. Anderson, No. 570, 933.

55. Anderson, No. 571, 934.

56. Anderson, No. 588, 946.

57. Anderson, No. 600, 955.

58. Anderson, No. 604, 958.

59. Anderson, No. 606, 959.

60. Anderson, No. 609, 961.

61. Anderson, No. 584, 942.

62. Viktor E. Frankl, *Man's Search for Meaning. An Introduction to Logotherapy*, London: Hodder & Stoughton 1982 (rev.), 97-136. Viktor Frankl is the founder of the third school of Viennese psychiatry, the School of Logotherapy.

63. Anderson, No. 580, 939.

64. For the details of the cuts and corrections in the autograph of *Così Fan Tutte*, see Tyson, 1984.

65. Anderson, No. 557, 918.

66. E. Slater and A. Meyer, "Contributions to a Pathography of the Musicians. 2. Organic and Psychotic Disorders," *Confinia Psychiatrica* 3 (1960), 130-31; Davies, 1983, 780.

67. H. I. Kaplan and B. J. Sadock, eds. *Comprehensive Text Book of Psychiatry*, Baltimore: Williams & Wilkins, 4th ed., 1985, 779-86.

68. I am most grateful to Dr. Rudolph Angermüller who searched the parish records at Salzburg for this information.

69. Paumgartner, 102.

70. For an excellent discussion of the effects of mental disorder on musical creativity, see W. H. Trethowan, "Music and Mental Disorder," in Critchley and Henson, 398-432.

71. Anderson, No. 299a, 519.

72. Anderson, No. 286a, 481-82. At this time Mozart was also composing the violin sonatas (K. 301-306) and a Kyrie in E-flat (K. 322).

73. Anderson, No. 307a, 544.

74. Anderson, No. 409, 742.

75. Anderson, No. 611, 963-64.

CHAPTER 17

1. Deutsch, 1966, 563-66. These recollections of a personal acquaintance of Mozart were published for the centenary of his birth in the *Morgen-Post Vienna*, 28 January 1856, 2.

2. Davies, 1983, 781-82; 1984b, 555-56; 1987d, 585.

3. The celebrated Dr. Closset was personal physician to Prince Kaunitz. In 1783, he had written an article on putrid fever: Joseph Mohrenheim, *Wienerische Beyträge zur Praktischen Arzneykunde*, Leipzig, 1783, 70.

4. Dr. Sallaba wrote a book, dedicated to Closset, in 1791: *Historia Naturalis Morborum*, Vienna, 1791.

5. Deutsch, 1966, 526.

6. A vivid and moving account of Mozart's last days was written by Sophie Haibel to Nikolaus von Nissen for his biography on 7 April 1825. See Anderson, 975-77; Deutsch, 1966, 524-27; Nissen, 573-75.

7. Medici and Hughes, 215.

8. Nissen, 572.

9. Deutsch, 1966, 416.

10. See Jahn, III, 359; Nohl, II, 304-6; Wilder, II, 377-79; A. Schurig, *W. A. Mozart: sein Leben, sein Werk*, Leipzig, 1923, II, 380; Paumgartner, 455; Abert, II, 697; Schenk, 446-47; Deutsch, 1966, 416-18.

11. Bär, 1972, 126-57; Sadie, 1982, 141-42; Komorzynski, 10-29; Braunbehrens, 436-48.

12. Nissen, 572-76. This passage was kindly translated by Erna Schwerin; see Davies, 1987c, 1.

13. Deutsch, 1966, 565.

14. See Davies, 1987c, 2.

15. Deutsch, 1966, 418.

16. Slonimsky, 17.

17. Deutsch, 1966, 416.

18. See Schwerin, 1981b, 2.

19. Kolb, 362.

20. Braunbehrens, 440-41.

21. Schenk, 447.

22. Braunbehrens, 439.

23. J. D. John, *Lexikon der k.k. Medizinalgesetze*, 6 vols., Prague, 1790: I, 177.

24. During November and December 1791 in Vienna there were seventy-four funerals: first class—5, second class—7, third class—51, and paupers—11. See Bär, 1972, 149.

25. Bär, 1972, 129-32.

26. *John's Lexicon*, 1790 (see note 23), I, 177; Bär, 1972, 135, translated by Erna Schwerin.

27. *John's Lexicon*, 1790, op. cit., II, 198; Bär, 1972, 135-36, translated by Erna Schwerin.

28. Deutsch, 1966, 522-23.

29. Medici and Hughes, 97.

30. Davies, 1987c, 5.

31. Jahn, III, 359; Abert, II, 697; Bär, 1972, 153-54; Schenk, 447.

32. Breakspeare, 253-56.

33. See "Wiener Fremdenblatt," 24 October 1875. Dr. John Horan, of Melbourne, has informed me that the quote is from: Horace, *Odes,* IV, viii, line 28.

34. Zenger & Deutsch, 368; Duda, 1985, 62.

35. The skull in the Mozarteum is illustrated in: Zenger & Deutsch, No. 597b, 284.

36. See Tichy G & Puech Pf: "Identification of a passing guest: Wolfgang Amadeus Mozart," *Journal of the Canadian Society of Forensic Science,* 20 (1987), 176-77.

37. Deutsch, 1966, 388-89.

38. Zenger and Deutsch, Nos. 514, 515, 516; 356-57.

39. See Anderson, 977.

40. See Bauer and Deutsch, No. 1342, VI, 571.

41. Arthur Schurig, "Constanze Mozart," *Opal Verlag,* Dresden, 1922, 26; Schenk, 446.

42. Breakspeare, 273; Anderson, 977.

43. Deutsch, 1966, 389.

44. Nohl, II, 302 n. 2.

45. The second-hand dealer in the Brauhausgasse was Anton Vorreith.

46. Duda, 1985, 56-57. Kauer was also a graphic artist, and an expert in life and death masks. In 1943, he was commissioned to remodel a Mozart mask for the film *Whom the Gods Love.* His model was based on Lange's portrait.

47. A purchase agreement, with the right to unlimited use, was signed.

48. The expert panel was headed by Professor Schwarzacher, the professor of forensic medicine and anthropology. The other members of the panel included Dr. Chiari, Dr. Nowak, Professor Warhanek, Professor J. Weninger, and the musicologist Dr. Erich Schenk.

49. G. Duda, "Eine ungelöste Frage: Mozarts Totenmaske," *Acta Mozartiana* 7 (1960), 23-24.

50. G. Duda, "Die Totenmaske Wolfgang Amadé Mozarts," *Die Therapie des Monats* 10 (1960), 237-39.

51. Duda, 1985, 66.

52. On 9 April 1949, Jelinek, accompanied by Schenk and four detectives, confronted Kauer in his apartment with a search warrant. The bronze mask and a plaster copy were confiscated. The hearing before the state prosecutor began on 23 May. See Duda, 1985, 68-70.

53. Duda, 1985, 70-71.

54. Duda, 1985, 127, 152.

55. Duda, 1985, 79. See also Zenger and Deutsch, No. 597a, 368.

56. Duda, 1985, 17.

57. Duda, 1985, 20, 23.

58. See *Mozart-Jahrbuch* 1986: Bärenreiter, Kassel. Basel, London, New York, 1987, 205-8.

CHAPTER 18

1. A mock "coroner's inquest" into the cause of Mozart's death was held at the Brighton Festival, England, on 14 May 1983. The findings were reported in the *Times* two days later. The 250 members of the "jury" voted as follows: death from natural causes 49 percent, murder by Franz Hofdemel 24 percent, murder by Franz Xaver Süssmayr 11 percent, and murder by Salieri 11 percent.

2. From Salieri's opera *La Fiera di Venezia* which was given its premiere in the Burgtheater on 29 January 1772.

3. See Anderson, No. 378, 693.

4. See Anderson, No. 398, 724.

5. See Anderson, No. 436, 782.

6. See Anderson, No. 450, 804.

7. See Anderson, No. 489, 848.

8. Anderson, No. 501, 863.

9. Anderson, No. 539, 897.

10. Kelly, 130.

11. Anderson, No. 579, 938-39.

12. Da Ponte, 100-1.

13. See Anderson, No. 591, 947-48. Operas by Salieri and Weigl were performed, and a concert, featuring works by Haydn and other composers, was given.

14. Possibly the second version, with clarinets, of the Symphony in G Minor, K. 550; see Deutsch, 1966, 393.

15. Anderson, No. 616, 970.

16. Deutsch, 1966, 432. This notice appeared in the *Musikalisches Wochenblatt*, Berlin, 31 December 1791(?).

17. Deutsch, 1966, 489. An editorial footnote to a poem on Mozart's death by Johann Isaak; and a letter written by an anonymous Englishman, who was residing in Vienna.

18. Jahn, II, 302.

19. Niemetschek, 1966, 43, 53.

20. Warrack, 153.

21. Deutsch, 1966, 515.

22. Slonimsky, 18.

23. Elliot Forbes, *Thayer's Life of Beethoven*, 2 vols., Princeton, N.J.: Princeton University Press, 1967, Vol. II, p. 805.

24. Rossini held one corner of the shroud during the *Requiem* at the Invalides Cathedral on 2 October 1835.

25. Francis Toye, *Rossini*, New York, 1963, 162.

26. Kerner, 1969, 744.

27. Deutsch, 1966, 522. Schickh's entries were made in November 1823, and the end of 1823.

28. Kerner, 1969, 744.

29. Kerner, 1969, 744.

30. Deutsch, 1966, 524.

31. Year IX, No. 35, Milan, August 1824, 275ff.

32. Deutsch, 1966, 522-23.

33. Kerner, 1969, 744.

34. Deutsch, 1966, 527.

35. Deutsch, 1966, 527.

36. Slonimsky, 19.

37. Slonimsky, 17.

38. Slonimsky, 19-20. Neukomm's article appeared in an English translation in the *Quarterly Music Magazine of London*, 1826, 336-38.

39. Nissen, Anhang, Ref. No. 43, p. 215: A. von Schaden, *Mozarts Tod, ein Original-Traverspiel*, Augsburg, 1825.

40. Nissen, 563.

41. Medici and Hughes, 127.

42. Medici and Hughes, 125, 128.

43. Kerner, 1969, 745.

44. Jahn, III, 353; Bauer and Deutsch, IV, No. 1460, 515.

45. Holmes, 349.

46. Niemetschek, 1808, 81; Jahn, III, 358 n.17.

47. Kerner, 1973, 72-73; Dalchow, Duda and Kerner, 1971, 229-33.

48. Jahn, III, 353.

49. Igor Boelza, *Mozart and Salieri*, Moscow, 1953.

50. Borowitz, 276-77.

51. Kerner, 1973, I, 60-80.

52. Cedric Glover, *The Mysterious Barricades*, London, 1946; David Weiss, *The Assassination of Mozart*, Coronet Books, London, 1972.

53. Medici and Hughes, 127.

54. *Amadeus* opened at the Olivier Theatre, London, on 2 November 1979.

55. Jahn, III, 354 n.7.

56. Borowitz, 278; G. F. Daumer, *Aus der Mansarde*, Mainz, 1861, IV, 1-284.

57. Daumer, 1-71.

58. Daumer, 73-110.

59. M. Ludendorff, *Der ungesühnte Frevel an Luther;* Lessing, *Mozart und Schiller,* 2nd ed., Munich, 1936, 65-76. "Mozarts Leben und Gewaltsamer Tod," Munich, 1936.

60. Borowitz, 278.

61. Duda, 1958, 12.

62. Dalchow, Duda, and Kerner, 1966; 1971.

63. Borowitz, 281-82.

64. King, 1970, 141-63. See also Landon, 1988, 122-47.

65. See Friedrich Blume, trans. Nathan Broder, "Requiem But no Peace," in Lang, 103-26.

66. Blom, 1957, 324. See also W. Scheidt, "Quecksilbervergiftung bei Mozart, Beethoven und Schubert? *Med Klin* 62 (1967), 195-96.

67. Hildesheimer, 358.

68. Fluker, 844.

69. Blom, 1957, 323.

70. Schickling, 265-76; Hildesheimer, 337; Carr, 104.

71. Mozart's letters to his wife: Dresden, 13 April 1789, Berlin, 23 May 1789, Vienna, mid-August 1789, Frankfurt, 15 October 1790.

72. Eibl, 277-80.

73. Deutsch, 1966, 426.

74. Carr, 145-56. The Hofdemel murder theory was proposed by Goetz: Wolfgang Goetz, *Franz Hofdemel*, Vienna, 1932.

75. William Osler, *Modern Medicine*, Philadelphia, 1907, 1, 114-23; Beeson and McDermott, 1688-92; Robert H. Dreisbach, *Handbook of Poisoning*, 11th ed., Los Altos, Calif.: 1983, Lange Medical Pub., 1983, 240-45, 252-61.

76. Davies, 1984b, 559; 1987c, 585.

77. Osler, 124-31; Beeson and McDermott, 1692-94; Dreisbach, 262-66 (see note 75).

78. Gerhard Böhme concluded that Mozart died in uremic coma. He argued that, because some of Mozart's symptoms were compatible with mercury poisoning, the possibility of murder or accidental poisoning should be considered. See Böhme, II, 35.

79. Fluker, 845.

80. Singer and Underwood, 816.

81. Lang, 107 n.7.

82. The autograph of Mozart's *Requiem* is in the Vienna Nationalbibliothek, M.S., 17561 a-b; a facsimile of bars 6-9 of the Lacrimosa is reproduced in Valentin, 1970, 128, and also in Baker, 128.

83. Mozart's *Verzeichnüss* is in the British Library, loan 42/1. Facsimiles of the last page are reproduced in Bauer and Deutsch, IV, 160-61, Schenk, opposite 446, and Zenger and Deutsch, No. 535, 252.

84. Davies, 1983, 783; 1984b, 560; 1987c, 585.

85. Peter J. Davies, BBC, *Music Weekly*, Radio 3, Programme on Salieri, 13 January 1985, 10:30-11:15 A.M., interviewer Michael Oliver, producer Andrew Lyle.

CHAPTER 19

1. Nissen, 572.

2. Deutsch, 1966, 416.

3. A facsimile from the Stadtarchiv, Vienna, is reproduced in Bär, 1972, 151.

4. A facsimile is reproduced in Bär, 1972, 152.

5. Bär, 1972, 50.

6. *The Musical Times*, Mozart supplement, 1 December 1891, 28.

7. Nissen, 575-76, in German.

8. *The Musical Times*, 1 December 1891, 20.

9. Diving accidents are a common cause of quadriplegia.

10. Russell Brain, *Clinical Neurology*, 2nd ed., London: Oxford University Press, 1964, 159.

11. Nissen, 570.

12. P. J. Vinken and G. W. Bruyn, *Handbook of Clinical Neurology*, Amsterdam: North-Holland Publishing Co., Vol. 33, 1978, 337.

13. Davies, 1983, 782.

14. See Kerner, 1971a, for a summary of 180 years of diagnoses of Mozart's fatal illness.

15. Gehring, 129.

16. Arthur Schurig, *Wolfgang Amade Mozart,* 2 vols., 2nd ed., Leipzig, 1923, Vol. II, 374.

17. Stein, 1088; Lyme arthritis was first noted near Lyme, Connecticut.

18. Shapiro, 20.

19. Bär, 1972, 88-118.

20. Franken, 302.

21. Davies, 1983, 784; 1984b, 561; 1987d, 585. See also S. T. Green, and F. A. M. Green, "The Great Composers: Their Premature Deaths," *J Royal College of Physicians of London* 21 (1987), 202-5, 204. See also Landon, 1988, 178-80.

22. Medici and Hughes, 215.

23. Clein, 44; Sakula, 6-9.

24. Davies, 1983, 784.

25. Sederholm, 345-48.

26. O. E. Deutsch considers Bosia's portrait to be spurious; see Landon and Mitchell, p. 8.

27. An exophthalmometer.

28. Schenk, 445; Deutsch, 1966, 415.

29. Barraud, 744; the articles by Casseroller, Holtz, Marx, and Willms are quoted by Greither: 1956b, 167.

30. Greither, 1956b, 169; 1967, 725-26; Clein, 44; Scarlett, 316; Carp, 279; Roe, 1320; Fluker, 844. The French author, Dr. B. Juhn, also favored a uremic coma resulting from chronic nephritis or malignant hypertension Juhn, 194. See also Gerhard Böhme, *Medizinische Porträts berühmter Komponisten,* Stuttgart: Gustav Fischer Verlag, 1981, II, 19-30; Arthur Rappoport, 220 (see chapter 8, note 14).

31. De Wardener, 206.

32. Bókay, 233-34.

33. Katner, 21-25; Stein and Schwerin, 332; Neumayr, 106-13.

34. Davies, 1985, 390.

35. Deutsch, 1966, 527.

36. Bär, 1972, 117-18.

37. Davies, 1983, 783-84.

38. Davies, 1983, 784-85; 1984b, 561; 1987d, 585.

39. Douglas Gairdner, "The Schönlein-Henoch Syndrome (Anaphylactoid Purpura)," *Quarterly Journal of Medicine* 17 (1948), 95-122, 110.

40. Stein, 1090.

41. Bywaters, Isdale, and Kempton, 167.

42. Professor J. F. Soothill, "Mozart's Illnesses and Death, Letter to the Editor," *Journal of the Royal Society of Medicine* 77 (1984), 436; Peter J. Davies, Letter to the Editor, *Journal of the Royal Society of Medicine* 77 (1984), 623.

43. T. R. Cupps, and A. S. Fauci, *The Vasculitides,* Philadelphia: W. B. Saunders, 1981, 64.

44. Gairdner (see note 39), 105-6.

45. Davies, 1983, 784-85.

46. Rappoport (see chapter 8, note 14).

47. D. J. Weatherall, J. G. G. Ledingham, and D. A. Warrell, *Oxford Textbook of Medicine,* Oxford University Press, 1983, 18-37.

48. M. Sturtevant and I. Graef, "Henoch-Schönlein Purpura with Paralytic

Ileus and Rheumatic Carditis," *Medical Clinics of North America* 17 (1933), 91-101; Gairdner, 107-9.

49. Davies, 1985, 391.

50. Jean Berger (see chapter 7, note 12); Davies, 1987d, 585.

51. Dalchow, Duda & Kerner, 1971, 231; Landon, 1988, 159-60.

52. See Pozzati E., Frank F., Frank G., Gaist G.: "Subacute and chronic extradural haematomas: A study of 30 cases," *Journal of Trauma 20*, (1980), 795-99; See also Bullock R., Smith R. M., Van Dellen J. R.: "Nonoperative Management of Extradural Haematoma," *Neurosurgery* 16 (1985), 602-6.

EPILOGUE

1. Deutsch, 1966, 449.

2. R. Angermüller, "Feuerstein, Jähndl und das Ehepaar Nissen." *Mozartgemeinde Wien, Wiener Figaro* 37 (1971), 9-15.

3. Schwerin, 1981, 28; Hildesheimer, 259.

4. Genovefa von Weber (1798), G. N. von Nissen (1826), and Constanze Nissen (1842) were also buried in Leopold Mozart's grave.

5. Niemetschek, 1966, 62-63.

BIBLIOGRAPHY

Abert, H. *Mozart's Don Giovanni*. Trans. P. Gellhorn. Ernst Eulenburg, London, 1976.

_____. *W. A. Mozart*. 2 vols., Breitkopf & Härtel, Leipzig, 1983.

Abraham, G., ed. *The Age of Beethoven, 1790-1830*. The New Oxford History of Music, vol. VIII. Oxford Univ. Press, London, 1982.

Adams, G. *Mozart*. Giants of the Past Series. Hasso Ebeling International, Luxembourg, 1981.

Allanbrook, W. J. *Rhythmic Gesture in Mozart: Le Nozze di Figaro and Don Giovanni*. Univ. of Chicago Press, Chicago, 1983.

Anderson, E. *The Letters of Mozart and His Family*, 3rd ed. Macmillan, London, 1985.

Angermüller, R. "Antonio Salieri." In *The New Grove Dictionary of Music and Musicians*, vol. 16, ed. Stanley Sadie. Macmillian, London, 1980, pp. 415-20.

_____. *"Auf ehre und Credit" die Finanzen des W. A. Mozart*. Int. Stift. Mozarteum—Bayerische Vereinsbank, Munich, 1983.

_____. *Antonio Salieri: Fatti e Documenti*. Cassa di Risparmio di Verona Vicenza e Belluno, 1985.

_____. *Figaro*. Int. Stift. Mozarteum—Bayerische Vereinsbank, Munich, 1986.

_____. *Don Juan-Register*. Int. Stift. Mozarteum—Bayerische Vereinsbank, Munich, 1987.

Angermüller, R., Berke, D., and Rehm, W., eds. *Mozart-Jahrbuch 1984-85*. Bärenreiter, Kassel, 1986.

Angermüller, R., Berke, D., and Rehm, W., eds. *Mozart-Jahrbuch 1986*. Bärenreiter, Kassel, 1987.

Angermüller, R., and Schneider, O., eds. *Mozart-Bibliographie 1981-1985*. Bärenreiter, Kassel, 1987.

Badura-Skoda, E. and Badura-Skoda, P. *Interpreting Mozart on the Keyboard*. Trans. Leo Black. Da Capo, New York, 1986.

Baker, R. *Mozart.* Thames & Hudson, London, 1982.

Bär, C. *Mozart: Krankheit Tod Begräbnis,* 2nd ed., Int. Stift. Mozarteum, Salzburg, 1972.

———. "Er war . . . kein guter Wirth." *Acta Mozartiana* 25 (1978), 30-53.

Barraud, J. "A quelle maladie a succombé Mozart?" *La Chronique Médicale* 12 (1905), 737-44.

Barth, K. *Wolfgang Amadeus Mozart.* Trans. Clarence K. Pott. William B. Eerdmans, Michigan, 1986.

Batley, E. M. *A Preface to the Magic Flute.* Dennis Dobson, London, 1969.

Bauer, W. A., and Deutsch, O. E. *Mozart Briefe und Aufzeichnungen,* 7 vols. Bärenreiter Kassel, Basel, 1962-75.

Beeson, P. B., and McDermott, W., eds. *Cecil-Loeb's Text Book of Medicine,* 12th ed. W. B. Saunders, Philadelphia, 1967.

Benn, C. *Mozart on the Stage.* Ernest Benn, London, 1946.

Bett, W. R. "W. A. Mozart: A Puzzling Case-history." *The Medical Press* 235 (1956), 90.

Bleiler, E. H. *Don Giovanni.* Dover, New York, 1964.

Blom, E. "Mozart's Death." *Music & Letters* 38 (1957), 320-26.

———. *Mozart.* J. M. Dent & Sons, London, 1976.

Bokay, J. "Mozart halalanak oka." *Orvosi Hetilap* (Budapest), 3 (1906), 233-34.

Borowitz, A. I. "Salieri and the 'Murder' of Mozart." *The Musical Quarterly* 59 (1973), 263-84.

Bory, R. *La Vie et L'oeuvre de Wolfgang-Amadeus Mozart par L'Image.* Editions du Journal de Genève, Genève, 1948.

Braunbehrens, V. *Mozart in Wien.* R. Piper, Munich, 1986.

Breakspeare, E. J. *Mozart.* J. M. Dent & Sons, London, 1931.

Broder, N. *The Great Operas of Mozart.* W. W. Norton, New York, 1962.

Brophy, B. *W. A. Mozart: Die Zauberflöte: Die Entführung aus dem Serail.* Cassell, London, 1971.

Buchner, A., Koval, K., Mikysa, K., and Cubr, A. *Mozart and Prague.* Trans. Daphne Rusbridge. Artia, Prague, 1956.

Burgess, A. *W. A. Mozart: Don Giovanni: Idomeneo.* Universe Books, New York, 1971.

Carp, L. "Mozart: His Tragic Life and Controversial Death." *Bulletin of the New York Academy of Medicine* 46 (1970), 267-80.

Carr, F. *Mozart & Constanze.* John Murray, London, 1983.

Clein, G. P. "Mozart: A Study in Renal Pathology." King's College Hospital, *Gazette* 37 (1959), 37-45.

Crankshaw, E. *Maria Theresa.* Constable, London, 1983.

Crompton, L. *The Great Composers. Reviews and Bombardments by Bernard Shaw.* Univ. of California Press, Berkeley, 1978.

Dalchow, J., Duda, G., and Kerner, D. *W. A. Mozart: Die Dokumentation seines Todes* Introd. I. Boelza. F. v. Bebenburg, Pähl, 1966.

Dalchow, J., Duda, G., and Kerner, D. *Mozarts Tod (1791-1971).* F. v. Bebenburg, Pähl, 1971.

Da Ponte, L. *The Memoirs of Lorenzo Da Ponte.* Trans. Elisabeth Abbot. Orion Press, New York, 1959.

_____. *Don Giovanni Libretto.* Trans. A. & A. Holden. Andre Deutsch, London, 1987.

Davenport, M. *Mozart.* Avon Books, New York, 1979.

Davies, P. J. "Mozart's Illnesses and Death." *Journal of the Royal Society of Medicine* 76 (1983), 776-85.

_____. "Mozart's Illnesses and Death I: The Illnesses 1756-90." *The Musical Times* 125 (1984), 437-42.

_____. "Mozart's Illnesses and Death II: The Last Year and the Fatal Illness." *The Musical Times* 125 (1984), 554-61.

_____. "Mozart's Illnesses. Letter to the Editor." *The Musical Times* 126 (1985), 390-91.

_____. "Mozart's Manic-Depressive Tendencies, in two parts:" *The Musical Times* 128 (1987), 123-26; 128 (1987), 191-96.

_____. "The Date of Mozart's Funeral." Friends of Mozart, New York, Newsletter No. 22, Fall 1987, pp. 1-6.

_____. "Mozart's Left Ear, Nephropathy and Death." *Medical Journal of Australia* 147 (1987), 581-86.

Dearing, R. *The Music of W. A. Mozart: The Symphonies.* Associated University Presses, London, 1982.

Dent, E. J. *Mozart's Operas.* 2nd ed. Oxford University Press, London, 1975.

Deutsch, O. E. *Mozart: A Documentary Biography.* Trans. Eric Blom, Peter Branscombe, and Jeremy Noble, 2nd ed. Adam & Charles Black, London, 1966.

_____. *Schubert. A Documentary Biography.* Trans. Eric Blom. Da Capo, New York, 1977.

De Wardener, H. E. *The Kidney: An Outline of Normal and Abnormal Function,* 5th ed. Churchill-Livingstone, London, 1985.

Duda, G. "Gewiss man hat mir Gift gegeben." F. v. Bebenburg, Pähl, 1958.

_____. "Der Echtheitsstreit um Mozarts Totenmaske." Verlag Hohe Warte, F. v. Bebenburg, Pähl, 1985.

Eibl, J. H. *Süssmayr und Constanze. Mozart Jahrbuch,* 1976-77, 277-80.

Einstein, A. *Mozart: His Character, His Work.* Trans. A. Mendel and N. Broder. 5th ed. Cassell, London, 1961.

Eisen, C. "Contributions to a New Mozart Documentary Biography." *JAMS* 39 (1986), 615-32.

Engel, C. *Musical Myths and Facts.* 2 vols. Novello, Ewer & Co., London, 1876.

English, H. B., and A. C. *A Comprehensive Dictionary of Psychological and Psychoanalytical Terms.* David McKay, New York, 1962.

Farmer, H. G., and Smith, H. *New Mozartiana: The Mozart Relics in the Zavertal Collection at the University of Glascow.* A.M.S. Press, New York, 1979.

Flothius, M. *Mozarts Bearbeitungen Eigener und Fremder Werke.* Int. Stift. Mozarteum, Salzburg, 1969.

Fluker, J. L. "Mozart: His Health and Death." *The Practitioner* 209 (1972), 841-45.

Forman, D. *Mozart's Concerto Form: The First Movements of the Piano Concertos.* Rupert Hart-Davis, London, 1971.

Franken, F. H. "Mozarts Todeskrankheit." *Fortschritte der Medizin* 98 (1980), 301-2.

Gal, H. *The Golden Age of Vienna.* Max Parrish, London, 1948.

Gammond, P. *The Magic Flute*. Barrie & Jenkins, London, 1979.

Gehring, F. *Wolfgang Amadeus Mozart*. Foreword by Francesco Berger, Sampson, Low, Marston & Co., London. Undated.

Gerber, P. H. "Mozarts Ohr." Deutsche. *Medizinische Wochenschrift* 24 (1898), 351-52.

Ghéon, H. *In Search of Mozart*. Trans. Alexander Dru. Sheed & Ward, London, 1934.

Gianturco, C. *Mozart's Early Operas*. B. T. Batsford, London, 1981.

Girdlestone, C. M. *Mozart's Piano Concertos*. 3rd. ed. Cassell, London, 1978.

Greither, A. "Mozart und die Ärzte, seine Krankheiten und sein Tod. In two parts." *Deutsche Medizinische Wochenschrift* 81 (1956), 121-24; 81 (1956), 165-69.

_____. "Die Todeskrankheit Mozarts." *Deutsche Medizinische Wochenschrift* 92 (1967), 723-26.

Haas, R. "Wolfgang Amadeus Mozart." *Akademische Verlagsgesellschaft Athenaion*, M.B.H. Potsdam, 1933.

Hanson, A. M. *Musical Life in Biedermeier*. Vienna, Cambridge Univ. Press, Cambridge, 1985.

Heartz, D. "Constructing *Le Nozze di Figaro*." *JRMA* 112 (1987), 77-98.

Higgins, J. *The Making of an Opera: Don Giovanni at Glyndebourne*. Secker & Warburg, London, 1978.

Hildesheimer, W. *Mozart*. Trans. Marion Faber. J. M. Dent & Sons, London, 1983.

Hill, R., ed. *The Symphony*. Penguin, Middlesex, 1956.

Hodges, S. *Lorenzo Da Ponte: The Life and Times of Mozart's Librettist*. Granada, London, 1985.

Holmes, E. *Life of Mozart, Including His Correspondence*. Chapman & Hall, London, 1845.

Hughes, S. *Famous Mozart Operas*. 2nd ed. Dover, New York, 1972.

Hussey, D. *Wolfgang Amade Mozart*. Kegan Paul, Trench, Trubner & Co., J. Curwen & Sons, London, 1933.

Hutchings, A. *A Companion to Mozart's Piano Concertos*, 2nd ed. Oxford Univ. Press, 1974.

_____. *Mozart: The Man. The Musician*. Thames & Hudson, London, 1976.

International Foundation Mozarteum. *Mozart Memorials in Salzburg*. Undated.

Jahn, O. *The Life of Mozart*. 3 vols. Trans. Pauline D. Townsend. Novello, Ewer & Co., London, 1882.

Jefferson, A. *Sir Thomas Beecham, World Records*. London, 1979.

Juhn, B. *Maladie et mort de Mozart*. Symposium, Ciba, (Paris), 3, (1956), 191-94.

Kaiser, J. *Who's Who in Mozart's Operas: From Alfonso to Zerlina*. Trans. Charles Kessler. Weidenfeld & Nicholson, London, 1986.

Kann, R. A. *A History of the Habsburg Empire, 1526-1918*. Univ. of California Press, Berkeley, 1980.

Katner, W. "Pathography of W. A. Mozart." *Boehringer Ingelheim Informa* 19, 1969, pp. 1-28.

Kay, J. *Mein Sohn Wolfgang Amadeus: Glück und Tragik des Vaters. Leopold Mozart*. Verlag Herold, Wien, München, 1965.

Kelly, M. *Reminiscences*. Roger Fiske, ed. Oxford Univ. Press, London, 1975.

Kenyon, M. *Mozart in Salzburg*. Putnam, London, 1952.

Kerner, D. "Mozarts Tod bei Alexander Pushkin." *Deutsches Medizinisches Journal* 20 (1969), 743-47.

———. "180 Jahre Mozart-Pathologie." *Münchener Medizinische Wochenschrift* 49 (1971), 1664-71.

———. *Mozarts Tod, 1791-1971.* 180 Jahre Missbrauch der Dokumentation, Mainz, 1971.

———. *Krankheiten Grosser Musiker,* 3rd ed. 2 vols. F. K. Schattauer Verlag, Stuttgart, 1973.

Kerst, F. *Mozart: The Man and the Artist Revealed in His Own Words.* Geoffrey Bles, London, 1926.

Keys, I. *Mozart: His Music in His Life.* Granada Publishing, London, 1980.

King, A. Hyatt. *Mozart.* Clive Bingley, London, 1970.

———. *Mozart in Retrospect. Studies in Criticism and Bibliography.* Oxford Univ. Press, London, 1970.

———. "Some Aspects of Recent Mozart Research. Royal Music Association Centenary Essays." *Proceedings of the Royal Musical Association* 100 (1974), 1-18.

———. *Mozart Chamber Music.* BBC Music Guides. BBC Publications, London, 1975.

———. *Mozart Wind and String Concertos.* BBC Music Guides. BBC Publications, London, 1978.

———. "The Mozarts at the British Museum." *Festschrift Albi Rosenthal,* 1984, pp. 157-79.

———. *A Mozart Legacy. Aspects of the British Library Collections.* The British Library, London, 1984.

Köchel, L. R. von. *Chronologisch-thematisches Verzeichnis sämtlicher Tonwerke Wolfgang Amade Mozarts,* 2nd ed., Ed. Paul Graf von Waldersee. Breitkopf & Härtel, Leipzig, 1905.

———. *Der Kleine Köchel. Mozarts Werke,* 7th ed. Ed. Hellmuth von Hase. Breitkopf & Härtel, Wiesbaden, 1979.

Kolb, A. *Mozart.* Trans. P. & T. Blewitt, Victor Gollancz, London, 1939.

Komorzynski, E. *Mozarts 'Einsames' Begräbnis.* Mozartgemeinde, Wien, December 1985, pp. 10-29.

Kraemer, U. "Wer hat Mozart Verhungern Lassen?" *Musica* 30 (1976), 203-11.

Kupferberg, H. *Amadeus. A Mozart Mosaic.* McGraw-Hill, New York, 1986.

Landon, H.C.R., and Mitchell, D. *The Mozart Companion.* Faber & Faber, London, 1977.

———. *Haydn: Chronicle and Works. Haydn at Eszterháza, 1766-1790.* Thames & Hudson, London, 1978.

———. *Haydn: A Documentary Study.* Thames & Hudson, London, 1981.

———. *Mozart and the Masons: New Light on the Lodge "Crowned Hope."* Thames & Hudson, London, 1982.

———. *1791: Mozart's Last Year.* Thames & Hudson, London, 1988.

Lang, P. H. *The Creative World of Mozart.* W. W. Norton, New York, 1963.

Layer, A. *Die Augsburger Künstlerfamilie Mozart.* Verlag Die Brigg, Augsburg. Undated.

Levey, M. *The Life and Death of Mozart.* Cardinal, London, 1973.

Liebner, J. *Mozart on the Stage.* Calder & Boyars, London, 1972.

Mann, W. *The Operas of Mozart.* Cassell, London, 1977.

Medici di Marignano, N. and Hughes, R. *A Mozart Pilgrimage: Being the Travel Diaries of Vincent and Mary Novello in the Year 1829.* Novello & Co., London, 1955.

Mersmann, H., ed. *Letters of Wolfgang Amadeus Mozart.* Trans. M. M. Bozman. J. M. Dent, London, 1928.

Mörike, E. *Mozart on the Way to Prague.* Trans. Walter and Catherine Alison Phillips. Basil Blackwell, Oxford, 1934.

Mozart, L. *A Treatise on the Fundamental Principles of Violin Playing,* 2nd. ed. Trans. Editha Knocker. Oxford University Press, London, 1978.

Mozart, W. A. *Neue Ausgabe sämtlicher Werke, Bärenreiter Kassel.* Basel, London, 1955.

_____. *Symphony in C, KV 551. Facsimile of the Autograph Manuscripts.* Introduction by Karl-Heinz Köhler. Bärenreiter Kassel, Basel, 1978.

_____. *Piano Concerto in C Minor, K. 491. Facsimile of the Autograph Manuscripts.* Foreword by Watkins Shaw, Introduction by Denis Matthews. Boethius Press, Kilkenny, 1979.

_____. *The Six "Haydn" String Quartets. Facsimile of the Autograph Manuscripts.* Introduction by Alan Tyson. British Library, London, 1985.

_____. *Piano Concerto in C, K. 467. Facsimile of the Autograph Score.* Introduction by Jan La Rue. Pierpont Morgan Library, Dover, New York, 1985.

Mueller von Asow, E. H. "Wolfgang Amadeus Mozart. Verzeichnis aller meine Werke und Leopold Mozart." *Verzeichnis der Jugendwerke W. A. Mozarts.* Verlag Doblinger, Wien, 1956.

Nettl, P. *Mozart.* Petite Bibliothèque Payot, Paris, 1955.

Neumann, F. *Ornamentation and Improvisation in Mozart.* Princeton University Press, Princeton, N.J., 1986.

Neumayr, A. *Musik und Medizin: Am Beispiel der Wiener Klassik.* Edition Wien, Wien, 1988.

Niemetschek, F. (F. X. Nemetschek). *Leben des K. K. Kapellmeisters Wolfgang Gottlieb Mozart,* 2nd ed. Prague, 1808.

_____. *Life of Mozart.* Trans. Helen Mautner. Introduction by A. H. King. Reprint, Hyperion Press, Westport, Conn., 1966.

Nissen, G. N. V. *Biographie W. A. Mozarts.* Foreword by Rudolph Angermüller. Georg Olms Verlag, Hildesheim, 1984.

Nohl, L. *The Life of Mozart.* 2 vols. Trans. Lady Wallace. Longmans, Green & Co., London, 1877.

Oldman, C. B. "Mozart and Modern Research." *P.R.M.A.* 58 (1931-32), 43.

Osborne, C. *The Complete Operas of Mozart: A Critical Guide.* Victor Gollancz, London, 1978.

Ottaway, H. *Mozart.* Orbis Publishing, London, 1979.

Paumgartner, B. *Mozart. Volksverband der Bücherfreunde Wegweiser.* Verlag G.M.B.H., Berlin, 1927.

Pestelli, G. *The Age of Mozart and Beethoven.* Trans. Eric Cross. Cambridge Univ. Press, 1984.

Pohl, C. F. *Mozart und Haydn in London.* Da Capo, New York, 1970.

Racek, J. *Neznama Mozartova Autografni Torsa.* Krajske Nakladatelstvi, Ostrava, 1959.

Radcliffe, P. *Mozart Piano Concertos*. BBC Music Guides. BBC Publications, London, 1978.

Raynor, H. *Mozart*. Macmillan, London, 1978.

Rech, G. *Das Salzburger Mozart Buch*. Residenz Verlag, Salzburg und Wien, 1986.

Roe, C. "Quaint Little Wolfgang." *Medical Journal of Australia*, 25 December 1971, pp. 1317-22.

Rothman, S. "Erythema Nodosum in the 18th Century: The Case of the Child Mozart." *Archives of Dermatology & Syphilology* 52 (1945), 33.

Rushton, J. W. A. *Mozart. Don Giovanni*. Cambridge Univ. Press, Cambridge, 1981.

Sadie, S. *Mozart*, 2nd ed. Calder & Boyars, London, 1970.

_____, ed. *The New Grove Dictionary of Music and Musicians*. 20 vols. Macmillan, London, 1980.

_____. *The New Grove Mozart*. Papermac, London, 1982.

_____. "Review of Hildesheimer's Mozart." *The Musical Times*, 124 (1983), 616-17.

_____. *Mozart Symphonies*. BBC Music Guides. BBC Publications, London, 1986.

_____. "Review of H. C. Robbins Landon's: Mozart's Last Year." *The Musical Times*, 129 (1988), 243-44.

Saint-Foix, G de. *The Symphonies of Mozart*. Trans. Leslie Orrey, Dennis Dobson, London, 1948.

Sakula, A. "Amadeus": Was Mozart Poisoned? *History of Medicine* (January-February 1980), pp. 6-9.

Scarlett, E. P. "The Illnesses and Death of Mozart." *Archives of Internal Medicine* 114 (1964), 311-16.

Schenk, E. *Mozart and His Times*. Trans. Richard and Clara Winston, Secker & Warburg, London, 1960.

Schickling, D. "Einige ungeklärte Fragen zur Geschichte der Requiem-Vollendung." *Mozart Jahrbuch*, 1976-77, 265-76.

Schlichtegroll, F. von. *Musiker-Nekrologe*. Bärenreiter, Kassel, 1939.

Scholes, P. A. *The Oxford Companion to Music*, 9th ed. Oxford Univ. Press, London, 1963.

Schonberg, H. C. *The Great Conductors*. Victor Gollancz, London, 1977.

_____. *The Great Pianists*. Victor Gollancz, London, 1978.

Schonholz, I. F. von, ed. *Wiener Allgemeine Musikalische Zeitung—1813*. Zentralantiquariat der Deutschen Demokratischen Republik, Leipzig, 1986.

Schwerin, E. "Some Thoughts About Mozart." *Musical Heritage Review* 2 (1978), 6-9.

_____. "Some Thoughts About Mozart's Relationship with His Father." Friends of Mozart, New York, Newsletter No. 4, Spring 1978, 1-4.

_____. "Mozart's Delicate Balance: Credits and Debits." Friends of Mozart, New York, Newsletter No. 5, Fall 1978, 1-11.

_____. "A précis of: Mozart, Vater und Sohn: Eine psychologische Untersuchung, by Florian Langegger." Friends of Mozart, New York, Newsletter No. 7, Summer 1979, 1-4.

_____. "Constanze Mozart: Woman and Wife of a Genius." Friends of Mozart, New York, 1981.

_____. "Maria Anna ('Nannerl') Mozart: A Profile of Mozart's Sister. In two parts." Friends of Mozart, New York, Newsletters Nos. 19, Fall 1985, 1-4; 20, Spring 1986, 1-5.

_____. "Leopold Mozart: Profile of a Personality." Friends of Mozart, New York, 1987.

_____. "Mozart's 'Don Giovanni': The Many Versions and Diversions." Friends of Mozart, New York, Newsletter No. 23, Winter 1988, 1-4.

_____. "Antonio Salieri: An Appraisal and Exoneration (Part I)." Friends of Mozart, New York, Newsletter No. 24, October 1988, 1-8.

Sederholm, C. G. "Mozart's Death." *Music and Letters* 32, (1951), 345-48.

Shaffer, P. *Amadeus.* Penguin, Harmondsworth, Middlesex, 1982.

Shapiro, S. L. "Medical History of W. A. Mozart." *The Eye, Ear, Nose & Throat Monthly* 47 (1968), 17-20.

Singer, C., and Underwood, E. A. *A Short History of Medicine,* 2nd ed. Oxford Univ. Press, Clarendon Press, 1962.

Singer, I. *Mozart & Beethoven: The Concept of Love in Their Operas.* Johns Hopkins Univ. Press, Baltimore, 1977.

Sitwell, S. *Mozart.* Greenwood Press, Westport, Conn. 1971.

Slonimsky, N. "The Weather at Mozart's Funeral." *The Musical Quarterly* 46 (1960), 12-21.

Smith, E. *Mozart Serenades, Divertimenti & Dances.* BBC Music Guides. BBC Publications, London, 1982.

Solomon, M. "Review of Mozart by Wolfgang Hildesheimer." *The Musical Quarterly* (Spring 1983), 270-79.

Stearns, M. *Wolfgang Amadeus Mozart: Master of Pure Music.* Franklin Watts, New York, 1968.

Stein, J. H., ed. *Internal Medicine.* Little, Brown, Boston, 1983.

Stein, W. G., and Schwerin, E. "Mozart's Death, Letter to the Editor." *The Musical Times* 126 (1985), 332.

Stendhal (Henri Beyle). *The Lives of Haydn, Mozart & Metastasio.* Trans. Richard Coe. Calder & Boyars, London, 1972.

Steptoe, A. "Mozart, Joseph II and Social Sensitivity." *The Music Review* 43 (1982), 109-20.

_____. "Mozart and Poverty." *The Musical Times* 125, (1984), 196-201.

Tobin, J. R. *Mozart and the Sonata Form.* William Reeves, London, 1916.

Tovey, D. F. *Essays in Musical Analysis,* 6 vols. and Supplement. Oxford Univ. Press, London, 1972.

Turner, W. J. *Mozart. The Man and His Works.* Greenwood Press, Westport, Conn. 1979.

Tyson, A. "'La Clemenza di Tito' and Its Chronology." *The Musical Times* 116 (1975), 221-27.

_____. "Mozart's Truthfulness. Letter to the Editor." *The Musical Times* 119 (1978), 938.

_____. "The Two Slow Movements of Mozart's Paris Symphony, K 297." *The Musical Times* 122 (1981), 17-21.

_____. "Le Nozze di Figaro. Lessons from the Autograph Score." *The Musical Times* 122 (1981), 456-61.

_____. "Notes on the Composition of Mozart's *Così Fan Tutte.*" *Journal of the American Musicological Society* 37 (1984), 356-401.

_____. "Some Problems in the Text of *Le Nozze di Figaro:* Did Mozart Have a Hand in Them?" *JRMA* 112 (1987), 99-131.

_____. *Mozart: Studies of the Autograph Scores.* Harvard Univ. Press, Cambridge, Mass., 1987.

Valentin, E. *Mozart and His World.* Thames & Hudson, London, 1970.

_____. *Lübbes Mozart Lexikon,* 2nd ed. Gustav Lübbe Verlag, Bergisch Gladbach, 1985.

_____. *Mozart: Weg und Welt.* Paul List Verlag, Munich, 1985.

_____. *Leopold Mozart.* Paul List Verlag, Munich, 1987.

Walter, B. *Theme and Variations: An Autobiography.* Hamish Hamilton, London, 1947.

Warrack, J. *Carl Maria von Weber,* 2nd ed. Cambridge Univ. Press, Cambridge, 1976.

Wellesz, E., and Sternfeld, F., eds. *The Age of Enlightenment: 1745-1790,* vol. 7. *The New Oxford History of Music,* 10 vols., Oxford Univ. Press, London, 1981.

Wilder, V. *Mozart.* 2 vols. Trans. Louise Liebich. William Reeves, London, 1907.

Wood, P. *Diseases of the Heart and Circulation,* 3rd ed. Eyre & Spottiswoode, London, 1968.

Woodford, P. *Mozart: His Life and Times.* Midas Books, Tunbridge Wells, 1978.

Wyzewa, T. de, and Saint-Foix, G. de. *Wolfgang Amadeus Mozart.* 2 vols. Robert Laffont, Paris, 1986.

Zeman, H. von H. *Wege zu Mozart: Don Giovanni.* Verlag Hölder, Pichler, Tempsky, Vienna, 1987.

Zenger, M., and Deutsch, O. E. *Mozart and His World in Contemporary Pictures.* Neue Ausgabe Sämlicher Werke, X, 32. Bärenreiter, Kassel, Basel, 1961.

GLOSSARY OF MEDICAL TERMS

Adenitis:	Inflammation of the lymphatic glands.
Afebrile:	Absence of an elevated body temperature.
Anomy:	The state of being without organization or system.
Brachycephalic:	Short-headed or broad-headed.
Calcified:	Hardening due to the deposition of calcium salts within tissue.
Cardiac:	Pertaining to the heart.
Catarrh:	Inflammation of the mucous membrane of the upper respiratory passages with free discharge.
Cerebral:	Pertaining to the brain.
Chorea:	Disorganized, bizarre involuntary movements.
Chronic:	Marked by long duration.
Collagen:	An insoluble, fibrous protein, that occurs in vertebrates, as the chief constituent of the fibrils of connective tissue, and of the organic substance of bone.
Coprolalia:	Irresistible desire to use obscene words.
Coprophilia:	Inordinate interest in feces.
Cornea:	The outer membrane of the eye.
Dura mater:	One of the meninges—the tough, fibrous membrane on the inner surface of the brain and spinal cord.

Edema:	Swelling due to an accumulation of tissue fluid.
Ego:	An aspect of the personality which is in contact with the external world by means of perception, thought, and reality-regulated striving.
Endemic:	Universal prevalence in a human community.
Epidural:	Situated upon or outside the dura mater.
Erythema marginatum:	A skin rash specific to rheumatic fever.
Extradural:	Situated or occurring outside the dura mater, but within the skull.
Gingivitis:	Inflammation of the gum.
Glabella:	The smooth prominence between the eyebrows.
Hematoma:	A swelling containing blood.
Hyperuricemia:	Elevation of the blood uric acid concentration.
Impetigo:	Infection of the skin with yellow crust formation.
Macule:	A flat, discolored spot on the skin.
Malaise:	A vague feeling of being unwell.
Mastoiditis:	Inflammation of the mastoid.
Meningeal:	Of, relating to, or affecting the meninges.
Meninges:	Any of the three membranes that cover the brain and spinal cord.
Metopic:	A suture uniting the frontal bones in the fetus, and sometimes persisting after birth.
Nephritis:	Inflammation of the kidney.
Nephrotic:	Kidney damage resulting in excessive leakage of proteins into the urine.
Neuropathy:	Functional disturbance of a peripheral nerve.
Orbit:	Eye socket.
Otitis media:	Inflammation of the middle ear.
Pancarditis:	Inflammation of all three layers of the heart.
Papule:	A small elevated lesion of the skin.
Paranoid trend:	A tendency to grandiose ideas and/or sensitivity to real or apparent criticism.
Paraphrasia:	A misuse of words or phrases.
Pathogenicity:	The ability of a microorganism to produce disease.
Polyarthritis:	Inflammation of more than one of the joints.

Pulmonary artery:	The major blood vessel supplying blood to the lung.
Somnambulistic:	A deep trance induced by hypnotism.
Streptococcus pyogenes:	A virulent gram-positive spherical bacterium which is classified further into the Group A Beta hemolytic strain.
Subcutaneous:	Beneath the skin.
Suppuration:	Formation of pus.
Synesthesia:	A condition found in some individuals in which perception of a certain type of object is regularly linked with particular images from another sensory mode.
Synostosis:	Union of two or more separate bones to form a single bone.
TAB:	A vaccine for prophylaxis against typhoid fever.
Temporoparietal:	Relating to the temporal and parietal bones.
Thrombosis:	Clotting of blood.
Varicose:	A distended, enlarged, tortuous vein.
Vasculitis:	Inflammation of a blood vessel.
Vesicle:	A small blister.

INDEX OF MOZART'S WORKS
IN THIS BOOK

Köchel
Number   Work

GENERAL INDEX

About the Author

PETER J. DAVIES is a Consultant Physician in Internal Medicine and Gastroenterology in private practice, in Melbourne, Australia. He is the author of many scholarly papers and articles published in the *Journal of the Royal Society of Medicine, The Musical Times, Speculum, Gut, Journal of Gastroenterology and Hepatology,* and *The Medical Journal of Australia.*

**Recent Titles in
Contributions to
the Study of Music and Dance**

Music and Musket: Bands and Bandsmen
of the American Civil War
Kenneth E. Olson

Edmund Thornton Jenkins: The Life and Times
of an American Black Composer, 1894-1926
Jeffrey P. Green

Born to Play: The Life and Career of
Hazel Harrison
Jean E. Cazort and Constance Tibbs Hobson

Titta Ruffo: An Anthology
Andrew Farkas, editor

Nellie Melba: A Contemporary Review
William R. Moran, compiler

Armseelchen: The Life and Music of Eric Zeisl
Malcolm S. Cole and Barbara Barclay

Busoni and the Piano: The Works, the Writings,
and the Recordings
Larry Sitsky

Music as Propaganda: Art to Persuade, Art to Control
Arnold Perris

A Most Wondrous Babble: American Art Composers, Their Music,
and the American Scene, 1950-1985
Nicholas E. Tawa

Voices of Combat: A Century of Liberty and War Songs, 1765-1865
Kent A. Bowman

Edison, Musicians, and the Phonograph: A Century in Retrospect
John Harvith and Susan Edwards Harvith, editors

The Dawning of American Keyboard Music
J. Bunker Clark